Annuals

How to Select, Grow and Enjoy

by Derek Fell

HPBooks®

Executive Editor
Rick Bailey

Editorial Director
Randy Summerlin

Editor
Scott Millard

Art Director
Don Burton

Book Design
Paul Fitzgerald

Photography
Derek Fell

Illustrations
Jane Barton

About the Author

Derek Fell is a widely published garden writer and plant photographer, and author of two HPBooks— *Vegetables: How to Select, Grow and Enjoy* and *How to Photograph Flowers, Plants & Landscapes.* He is a contributor to *Woman's Day, Architectural Digest* and *Encyclopaedia Britannica,* and has appeared on the *Good Morning, America* TV show as a gardening expert.

He first began growing annuals in 1964, working with Europe's largest flower-breeding establishment. He later served as manager for the largest mail-order seed house in the United States. He has been director of All-America Selections—the national seed trials—and director of the National Garden Bureau—an information office sponsored by the American seed industry. Fell tests new flower varieties and growing techniques on his 2-acre farm in Bucks County, Pennsylvania.

Contents

Published by HPBooks
a division of Price Stern Sloan, Inc.
360 N. La Cienega Blvd.
Los Angeles, CA 90048
ISBN: 0-89586-240-9
Library of Congress Catalog Card Number: 83-82466
©1983 Fisher Publishing Inc.
Printed in U.S.A.
9 8 7 6 5 4 3

Cover photo: 'Sombrero' zinnia, by Derek Fell.
Actual size of blossom is 2-1/2 inches in
diameter.

1

Pleasures of Flowering Annuals

Flowering annuals are synonymous with dramatic garden color, and it is no wonder. No other plants will give you more color over a longer period at less cost than flowering annuals. The vibrant pinks of petunias, the shimmering reds of zinnias and the glowing yellows of marigolds equal the most colorful tulips. As a bonus, annuals put on a far-longer flowering display, lasting for weeks or even months.

On a per-plant basis, annuals are less expensive than perennials or flowering bulbs. One daffodil bulb, blooming for about 10 days each year, costs approximately 50¢. A packet of marigold seeds for the same money can produce more than 100 plants, flowering non-stop for 100 days or more. You can see why annuals have such universal appeal.

ANNUALS, BIENNIALS, PERENNIALS
Technically, *annuals* are a large group of plants that complete their life

cycles in a single growing season. An annual germinates, flowers, sets seeds and dies with the first frost. In nature, plants grow from these seeds that remain dormant until conditions are right for germination. When light, temperature, moisture and other factors are correct for the particular annual, the life cycle begins all over again.

Because they must complete their life cycle in a single season, flowers of most annuals are bright and colorful. The colorful flowers attract the attention of pollinating insects, to help ensure a good crop of seeds for the next cycle of life.

A few *biennials*—plants needing two seasons to produce flowers and then die—can be grown to bloom the first year. The trick is to start seeds early in the year so they have enough time to mature and flower. Some of these, such as foxglove 'Foxy' and sweet William 'Wee Willie', have been specially bred to possess this

first-season quality.

A few *perennials*—plants that require two seasons to flower and live year after year—can be grown to flower as annuals. One example is gloriosa daisy. Seeds started early in the season will flower the first year. Plants then perform as hardy perennials thereafter, flowering year after year.

ANNUALS IN THE LANDSCAPE
Annuals are such a diverse group of plants they can be used in many ways. Because they have varied cultural requirements, certain annuals do better in certain climates or locations. Some prefer cool conditions, producing the best blooms either early or late during the growing season. Pansies, sweet peas and snapdragons are representative of this group. Other annuals bloom more spectacularly during warm, sunny periods. Many of these originate from desert areas. Marigolds, zinnias and portulacas are examples of heat-lovers. Some

A garden of annuals can take many forms. Left: Large-scale planting of different annuals is as colorful as any garden. Above: Close-up view of 'Irish Eyes' gloriosa daisy shows striking simplicity.

annuals, such as impatiens and begonias, prefer shade but the majority do best in an open, sunny location.

Annuals can be used to create beautiful, temporary ground covers. Others make spectacular hanging baskets—striking in entryways. Some are best adapted to containers as greenhouse plants, or planted in tubs for placement on decks and patios. Certain ones are valued for drying to make dried arrangements. Some thrive in dry walls and rock gardens. Some annuals are suitable for cutting to make spectacular fresh-flower arrangements. In fact, a *cutting garden*—a rectangular plot of annuals resembling a vegetable garden—is becoming a popular feature among homeowners.

Many kinds of annuals are used as *bedding plants.* This is a term used frequently in the book. It refers to annuals commonly planted in flower beds and borders along walks and paths. Petunias, impatiens and marigolds are the most popular in the group. They are widely available as transplants from garden centers.

Annuals also play an important role in wildflower or naturalistic landscapes. Meadows, banks, hillsides and roadsides sparkle when planted with coreopsis, gaillardias, poppies, godetias and larkspur.

For a guide to which annuals do best in special situations, see the lists on pages 17 to 21.

ABOUT THIS BOOK
The following pages provide a complete guide to growing annuals successfully. Emphasis has been placed on 10 important factors:

1. Selection of a Good Site—Some annuals tolerate shade but most do best with full sun. A location receiving full sun allows you to plant the widest selection and most colorful kinds of annuals. If you have no choice and some of your garden is in partial shade, grow impatiens. It is the best annual for shade. See page 106.

2. Garden Layout and Design—Beds, borders and cutting gardens are the most popular ways to grow flowering annuals. Sample plans are given on pages 12 and 13. Also, there are many outstanding public display gardens and test gardens you can visit. These are great places for ideas. Use them to make your planting plans and variety selections. Many of these gardens are All-America display gardens, where recent award winners can be seen and evaluated.

If space is at a premium, consider container plantings. Information on how to grow plants in containers and small spaces is given on pages 23 to 27.

Annuals are popular for creating wildflower meadows. Field of annual calliopsis and Queen-Anne's lace was established in one season.

A single color can be dramatic. This is a seed-production field of French marigolds near Lompoc, California. The same effect can be achieved on a smaller scale in the home landscape.

'Springtime' verbena creates a multicolor carpet in this island bed.

3. Principles of Color—Like an artist, the gardener uses the colors of flowers and foliage to paint and accent the landscape. Use a color wheel like the one shown on page 10 to guide you in making color selections.

4. Recommended Varieties—The Gallery of Garden Annuals, pages 59 to 157, includes recommended varieties for almost every class of annuals. Strongly consider *hybrids* and those that have won awards in the All-America Selections, the national seed trials.

5. Soil Preparation—Soil quality is not as necessary as it is for growing vegetables, but good soil will increase your flower-garden success. Testing soil, adding amendments and increasing soil fertility will ensure best results for most annuals. Step-by-step instructions for soil preparation are given on page 31.

6. Seeds, Plants and Supplies— After investing time, materials and effort in locating, planning and preparing your garden, you should plant quality seeds or transplants. This is usually the least expensive part of your entire investment. Learn how to buy quality transplants. See page 44. Purchase seeds from reputable companies, either from a seed rack or mail-order catalog. See page 38 for addresses of mail-order sources.

7. When and How to Plant— Annuals can be grouped into two categories: *hardy annuals* that tolerate mild frosts, and *tender annuals* that are damaged by frost. Also, knowing whether a plant is a *cool-season* annual or a *warm-season* annual is helpful. The climate map on pages 46 and 47 shows average frost dates for North America, and is useful as a guide to planting dates.

8. Irrigation—Some annuals are drought resistant. Regular amounts of water ensure earliest flowers, largest flower size and prolific bloom over a longer period. The different ways to water are described on page 50. Drip irrigation as a watering method is becoming more popular. See page 51 for information on installing an efficient drip-irrigation system.

9. Weed Control—Weeds can dampen your enthusiasm for gardening faster than anything. Mulching is a simple method of weed control. Decorative mulches will not detract from the beauty of your flower garden. See page 52 for information on mulches.

10. Pest and Disease Control— Prevention is the best method of pest and disease control. Keeping your garden clean avoids most problems. Being alert for early signs of trouble is important. For information on identifying and treating common plant pests and diseases, see pages 54 to 57.

2

Planning Your Color Garden

Winter is the best time to plan your displays of flowering annuals. Seed catalogs generally arrive soon after the holidays, and stores begin to set out their seed-packet displays. Planning early, before spring arrives, allows you time to decide what to plant and where.

The first decision you should make is whether to grow plants from seeds, or wait until planting time and buy ready-grown transplants. Growing your own plants from seeds gives you greatest freedom of choice. Major seed catalogs offer up to 2,000 varieties of flowers. This compares to about 50 varieties of transplants from a well-stocked garden center.

If you plan to raise plants from seeds purchased from a mail-order catalog, order before February 15. If you live in a mild-climate area, order earlier. You must provide sufficient time for seeds of slow-growing plants such as begonias and coleus to grow to transplant-size for early flowering. As

a bonus, many mail-order seed suppliers give discounts for early orders.

PLAN ON PAPER
To help you decide the number of plants and type of plants—sun-loving or shade-loving for example—make a plan of your outdoor planting areas. Graph paper is commonly used, with one square on the graph equal to one square foot of actual garden space.

Draw beds, borders and gardens to scale, using colored felt pens to represent groups of plants. You can then count the squares within the colored areas to determine number of plants needed. For most flowering annuals, figure on planting one plant for every square foot—the same as the squares in your graph-paper plan. Some spreading kinds need more space, and some edging plants can be planted more closely. For exact spacing requirements, refer to descriptions in Gallery of Garden Annuals, pages 59 to 157.

Make a list of the different annuals you need to match your planting plans. Decide which you wish to start from seeds and which you plan to buy as ready-grown transplants. Many gardeners prefer to start large-seed, quick-growing varieties such as marigolds, zinnias, dahlias and calendulas. They buy ready-grown transplants of slow-growing, fine-seed kinds such as begonias, impatiens and coleus from a garden center.

Use your list to decide when to start seeds indoors and when to sow those that can be planted directly in the garden. For example, coleus and begonia seeds should be planted indoors 10 to 12 weeks before your last frost date. They will then have enough time to become decent-size transplants. Marigolds and asters require only 4 to 6 weeks to reach transplant size. Nasturtiums, poppies and sweet peas can be sown directly in the garden as soon as soil can be worked in spring.

Left: Landscape at Filoli Estate, Woodside, California, has spectacular displays of flowering annuals. 'Yellow Sun' zinnias combine with cosmos, phlox and white nicotiana in massed bed. Above: Border planting features tall orange calendulas, dwarf blue ageratum, blue lobelia, white wax begonias, white alyssum, dwarf French marigolds and mixed zinnias.

Principles of Color

Like an artist daubing a canvas with bold or subtle strokes of paint, you can use flowers and foliage to paint your landscape. Many principles of color that apply to art also apply to flower gardening.

It's easier to select colors for harmony or contrast if you know how to use a color wheel such as the one shown below. The wheel is divided into *cool* and *warm* hues, or "pure" colors using three *primary* colors—red, yellow and blue. Cool colors such as blue, green and violet are subdued. Warm colors such as red, yellow and orange tend to catch the eye more easily.

The primary colors are the source of all other colors. Primary colors cannot be made by mixing other colors together. A primary color mixed with another primary color makes a *secondary* color. For example, red and yellow make orange, yellow and blue make green and blue and red make violet. When mixed with black, gray or white, tints, shades and tones are created.

Color groupings of flowers can be *harmonious* or *contrasting. Hues* are particular shades of colors. Hues in any neighboring group on the color wheel are harmonious or *analogous.* You can create *complementary* contrasts by selecting colors at opposite sides of the color wheel. These complementary colors produce the most dramatic companion plantings in beds and borders. The photo on page 59 is a vivid example. Plantings such as these are often enhanced by using white flowers as a divider or edging.

Examples of effective combinations using complementary color contrasts include spring-blooming, orange Siberian wallflowers and blue forget-me-nots. Try yellow French marigolds and violet petunias in midsummer. Red impatiens and green coleus are good combinations in late summer.

The concept of coordinating cool and warm colors can be applied to the different seasons of the year.

For example, annuals with white and blue flowers are most appealing if they bloom in early summer—when these colors naturally predominate. Follow these with vibrant yellow and red flowers timed to bloom in midsummer. They will come into their best bloom at this time, and are most effective at reflecting the increased sunlight.

Planting *monochromatic* theme gardens—those using a single color—is an effective way to use annuals. All-white, all-blue, all-gold and all-pink are just a few examples. Photos of these kinds of plantings can be seen throughout this book.

"Rainbow" plantings of several colors are probably most widely used when seeking a brilliant mixture of colors. Many seed companies offer inexpensive mixtures of popular, long-lasting annuals. However, a more spectacular effect can be produced by planting a mixed border of separate colors.

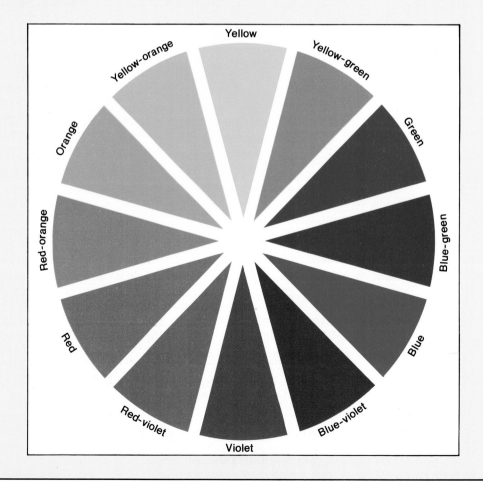

SUCCESSION PLANTING

If you want continual color from early spring to fall frosts, you might have to plant more than one kind of annual in a particular location. For example, Siberian wallflowers, forget-me-nots and pansies bloom prolifically in spring yet are often exhausted by summer. They can be replaced with heat-tolerant plants such as zinnias and marigolds to finish the season. Similarly, beds of petunias that flower poorly after midsummer can be removed and replanted with chrysanthemums or scarlet sage for fall displays.

PLANTING DESIGNS

The scope of your flower garden is often dictated by the amount of land available. In small back yards, borders can be planted along fences, hedges or walls. In larger spaces, consider planting *island beds*. These are areas planted within a lawn or ground-cover planting. Island beds allow plants to be seen from all sides. Plants are also easy to reach so weeding and watering is easier. An open, well-ventilated, evenly lighted location tends to produce the best flowering displays.

BEDS AND BORDERS

Flower beds are most effective when located at the edge of a lawn, alongside the house or as islands of color in a lawn. Located on either side of a driveway, a border makes an attractive ribbon of color leading to the house.

When starting a bed from scratch, follow the instructions for soil preparation, page 31. Stake out the area of your proposed bed with string and stakes. Use a spade to make a crisp, clean border at the edge of the lawn. In the center of the bed, mound soil so it is several inches above the surrounding surface, sloping at the edges. This displays the flowers better and allows excess water to drain away. When a border is made alongside a fence or wall, soil can be made higher at the back, sloping slightly forward.

After plants are in position, you may want to lay down a decorative mulch of pine bark or coco bean hulls. It will help discourage weeds and is more attractive than the bare earth.

When selecting annuals, you should have some idea which plants can be grown successfully in your region. Visit local parks and botanical gardens. Make note of the good gardens in your neighborhood. These will help give you ideas you can copy or improve for your own garden.

With beds of annuals, it is best to keep the design simple. Avoid creating a hodgepodge of unrelated heights and colors. Check the seed-packet description so you will know whether a variety is tall, intermediate or dwarf in height. You can then plant them correctly so tall plants do not obstruct your view of shorter plants. Although plant mixtures can be effective, it's best to plant separate colors when combining different flower classes in the same bed.

Beds and borders planted in shades of a single color can be especially effective. For example, consider planting an all-white garden using plants with silver foliage and white flowers, or a striking, all-blue garden.

Island Beds—Square, rectangular, round or kidney-shape island beds are viewed from all directions. They look best if completely edged with a low-growing annual such as ageratum, portulaca or alyssum. A short, evergreen hedge such as dwarf boxwood, dwarf barberry or germander also makes an effective edging. For simplicity, the center of the island bed can be planted with a single color or mixture of one variety. If a bed of mixed annuals is desired, place tall varieties in the center, intermediate-height varieties next, and dwarf varieties around the edge. This way no plant blocks the view or shades another plant.

Island beds are usually located in sunny locations, surrounded by open lawn. They can be shaded by high trees or by a tree located in the middle of the bed. This way the bed forms a "collar" around the tree.

Borders—The only difference between a bed and a border is that borders usually have a solid backdrop such as a hedge, fence or wall. They are generally of one or two types: sunny borders facing east or south and shady borders facing north or west.

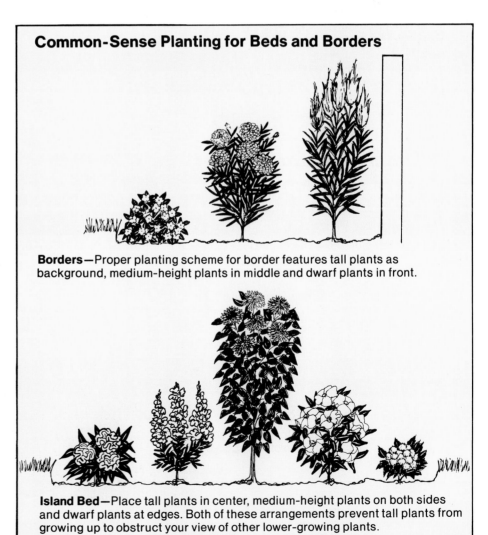

Common-Sense Planting for Beds and Borders

Borders—Proper planting scheme for border features tall plants as background, medium-height plants in middle and dwarf plants in front.

Island Bed—Place tall plants in center, medium-height plants on both sides and dwarf plants at edges. Both of these arrangements prevent tall plants from growing up to obstruct your view of other lower-growing plants.

Designs for a Cutting Garden

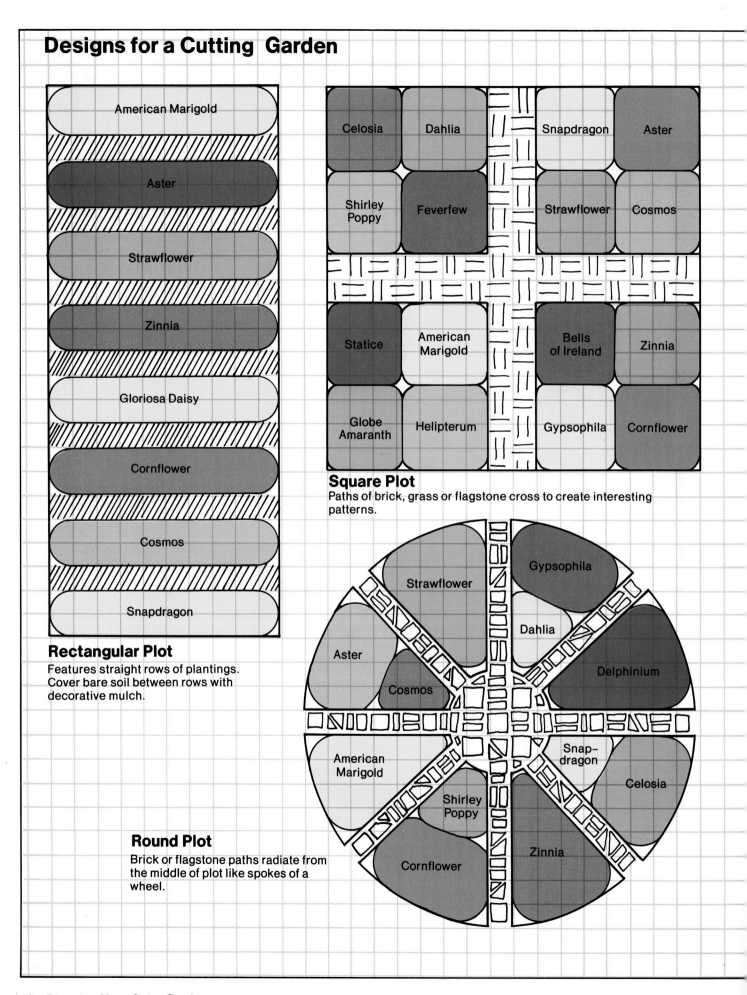

American Marigold

Aster

Strawflower

Zinnia

Gloriosa Daisy

Cornflower

Cosmos

Snapdragon

Rectangular Plot
Features straight rows of plantings. Cover bare soil between rows with decorative mulch.

Celosia | Dahlia

Shirley Poppy | Feverfew

Snapdragon | Aster

Strawflower | Cosmos

Statice | American Marigold

Globe Amaranth | Helipterum

Bells of Ireland | Zinnia

Gypsophila | Cornflower

Square Plot
Paths of brick, grass or flagstone cross to create interesting patterns.

Strawflower

Gypsophila

Aster

Dahlia

Cosmos

Delphinium

American Marigold

Snap-dragon

Shirley Poppy

Celosia

Cornflower

Zinnia

Round Plot
Brick or flagstone paths radiate from the middle of plot like spokes of a wheel.

Designs for Beds and Borders

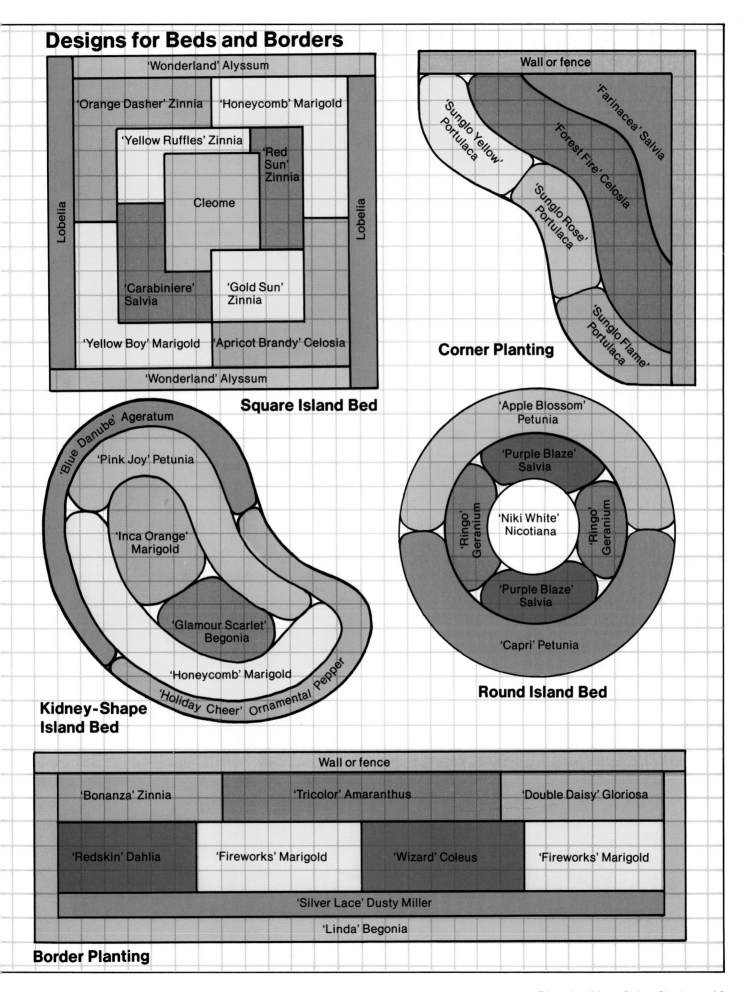

'Wonderland' Alyssum

'Orange Dasher' Zinnia

'Honeycomb' Marigold

'Yellow Ruffles' Zinnia

'Red Sun' Zinnia

Cleome

Lobelia

Lobelia

'Carabiniere' Salvia

'Gold Sun' Zinnia

'Yellow Boy' Marigold

'Apricot Brandy' Celosia

'Wonderland' Alyssum

Square Island Bed

Wall or fence

'Sunglo Yellow' Portulaca

'Farinacea' Salvia

'Forest Fire' Celosia

'Sunglo Rose' Portulaca

'Sunglo Flame' Portulaca

Corner Planting

'Blue Danube' Ageratum

'Pink Joy' Petunia

'Inca Orange' Marigold

'Glamour Scarlet' Begonia

'Honeycomb' Marigold

'Holiday Cheer' Ornamental Pepper

Kidney-Shape Island Bed

'Apple Blossom' Petunia

'Purple Blaze' Salvia

'Ringo' Geranium

'Niki White' Nicotiana

'Ringo' Geranium

'Purple Blaze' Salvia

'Capri' Petunia

Round Island Bed

Wall or fence

'Bonanza' Zinnia

'Tricolor' Amaranthus

'Double Daisy' Gloriosa

'Redskin' Dahlia

'Fireworks' Marigold

'Wizard' Coleus

'Fireworks' Marigold

'Silver Lace' Dusty Miller

'Linda' Begonia

Border Planting

Like island beds, borders can be planted with a single variety in one color or a mixture. An edging around the border is generally desirable. It serves as a frame for the planting. Dwarf annuals or dwarf evergreen plants clipped to make a low hedge can form the frame.

Position tallest plants at the rear against the backdrop. Intermediate-height plants should be placed next, with dwarf varieties planted in front. All plants will be displayed in full view and no plant will shade another.

Corner Plantings—These generally form a triangle. The leading side can be straight but looks more natural if it curves. Corner plantings are especially effective if soil is terraced. Use lumber, stone or railroad ties to form the terraces. This allows dwarf annuals to be used on different levels to create uniform "steps" of color. Unless they face due south, corner plantings are likely to be shady.

CUTTING GARDENS
These are gardens designed primarily for utility. Annuals are planted so they can be "harvested" and brought indoors so you can enjoy their beauty. Three ideas for cutting gardens are shown on page 12. Each group of plants should be attractive for display purposes and accessible for cutting.

The first and simplest plan is a rectangular plot featuring straight rows with pathways between—just like a traditional vegetable plot. To keep pathways from becoming muddy, cover with an organic mulch such as pine needles, straw, grass clippings or wood chips. For decorative appeal, frame the entire area with a white picket fence or dwarf evergreen hedge.

The square or rectangular plot features planting squares within the garden. Paths cross to provide easy access to planting areas. Paths can be bare soil but are more attractive and clean when covered with an organic mulch. For even greater decorative appeal, plant grass pathways. They should be at least as wide as your mower will cut. Or install a gravel, rock or brick path. To enhance each planting square, frame with dwarf edging plants or dwarf evergreens such as boxwood to create a low hedge. This creates what the French call a *parterre,* a garden separated by paths.

All the planting area can be enclosed in a regular hedge or picket fence. A trellised arbor at the entrance decorated with vining annuals makes a spectacular and inviting entry.

The round cutting garden is laid out like a wagonwheel. Spokes of the wheel form narrow pathways with spaces between, creating pie-shape beds. For a decorative touch, pathways can be covered with flagstone or gravel. The circumference of the circle can be planted with dwarf boxwood. By enclosing each pie-shape bed with a low boxwood hedge, you can create a *parterre* garden.

SELECTING A SITE
Consider several factors before choosing a planting site. These include amounts of sun and shade, heat and reflected light, winds and soil condition. Make note of these on your graph-paper plan.

Sunlight and Shade—Amount of available sunlight is the most important factor when choosing a location for your annuals. Most flowering annuals do best in full sun—a minimum of 7 hours is required for good flower production. Some, such as portulaca and gazanias, close their flowers on cloudy days.

When choosing a location, avoid shady sites. Relatively few flowering annuals do well in shade. Select a site that receives plenty of sun. For sun-

Pink wax begonias with bronze foliage and dusty miller with silvery foliage produce an unusual but striking combination.

Sunny border does double-duty as cutting garden. Yellow gloriosa daisies and red, dahlia-flower zinnias have long stems. Dwarf, compact, triploid-hybrid marigolds and white grandiflora petunias provide lower level of color at edges of border.

loving annuals, do not plant in a location that is shaded during noon hours. If shadows from a tall building or tree block the sun during midday, it may be better to choose shade-tolerant plants for the location. This is true even if the site receives 7 hours sunlight daily.

Keep in mind that plants recommended for shaded areas perform best in a *partially* or *lightly* shaded area. In deep shade or locations that do not receive any direct sun, even shade-tolerant plants may come under stress and fail to flower.

I once planted some impatiens and coleus in a raised planter under a dense maple tree. They performed poorly. I selectively pruned a few tree limbs from the tree's interior. It didn't hurt the appearance of the tree, but greatly increased the amount of light reaching the planter. Soon after, both impatiens and coleus began to thrive.

Heat—Temperature is the second most important factor for plant adaptation. Most flowering annuals can be classified as *cool-season* or *warm-season* plants. Warm-season plants generally thrive in heat if they are irrigated. Cool-season plants burn up if temperatures get too high. In hot-summer areas, you can grow many desirable cool-season plants if you time plantings so they mature during cool weather.

Some plants don't mind the heat as long as their roots are cool. One way to reduce temperatures in a hot, dry location is to add lots of organic matter to the soil. Leaf mold, peat moss or garden compost are good soil amendments. Organic matter in the soil significantly increases its moisture-holding capacity. Adding a light covering of organic mulch helps reduce evaporation of moisture and cools the soil even more.

Deeply dug soils are also cooler than shallow soils. For sweet peas, dig a trench and fill it with good soil. Roots penetrate deep and remain cool.

An experience I had growing Shirley poppies is an example of putting this practice to work. I never had much success growing these plants. Just as they came into flower, the hot, summer sun would burn them up. One year I made a raised bed for a planting of the poppies. I added large quantities of compost to the soil for moisture retention. I installed drip

irrigation and covered the soil surface with a mulch of pine needles. The drip irrigation combined with the mulch kept the soil moist and cool. The results were fantastic. I had displays of Shirley poppies like I have never seen before.

Reflected Light and Heat—Locations with insufficient light or heat can sometimes be modified by reflecting heat and light toward plants. Painting a dark wall white increases the amount of reflected heat and light. Surrounding a shaded planter with white landscape stone reflects light upward to plants.

Reflected heat and light can be a detriment. In hot-summer areas, planting against a south or west wall may be too much for certain plants. In desert regions, plants do best with some afternoon shade in summer months.

Shelter and Protection—Flowers exposed to the drying effects of summer winds can suffer rapid moisture loss. Warm-season plants exposed to cool winds can be damaged. Many annuals with tall, brittle stems will topple over in high winds or stems may break. If your planting area is exposed to winds, a windbreak may be necessary. A row of evergreen shrubs or trees is more effective than a solid fence or wall. When wind hits a solid barrier it flows over and down with severe force. A windbreak of evergreen shrubs or trees filters the force of the wind and dissipates it.

Protection from animals is also important. A stray dog can destroy a flower bed. Rabbits, quail and deer enjoy the tender transplants of many annuals. You may need to concentrate your plantings in a special area, fencing it in to keep animal pests away. For more on pest control, see pages 54 to 57.

Soil Drainage—Most flowering annuals require good soil drainage. Both air and moisture are needed in the root zone for health and growth. How well the soil drains depends on its composition. Clay soil tends to drain slowly. Sandy soil drains rapidly. Both can be improved with the addition of large quantities of organic matter such as peat moss, compost and leaf mold.

In certain regions, soil drainage may be so poor that the soil is constantly waterlogged. In these conditions, plants are doomed to fail. Ditches lined with drainage tiles can

be installed to channel excess water away. This can become costly or impractical. As an alternative, consider building a raised planting bed on a foundation of crushed stones.

SELECTING ANNUALS
Annuals comprise a diverse group of plants, with wide applications around the home and garden. Plants are available that grow 3 to 4 inches high, suitable as ground covers. Annual vines grow to 10 feet long, useful for decorating walls or as screening. Most annuals prefer sun but some tolerate shade. In recent years, annuals for shady locations have greatly increased in popularity. Impatiens, one of the best shade-adapted plants, is a top-selling bedding plant for this reason.

Flowering *height* is important, as well as *color*. Red is the favorite of seed buyers, closely followed by yellow, orange, pink and white. Blue is an uncommon flower color because it is the color of the sky. Most flowers contrast with the sky so they will be seen by pollinating insects. Green flowers are even more scarce because green is the common color of leaves and stems. Brown and black are extremely rare.

All white, all blue, all red and pink and all yellow and orange are popular color schemes for beds and borders. Unusual flower colors such as brown, green and black have poor display value, but are in great demand among flower arrangers.

Most annuals adapt to various kinds of soils and grow acceptably without much fertilizer. However, heat and drought tolerance are important considerations when selecting plants. Where conditions are hot and dry it is unwise to plant cool, moisture-loving plants. That is the reason for the following special applications and lists. Use them as a ready reference. If you are interested in a plant and want to know more about it, refer to the descriptions on pages 59 to 157.

Plant and Flower Forms

Most annuals are available in dwarf and tall forms, and sizes in between. The illustration below compares relative sizes of a tall gloriosa daisy, left, to a dwarf variety.

Single flower, top right, means the flower has a single layer of petals. This is 'Golden Daisy' gloriosa daisy.

Double flower, second right, has more than one layer of petals. If the multilayers of petals form a complete globe, the flower is *fully double.* If the flower forms a partial globe, it is a *semidouble.* This fully double variety is 'Double Gold' gloriosa daisy.

Bicolor flower, third right, has two distinct color patterns in the petals. This 'Pinwheel' gloriosa daisy has a mahogany-color zone around a dark *eye,* or center, creating a beautiful contrast to the yellow petal tips.

Star flower, fourth right, is created if a bicolor flower has bands meeting at the center. This is 'Star Joy' petunia.

Picotee flower, fifth right, is a bicolor with contrasting petal edges. This is 'Red Picotee' petunia, winner of an All-America award.

Annuals Selection Guide

Annuals for Beds and Borders

An annual bed is usually an island of soil—either square, round, rectangular or kidney shape—surrounded by paving or lawn. An annual border is usually a long, narrow strip—either straight or free-form—backed by a wall, fence or hedge.

The most important considerations when planning beds and borders are *height* and *color.* See planting plans for beds and borders, page 13.

The following flowering annuals are noted for long-lasting displays in beds and borders under a wide range of conditions. Those marked with an asterisk are widely available as bedding plants from garden centers.

*Begonia, Wax	Nicotiana
Cleome	*Pansy
Celosia	Pepper, Ornamental
Chrysanthemum	*Petunia
*Coleus	*Portulaca
*Dahlia	*Snapdragon
*Dusty miller	*Salvia
*Geranium	Torenia (Wishbone flower)
Gloriosa daisy	Verbena
*Impatiens	Viola
*Lobelia	Vinca
*Marigold	*Zinnia
Nasturtium	

Annuals for Cutting

By choosing the right varieties, annuals planted in beds and borders can be used for cutting fresh flowers. Certain kinds are stimulated into producing more blooms the more they are cut. These are called *cut-and-come-again.* It's not always easy to step into formal beds and borders to cut flowers without causing damage. It makes sense to have a special cutting garden in a separate section of the garden. Three planting plans for cutting gardens are shown on page 12.

Those plants marked with an asterisk are cut-and-come-again varieties.

*Ageratum	*Larkspur
*Aster	Lavatera
Arcotis	*Marigold
Bells of Ireland	Mignonette
Calliopsis	Penstemon
*Calendula	Phlox
*Carnation	*Poppy, Iceland
*Celosia	Salpiglossis
*Chrysanthemum	*Scabiosa
Cleome	Schizanthus
Columbine	*Shasta daisy
*Cornflower	*Snapdragon
*Cosmos	Statice
*Cynoglossum	Stocks
*Dahlia	*Strawflower
Delphinium	Sunflower
Dianthus	Sweet pea
Feverfew	Sweet William
Foxglove	Tidy tips
*Gaillardia	Tigridia
Gerbera	*Tithonia
*Gloriosa daisy	Venidium
*Gypsophila	Verbena
Helipterum	Wallflower, Siberian
Hunnemannia (Mexican	Xeranthemum
tulip poppy)	*Zinnia

'Inca Orange' marigold edged with dusty miller makes a magnificent border.

Annuals for Edging

A flower bed or border featuring tall annuals looks best with a well-defined edge. This can be created by low-growing flowering annuals, which fill in the base of the planting with color. Even low beds and borders used to create a carpet effect generally look better framed with colorful edging plants.

Listed below are some good, low-growing plants for edging. Those marked with an asterisk are extremely compact and especially desirable for this use.

*Ageratum	*Nierembergia
*Alyssum	*Pansy
Anchusa (Dwarf types)	*Pepper, Ornamental
Aster (Dwarf border	Petunia
types)	Phacelia
*Begonia, Wax (Dwarf	Phlox (Dwarf types)
types	Portulaca
Browallia (Dwarf types)	*Sanvitalia
Candytuft	Schizanthus
Cuphia (Cigar plant)	*Snapdragon (Miniature
*Dahlberg daisy	kinds)
*Dianthus	Sweet William (Dwarf
*Dusty miller	kinds)
*Felicia (Dwarf types)	Torenia
*Forget-me-not	Vinca
Gazania	*Viola
Impatiens (Dwarf types)	Zinnia (Miniature kinds)
Kale, Ornamental	
Linaria	
Livingstone daisy	
*Lobelia	
*Marigold, French (Dwarf	
types)	
*Marigold, Signet	
Mimulus	
*Nemesia	
Nemophila	

Shade-Loving Annuals

There are many kinds of shade—light shade, deep shade, low shade, high shade, shade with moist soil, shade with dry soil, morning shade, afternoon shade and others. The worst kinds of shade are deep shade and shade with dry soils. Annuals recommended for shade generally do not tolerate these difficult conditions. Dense shade can sometimes be improved by pruning tree branches to allow more penetration of sunlight.

Impatiens are by far the most popular flowering annual for shade. The best shade is a moist, partially shaded area, either from high, light leaf cover or from a few hours of morning or afternoon shade.

In the following, annuals most tolerant of shade are noted with an asterisk.

Anchusa
*Begonia
Browallia
Canterbury bells
*Coleus
*Impatiens
Lobelia
*Mimulus (Monkey flower)
Forget-me-not
Nemophila (Baby blue-eyes)
Nicotiana
Primula
Salvia splendens (Scarlet sage)
Thunbergia (Black-eyed Susan vine)
*Torenia (Wishbone flower)
Viola

'Futura' impatiens add bright spot of color in the shade.

Annuals for Dry Places and Rock Gardens

Exposed, dry slopes and expanses of flat, open ground are common problem areas around a home. Lawn grasses and perennial ground covers are the first plants to consider for these sites. But many flowering annuals—most from desert areas of Mexico, South America and South Africa—can be used to create a dramatic color scheme. Problem dry areas can be found along the south-facing wall of a house, edging of a driveway, edge of a retaining wall and along property lines. A particular problem spot is where the soil meets hot pavement.

The best rock gardens rely heavily on three natural elements—*plants, rocks* and *water.* If water is unavailable, plants and rocks can work well together. Usually rock gardens feature perennials and flowering bulbs as the main plantings. These remain in permanent positions from year to year. Annuals are added in clumps and pockets for extra color. Particularly effective are ground-hugging annuals, and those that form bushy, compact clumps.

If possible, locate rock gardens on slopes. Good drainage is essential. In choosing rocks for the garden, use those prevalent locally to give your garden a more natural appearance.

Prepare the site before setting stones into place. Dig over the original soil and remove weed roots and other obstructions. Move in some good topsoil and grade the site. You may need to use railroad ties to create a retaining wall.

Begin laying rocks at the lowest level. Try to create natural ridges and outcrops. Place flat-top rocks where they can be used for steppingstones to gain access to different parts of the garden. Group rocks into natural-looking clusters to create bluffs. Place broadest-side facing down and set it firmly in soil. Stones that wobble when stepped on can cause injury.

The following plants are "survivors." They do well in dry places and are especially suited for growing in rock gardens and along dry walls. Many are at home planted with dwarf evergreens and perennials. Varieties with asterisks are specially recommended for rock gardens and dry walls. For ground-cover plants, see list on page 20.

Amaranthus
*Arctotis
Brachycome
*California poppy
*Calliopsis
*Candytuft
Cornflower
*Dahlberg daisy
*Dianthus
*Dimorphotheca
*Dusty miller (especially cineraria)
Euphorbia marginata (Snow-on-the-mountain)
Four o'clock
Gaillardia
*Gazania
Globe amaranth (Gomphrena)
Gloriosa daisy
Grasses, Ornamental
*Gypsophila
Kochia (Burning bush)
*Marigold
*Mesembryanthemum (Livingstone daisy)
Morning glory (Dwarf kinds)
*Nasturtium
Petunia
Phlox
*Polygonum (Knotweed)
*Portulaca
Salvia (Scarlet sage)
*Sanvitalia (Creeping zinnia)
Tidy tips
Tithonia (Mexican sunflower)
Venidium
*Verbena
*Vinca
Zinnia (Dwarf kinds)

Annuals for Naturalizing and Wildflower Plantings

Many annuals are native to North America. Because they reseed themselves freely, they are suitable for planting in open meadows, along slopes for erosion control and in vacant lots. Some types tolerate shade and can be planted in woodland. Many non-natives will adapt and naturalize.

When planting mixtures, it's best to plant at least 75% native plants. Choose plants adapted to your particular climate. Some seed companies sell special mixtures with local conditions in mind. For example, a Western wildflower mixture might contain godetias, scarlet flax, cornflowers, Shirley poppies, wild larkspur, California poppies and other native species. A Southern wildflower mixture might be made up of cosmos, calliopsis, gaillardias and black-eyed Susans. Mountain mixtures, desert mixtures and shade mixtures are also available.

Wildflower mixtures generally contain plants of different vigor. Sometimes a particular species dominates and crowds out the other wildflowers after the first year. Most commercial mixtures contain some perennial species. The annuals provide instant color. If a mixture effect is desired each year, it is often better to dig the planting area each spring and reseed exclusively with annuals. The best wildflower meadows are planted this way.

Sow seeds of mixtures alone or with non-spreading clump grasses such as blue fescue or chewing fescue. Plant at the rate of 1/2 pound of grass seed per 1,000 square feet—20 to 25 pounds per acre. The fescue grass grows quickly and helps to stabilize the soil. An appropriate planting rate for most wildflower mixtures is 4 ounces per 1,000 square feet—4 to 7 pounds per acre.

Pasture grasses—bluegrass, bromegrass, crested wheatgrass and annual ryegrass—will dominate and crowd out your wildflowers. Such grasses are planted where only a green ground cover is desired.

On steep slopes and in sandy, non-irrigated areas, add a layer of coarse gravel or 1- to 2-inch lava rock before sowing. These materials help control erosion and keep soil moist. Till soil and apply rock. Then broadcast seeds and soak thoroughly with water. Seeds will sprout in crevices where they are in contact with moist soil.

Do not fertilize wildflower plantings unless soil is extremely poor. Fertilizers generally encourage excessive weed and grass growth at the expense of wildflower plants. Provide adequate moisture and recommended seeding rates for wildflowers. This allows wildflowers to germinate rapidly and compete with seeds and grasses, crowding them out.

Plants in this list marked with an asterisk are *warm-season* annuals. They do well where summers are hot. Others are *cool-season* annuals that do best in most coastal locations and wherever summers are cool. Most reseed and overwinter in locations where the ground does not freeze.

Alyssum
Brachycome (Swan River daisy)
Calendula
*Calliopsis
Chrysanthemum carinatum
Chrysanthemum coronarium
Clarkia
Cornflower
*Cosmos
Daisy, Shasta
Dimorphotheca (African daisy)
Forget-me-not
*Four o'clock
Foxglove
*Gaillardia
*Gazania
Gilia tricolor (Bird's eyes)
*Gloriosa daisy
Godetia
Gypsophila (Baby's breath)
Hunnemannia (Mexican tulip poppy)
Larkspur, Rocket
*Lavatera
Linaria
Nasturtium
Nemophila
Pennisetum ruppelii (Ornamental grass)
Phacelia
Phlox drummondii
Poppy, California
Poppy, Iceland
Poppy, Shirley
*Salvia farinacea
Scarlet flax
*Sunflower
Tidy tips
Wallflower

Dry slope is planted with annual statice. Rock border helps reduce soil erosion.

California poppies are popular in Western wildflower mixes.

Annuals for Ground Covers

Many locations exist around the home where a carpet effect is desired. Annual ground covers can be used to cover a slope, edge a driveway and frame a flower bed. The following are especially useful as flowering ground covers. Those that last the longest are noted with an asterisk.

African daisy
  (Dimorphotheca)
Cuphea (Cigar flower)
*Dahlberg daisy
Dianthus barbatus (Sweet
  William)
Dianthus chinensis
  (China pinks)
Gazania
Livingstone daisy

*Nasturtium
Phlox
*Polygonum capitatum
  (Knotweed)
*Portulaca
*Sanvitalia (Creeping
  zinnia)
*Vinca
*Zinnia angustifolia

'Fordhook Finest' annual phlox makes a spectacular, flowering ground cover for cool, sunny locations.

Annuals for Moist Soils

No flowering annual can tolerate constantly wet roots like waterlilies and other "aquatic" plants. Some can be grown in moist soil such as at the edge of ponds, lakes and stream banks. The best are marked with an asterisk.

Cleome (Spider plant)
Euphorbia marginata
  (Snow-on-the-mountain)
*Forget-me-not
*Mignonette
Mimulus (Monkey flower)

Nasturtium
*Primula
Ricinus (Castor bean
  plant)
Vinca
Viola

Annuals for Indoors

Any flowering annual suited for growth indoors in a greenhouse or sunroom is known as a *pot plant.* Some do well only in a sheltered indoor environment. Others grow well outdoors and indoors. When fall frost dates approach, it's possible to dig up some of your outdoor plants and transfer them to pots for flowers indoors. It may take a little grooming to make them presentable, but it is usually worth it. Plants marked with an asterisk below can be treated this way. To prepare them for an extended life indoors, follow this step-by-step procedure.

1. Select bushy, compact plants. These can be dug before frost, placed in pots, trimmed a bit and taken indoors.
2. If plants are tall and straggly, you can often take *stem cuttings.* This is possible with impatiens, coleus, geraniums and wax begonias. Using a sharp knife, remove a non-flowering shoot with 6 inches of stem. Dip the base in rooting hormone and plant in moist potting soil.
3. You can revive straggly plants for indoor flowering—especially petunias and wax begonias—by pruning away top growth to within 3 inches of stem. Prune roots so you have a rootball that will fit comfortably into a 5-inch pot. Add about 1 inch of new potting soil, surrounding the original rootball. Water and fertilize every 2 weeks with liquid house-plant fertilizer.

*Begonia, Wax
*Browallia
Calceolaria
Calendula
Candytuft
Carnation
*Chrysanthemum
Cineraria
*Coleus
*Cuphea
Felicia
Forget-me-not
*Geranium
Gerbera
Heliotrope
*Impatiens
*Lobelia
Marigold

Mesembryanthemum
  (Livingstone daisies)
*Nasturtium
Pansy
*Pepper, Ornamental
*Petunia
Primula
Salpiglossis
Salvia
Schizanthus
Snapdragon
*Solanum, Ornamental
Stocks
*Thunbergia
*Torenia
*Vinca
*Viola

Annuals for Fragrance

An unfortunate side effect of plant breeding has been the loss of fragrance in many modern varieties. Modern sweet peas, for example, are fragrant but do not have the strong fragrance of old-fashion varieties. To correct the situation, some seedsmen now offer special collections of old-fashion varieties noted for intense fragrance.

Although sweet peas are the most popular flowers grown for fragrance, carnations, mignonette, sweet William and stocks are other favorites. Strongly fragrant annuals are noted with an asterisk.

Brachycome (Swan River
  daisy)
*Carnation
Four o'clock
*Heliotrope
*Mignonette
Nasturtium
Nicotiana
*Night-blooming stocks

Petunia
Primula
Siberian wallflower
Snapdragon
*Stocks
Sweet alyssum
*Sweet pea
Sweet sultan
*Sweet William

Annual Vines

Climbing plants are often needed to decorate a bare wall. If surfaces are smooth, a trellis may be necessary for vines to climb. Vines are also popular for covering fences—especially chain-link and split-rail—or to cover unsightly utility poles. Those with an asterisk in the following list produce thick foliage cover, sufficient to create a screen for privacy. Morning glories are the most popular, all-purpose, flowering vine.

Canary creeper
*Cypress vine
Geranium (Vining, ivy-leaf)
*Gourds, Ornamental
Hyacinth bean
*Moonflower
*Morning glory
Nasturtium (Tall kinds)
Sweet pea
*Thunbergia (Black-eyed Susan vine)

'Heavenly Blue' Morning glory is North America's most popular flowering vine.

Annuals For Dried Arrangements

Dried-flower arrangements can be expensive to buy in flower shops and gift stores. Quality-made arrangements retain their colors for years.

Using special commercial drying agents such as silica gel, it's possible to dry any flowering annual. In addition, some plants can be preserved simply by *air drying,* hanging them upside down in bunches in a cool, dry, dark place. These have papery petals and are called *everlasting* flowers. The most popular are strawflowers.

To preserve flowers by using a drying agent, follow these steps:

1. Cut flowers on a dry, sunny day when they are in peak bloom. Avoid flowers that are wilted or blemished.
2. Exclude light during drying process because it fades petal colors quickly.
3. Place flowers face down in deep bowl filled with *drying agent.* A drying agent can be any dry, absorbent powder, but silica gel works best. Flowers on spikes can be placed horizontally. Cover flowers with more drying agent, filling in all contours until flower is completely covered.
4. How long to dry depends on the variety. Usually the process is complete in 4 to 6 days. Depth of color and natural petal formation depends on how fast moisture is removed.

Pressed Flowers—Making floral prints with pressed flowers is also fun. Place flowers between pages of blotting paper. Insert them in a flower press or between the pages of a heavy book. Leave there for up to 7 days until dry. Flowers with flat faces such as violas, pansies, daisies and calliopsis are good subjects. Gently lift dried flowers from blotting paper and arrange them on cards for framing. Stick them in place with glue.

Flowers marked with an asterisk can be air-dried. Others require use of a drying agent.

Aster
*Bells of Ireland
Blue-lace flower
Calendula
*Celosia, Crested
*Chinese lantern
Chrysanthemum
Cornflower
Cosmos
Dahlia
Daisy, Shasta
*Globe amaranth
Gloriosa daisy
*Gourds, Ornamental
*Grasses, Ornamental
Gypsophila
Larkspur
Marigold
Pansy
*Statice
*Star flower (Scabiosa stellata)
*Strawflowers (Helichrysum)
Sweet sultan
Tahoka daisy

Strawflowers are the most popular annuals for dried arrangements.

3

Containers and Small Spaces

Plant breeders have recognized the great appeal of container gardening. Many varieties of flowering annuals specially suited to container culture have been developed. "Cascade" petunias and cascade lobelias are popular annuals because of their beauty in hanging baskets, tubs and window boxes.

Many gardeners grow annuals in containers because they have little garden space. Others with acres of gardening room enjoy having colorful container plantings close to the house—on decks, patios, terraces and in entryways.

CONTAINER CHOICES

A large assortment of containers is available at garden centers. But part of the fun of container gardening is hunting for offbeat pots, tubs and other containers at junk shops, auctions and garage sales.

Be sure the mature size of the plant is in scale with the size of the container. Annuals that grow to 10 inches high will look good in an 8-inch pot. But if plants grow to 3 feet high at maturity, they will look tall and gangly. Most popular annuals are available in dwarf and full-size varieties. Use the mature heights listed in the Gallery of Garden Annuals, pages 59 to 157, as a guide to matching plants with pots.

When choosing containers for your flowering annuals, keep in mind the two conditions that often cause failure with container gardening—*rapid moisture loss* and *overheating*. The more insulation against heat and cold, the longer the flowering display. A container with a double wall has better insulation than one with a single wall. If you make your own containers out of wood, it is a good idea to construct double walls. Air space between the two walls supplies insulation.

Moisture loss is avoided by choosing a roomy container in relation to size of the plants, and by watering regularly. A soil mix that drains well yet *retains* moisture in the root zone long enough for roots to absorb it is important.

Overheating of the container soil, which causes root damage, can be avoided by choosing the right kind of container. Wood and clay containers are best because they insulate the soil, helping to keep it cool. Steel and plastic are least desirable because they offer little insulation and overheat quickly.

All containers—wood, plastic, clay, ceramic or steel—should have drainage holes in the bottom. Place stones, screens or pieces of broken clay pot over drainage holes to keep soil mix from being washed out with waterings. Window boxes used as floor units around patio areas or on balconies should have trays or pans placed under them to collect water. Otherwise water will run out of pots to spill on your neighbor's patio below.

If it is not possible to punch holes, such as with steel cauldrons and certain window-box containers, create a drainage area within the container. Line the bottom with several inches of horticultural charcoal or volcanic rock.

Left: 'Rose Cloud' grandiflora petunias create spectacular display in raised redwood container. Above: 'Futura' impatiens planted in an old wheelbarrow add interest and whimsy to this small space.

Wooden barrels and tubs make excellent planters. They not only have a natural appearance, they are well insulated. Heartwood of redwood and red cedar resist rot and last longer than other woods. It is still best to line them with a sheet of plastic such as a garbage bag to prevent rot.

A coat of asphalt emulsion can also be used as a rot-resistant barrier. Raise wooden containers several inches above ground to prevent the base from rotting.

Whiskey half-barrels make particularly good planters. These can be purchased cut in half, sometimes fitted with rope handles, and with drainage holes already drilled. If you use a plastic liner be sure plastic has holes punched to correspond with the barrel's drainage holes.

Unglazed clay pots and concrete urns generally make excellent planters. Because the containers are porous, water, air and carbon dioxide move through the sides of the container. Because moisture evaporates through the sides of the pot, more-frequent watering is required.

A particularly attractive clay container is the strawberry pot. It is shaped like a small barrel with pockets around the sides for holding plants.

Plastic pots are prone to overheating. Glazed ceramic pots do not heat up as rapidly as plastic. Because the sides of pots are sealed, evaporation of moisture and movement of air in container soil is restricted. Some plastic containers have a liner that creates a humid air space between potting soil and plastic pot. These are better than regular plastic pots.

Steel cauldrons and other metal containers are prone to overheating but are popular for ornamental reasons. These are best used in areas out of intense sun, planted with shade-loving plants. Few steel containers have drainage holes. Be sure to add drainage material.

Wire baskets lined with sphagnum moss are readily available from garden-supply centers. These hanging baskets make striking displays in entryways and on patios—anywhere plants can be seen close-up.

Exposure to wind and sun is a problem, causing dehydration and overheating. If sphagnum moss is kept moist, it helps create a humid air space around the root zone.

Plants that drape and trail are naturals for hanging baskets. Plants that do not have a natural, cascading effect can be used by planting them around the sides of basket through the moss. Pansies and petunias are especially attractive planted this way.

Baskets should be at least 9 inches in diameter, but bigger is better—up to 16 inches. To fill a wire basket, place it on a flower pot or bucket to hold it in place. Line bottom and sides with moistened sphagnum moss to a thickness of 1 inch. This creates a planting nest. Fill center area of basket with potting soil. Or make a mix of equal parts peat, sifted garden topsoil and sand. Place plants in position. Create planting holes in the side by poking holes through moss with a pencil or other sharp instrument. Water plants daily. Feed with diluted liquid fertilizer at least once a week when you water.

SOIL FOR CONTAINERS
Container soil should provide plants with three primary functions: *adequate anchorage, moisture- and nutrient-holding capacity* and *drainage*. Brands of specially formulated soilless mixes

Wooden window boxes serve as planters for blue lobelia and white alyssum. These two annuals are among the best for a cascading effect.

are available from garden centers. They are called *soilless* because they do not contain garden soil. They are made up of materials such as peat moss, ground bark and other organic products. Usually materials are sterilized and fertilizer and trace elements are added to the mix.

Two ingredients commonly included in potting soils are *vermiculite*—lightweight, expanded mica, and *perlite*—porous, volcanic rock. Both are granular materials capable of holding many times their own weight in moisture. Because of their structure they also add valuable air space to the mix.

Although these mixes can be used as-is from the bag, they are expensive. In some instances they are too light and plants can be toppled by gusts of wind. Like many gardeners, I prefer to add some garden loam to the mix. This gives plants better anchorage and reduces evaporation of moisture. It also makes the mixes go further.

Be aware that by adding garden loam the mix is no longer sterile. In addition, soil drainage is reduced. Consider the plant's requirements for soil drainage and water requirements before adding garden loam. Amount of loam to add depends on its condition, but in most situations 1/3 loam to 2/3 soilless mix is a good ratio.

MAKING YOUR OWN SOIL MIX

The most popular container mixes are available in two basic formulations. One has been developed for the East, where peat moss is available and relatively inexpensive. The other is more common in the South and West, where ground pine, fir bark or redwood sawdust is more available.

Cornell Mixes—for the East: After many years of research, Cornell University developed several lightweight soil mixes, primarily for professional growers. Many planter mixes available to gardeners today are based on the Cornell formula. A typical Cornell mix contains by volume:

• 1/2 sphagnum peat moss, coarse
• 1/2 vermiculite No. 2, 3 or 4 size
• Add *chelated* micronutrients to the water used for moistening the mix. Micronutrients contain elements needed in trace amounts by plants. Lightly moisten ingredients and mix thoroughly. It helps if water is warm. Allow to stand in a pile for 24 to 48

Wood half-barrels make excellent containers for annuals. These are 'Showboat' triploid hybrid marigolds.

Hanging baskets and tubs filled with grandiflora petunias decorate entrance to swimming-pool bathhouse.

hours so the dry peat will soak up moisture. To a cubic yard add:

• 5 pounds ground limestone, preferably *dolomitic lime,* which contains both calcium and magnesium
• 2 pounds single superphosphate fertilizer
• 1 pound calcium nitrate or 1/2 pound ammonium-nitrate fertilizer

U.C. Mixes—for the South and West: The University of California developed this family of mixes for growers in the West, primarily for containers. A typical U.C. mix contains by volume:

• 1/4 small particles of fir or pine bark—1/2 inch or less diameter.
• 1/2 aged or composted redwood sawdust, or "forest compost"—a sawmill mix of fine and coarse sawdust composted with a little nitrogen fertilizer. Or pulverized pine bark.
• 1/8 coarse sphagnum peat moss
• 1/8 graded, 30-mesh, fine, sharp sand. Do not use sand from beaches. Omit sand or substitute perlite if weight of mix will be a problem.
• To a cubic yard of the above, add chelated micronutrients and the same starter ingredients as for the Cornell mix.

Mixing Tips—For small lots, keep in mind that a *cubic foot* fills about 7 to 10 1-gallon cans. Count on about a 15% to 20% loss of volume when you mix ingredients. The small particles simply fill in between the larger ones.

To keep the soil mix sterile, blend materials on a plastic sheet or concrete pad that has been washed with a solution of 1 part bleach and 10 parts water. Use clean, sterile tools for mixing. To mix thoroughly, shovel ingredients into cone-shape piles. Drop material on top of pile so it cascades evenly down sides of cone. Build cone three times to ensure a complete mix. Store unused mix in plastic garbage cans or heavy-duty plastic bags to prevent contamination.

Moisten soil mix before adding it to container so it is thoroughly saturated. Dry potting soil is difficult to moisten after it's in the container. Don't rely on available fertilizer to last through the season. After plants begin to flower, feed regularly with diluted liquid fertilizer every 2 weeks.

WATERING

Watering may be necessary every day, depending on the size of the container. Test for soil moisture by taking a pinch of topsoil and rubbing it between your fingers. Hanging-basket plants, because they are more exposed than container plants to heat and wind, are especially susceptible to drying out. They may need watering as often as three times a day to keep plants from wilting.

Viterra Hydrogel is a product that can be added to soil mixes to prevent rapid drying out and dehydration. It is a granular material that is capable of absorbing up to 20 times its own weight in moisture. This product is useful when added to hanging-basket soils and seed flats, which tend to dry out rapidly.

Drip-irrigation systems are well adapted to container gardening. Systems with "spaghetti" hoses work well. These have small, numerous hoses projecting from a main hose. Each small hose supplies water to individual containers or hanging baskets. Emitters at the end of each small tube supply water slowly to soil around root area.

FERTILIZING CONTAINER PLANTS

Most annuals in containers require regular amounts of fertilizer. Nutrients, especially nitrogen, are continually being washed out of the soil. A timed-release fertilizer, see page 32, distributes plant nutrients for an extended period. But you will probably have better results by adding a diluted liquid fertilizer about once a week when you water. Plant foods designed to be mixed with water can be purchased in concentrated form as liquid or crystals.

Premium-quality soil mixes are fortified with starter fertilizer and minor elements such as iron. If you use such mixes, do not feed plants for 3 to 4 weeks after seeding or transplanting. If you feed right away, the extra dose could injure your plants.

RAISED PLANTING BEDS

Raised beds are planting areas elevated above the normal soil level. They

Long-handle watering wand makes it easy to water hanging baskets. These are 'Grande' and 'Twinkles' impatiens.

help create a neat, tidy appearance in the home landscape. Many are bordered by wood, brick or stone. Because they are above ground level, the soil warms faster in spring and drainage is improved. Soil depth is increased, providing extra room for root growth.

Heartwood of redwood and red cedar are good materials for building raised beds. Sturdy railroad ties are popular for a rustic appearance. For long raised beds, telephone poles laid on their sides work well. These can be island beds or butted against a fence or wall.

The width of a raised bed should not be more than 6 feet. This represents the distance a person can comfortably reach with his hands from either side of the bed. If beds are butted against a wall, width should be reduced to 3 feet or less.

VERTICAL GARDENS
A number of commercially available planters called high-rise gardens or wall gardens allow you to grow flowers in a column. You plant in pockets located in the side of vertical plastic panels. It's possible to construct your own tower or wall using galvanized fencing. Set fencing 3 to 5 inches apart and parallel. Line the center with plastic sheeting and fill with potting soil. Punch planting holes through plastic between mesh and insert trailing annuals. Water from the top.

Usually, commercial high-rise gardens have a built-in irrigation system so water penetrates all parts of the soil. In constructing your own high-rise garden, use a length of plastic PVC pipe or similar tubing, with holes drilled to allow distribution of water.

For more information about vertical gardens, write Living Wall Gardens, Curious Research Inc., 2044 Chili Ave., Rochester, NY 14624.

GREENHOUSES
Don't think of a greenhouse as a luxury—it's a gardening tool that can bring you greater success and enjoyment. With a greenhouse you can grow *hundreds* of healthy plants that wouldn't fit on cramped windowsills. You can also be more successful at growing hard-to-start seeds because you can have precise control of temperature, moisture and light.

Also, you can grow flowering container plants year-round. Keep them in the greenhouse or wait until plants reach peak bloom and transfer them indoors to provide colorful table centerpieces. Calceolarias, cinerarias, ornamental peppers, Mexican cigar plants, gerberas and geraniums are a sampling of the flowering annuals that are good subjects as greenhouse container plants.

Important features to consider when buying a greenhouse are quality construction and style. Generally, a free-standing unit will provide better light than a lean-to. Glass, particularly safety glass, allows more light to be transmitted than other coverings. Wood and galvanized steel frames do not have the life span of an aluminum frame.

Hanging baskets, window boxes and pots planted with several kinds of annuals add color to back yard. Plants include pink and red 'Flash' geraniums, pink 'Glamour' begonias, 'Blue Bells' browallia and red 'Fiji' coleus.

4

Soil Preparation

Soil is an important factor for a successful flower garden. Soil anchors plants and supplies them with nutrients and moisture. Because nutrients are absorbed by plant roots in *soluble form*—dissolved by moisture—soil should have good moisture-holding capacity. This is created by air spaces between soil particles. Air is also necessary for plant roots to grow and remain healthy. A good soil allows excess moisture to drain away. Without air in the soil, plant roots suffocate and die.

SOIL TYPES
Garden soil comes in three basic types—*clay, sand* and *loam*—which describe its texture and consistency.
Sandy soil is composed of large mineral particles. It drains quickly and has a tendency to dry out fast. If you squeeze a handful of moist, sandy soil, it crumbles when released. It holds plenty of oxygen. Sandy soil is a good growing medium for most plants because plant roots can penetrate it freely. The drawback of sandy soil is that water and nutrients drain away quickly. Also, sandy soils tend to be alkaline, which many flowering annuals dislike.

You can improve sandy soil by adding lots of *organic matter.* Compost, leaf mold, well-decomposed manure, peat moss and ground-bark products are examples of organic matter commonly used.
Clay soil is difficult to work with. It is composed of small mineral particles that tend to pack tightly together. If you squeeze a handful of moist clay soil it feels slimy and sticky, and compacts into a thick, heavy mass. Clay soil is heavy and cold in spring and can bake into a hard crust in summer. It drains slowly, and acts as a barrier to plant roots. Water tends to form puddles on its surface.

You can improve clay soil by adding organic matter—the same as for sandy soil. Sometimes the addition of sand is recommended for clay soils, but sand alone will not improve clay soil without also adding organic matter.
Loam soil is the best garden soil. It contains proportionate amounts of sand, clay and rock particles and usually lots of organic matter. Loam soil retains moisture and nutrients in the root zone, yet drains well. If you squeeze a handful, it forms a loosely packed ball in your hand.

TESTING YOUR SOIL
In addition to its physical makeup, soil can be classified as *acid, alkaline* or *neutral,* referring to its pH content. Extremes of high acidity or high alkalinity are harmful to plants.

Generally, acid soils are concentrated in forested areas of the country. Alkaline soils predominate in low-rainfall regions. In either case, materials can be added to adjust the pH. Usually, lime is added to decrease soil acidity. Sulfur or peat moss is added to decrease soil alkalinity.

Left: Thorough soil preparation and use of an organic mulch are greatly responsible for the healthy growth of these begonias. Above: A close look at composted ground bark, a commonly used soil amendment. Adding organic matter such as this to the soil helps increase retention of water and nutrients in the root zone of plants.

There are many kinds of soil, generally due to differences in mineral content and organic matter. These are the three basic types. Sandy soil at left is composed of large mineral particles. It drains well but is not efficient at holding moisture and nutrients in the root zone. Clay soil at center is composed of small particles. It is dense, has poor drainage and is difficult to work. Loam soil at right has good balance of mineral particles and contains a lot of organic matter. It drains well yet spaces between particles hold moisture and nutrients in root zone.

The pH scale extends from 1 to 14, with extremely high acidity at the low end of the scale and extremely high alkalinity at the high end. A reading of 7.0 is considered *neutral*. A neutral to slightly acid soil is best for most flowering annuals.

In addition to soil pH, it's useful to know the availability of nutrients in your soil, although soil fertility for annuals is not as important as for growing vegetables.

Do-It-Yourself pH Test Kit—This kind of kit is usually inexpensive and available from garden centers and mail-order garden catalogs. It is not as accurate as a laboratory test, but is simple to use and usually reliable. You mix small samples of soil from different parts of your planting area into a test tube, pour in a solution, shake well and allow it to settle. You then compare the color of the solution with a chart provided with the kit to determine the pH range.

Laboratory Soil Test—A laboratory soil test is more precise than a test kit. A technician interprets the test results. It is more expensive. With the exceptions of California and Illinois, all states perform laboratory soil tests for the gardening public. Look in your phone book under "U.S. Government," "Department of Agriculture," "County Agent" or "Cooperative Extension Service" to determine the agency in your state responsible for soil testing. Call and tell them you wish to have your soil tested. For a fee they mail you a package of instructions that contains a pouch for including a sample of your soil. As an option, you can contact the soil-test laboratory directly for information.

If you live in California or Illinois, you must have your soil tested by a private lab. Look in the phone book under "Soil Laboratories" or "Soil Services."

MODIFYING SOIL pH

Acid soils are common in forested areas. Over the years, through composting of woody and other organic materials, soil increases in acidity. High acidity is not good because it chemically "locks up" nutrients in the soil, preventing them from becoming available to plants. The easiest way to adjust acidity to acceptable levels is through application of lime.

Lime is available in several forms. *Ground limestone*, also known as *dolomitic limestone*, is usually recommended. It is high in calcium, a trace element, and its effects are long lasting. Generally, lime is required every 3 years in acid-soil areas, applied at the rate of 5 pounds per 100 square feet. This amount lowers the pH one point.

Other materials that lower soil acidity are wood ashes and oyster shells. Oyster shells are high in lime and phosphorus. Wood ashes are also rich in potash.

Alkaline soils are common in the Southwest. They are usually neutralized by adding sulfur, peat moss or other highly acid organic matter such as leaf mold. Technically, the sulfur oxidizes and becomes sulfuric acid, which acidifies and neutralizes the alkaline compounds. Compost made from decomposed wood products is also used. All of these are normally available from nurseries and garden-supply centers.

Use sulfur carefully to acidify an alkaline soil. Have the soil tested by a soil-testing laboratory if you suspect your soil is alkaline. You will then receive an expert recommendation on amounts of sulfur to use.

Another product that is often recommended for acidifying soil is aluminum sulfate. It is generally applied at the rate of 1-1/4 pounds per 100 square feet in slightly alkaline soils. Be sure to read package directions and follow them precisely to avoid an overdose.

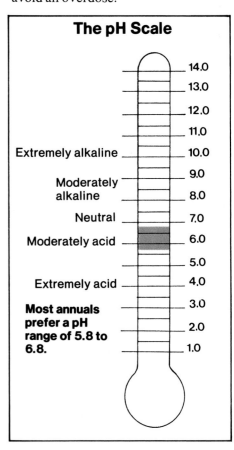

The pH Scale

	14.0
	13.0
	12.0
	11.0
Extremely alkaline	10.0
	9.0
Moderately alkaline	8.0
Neutral	7.0
Moderately acid	6.0
	5.0
Extremely acid	4.0
	3.0
Most annuals prefer a pH range of 5.8 to 6.8.	2.0
	1.0

PREPARING THE SOIL

A soil test is not the answer to all soil problems. Lack of organic matter can make it difficult for plants to make use of available nutrients. Organic matter also encourages beneficial soil microorganisms. If your soil is sandy, organic matter will improve its water- and nutrient-holding capacity. If your soil is clay, it will improve its drainage. Compost, leaf mold, peat moss, decomposed manure and bark products are common sources of organic matter.

As a guide, garden soil should be approximately 1/3 organic matter. Apply 3 to 6 inches of soil amendment over the existing soil. Till or spade all materials thoroughly to a depth of 8 to 12 inches.

The actions of wind, sun and footsteps on a garden lead to soil compaction and dissipation of organic material. For these reasons, it is wise to add soil amendments every year.

Preparing a New Garden—If possible, prepare soil for a new plot in the fall. Fall preparation allows amendments to blend with soil prior to spring planting. Soil preparation in fall also uncovers eggs and larvae of harmful insects.

Fall is the time to adjust the soil pH. If required, spread the recommended amount of lime, peat moss or other neutralizing material evenly over soil. If you don't have the opportunity to prepare your soil in fall, do it in spring as soon as ground is dry and can be worked.

Digging a new plot is much different from preparing an established area, especially if the area you want to plant is covered with lawn or weeds. If your soil is manageable, small gardens can be dug by hand.

The easiest method is to stake out the site you wish to dig. If rains haven't done it for you, thoroughly moisten soil the day before area is to be dug. Don't dig or prepare soil when it is wet or dry—try for that moist, crumbly, in-between stage. Remove squares of sod with a spade and shake valuable topsoil from roots. If there is heavy grass, sod or weeds, remove them first—don't turn them under. Clumps of turf are difficult to break up and restrict planting. Also, some grasses such as bermudagrass can infest your garden if turned under.

In preparing soil for a new site, you may *single dig* or *double dig*. Single digging is simply turning over soil to a depth of about 12 inches—length of your spade blade. You then work that 12 inches of soil with a garden fork and rake to remove rocks, clods and other debris.

Double digging is more work, but plants with deep root systems respond to additional depth of loose, fertile soil. First, dig a trench in soil to the depth of your spade. Then dig down farther with a garden fork to loosen the soil so you have a double depth of loose soil. Compost can be worked into the bottom level for more soil improvement.

As you turn over soil, remove weed or grass roots and stones. Keep a sharp eye open for any insect pests such as wireworms and cutworms and remove them by hand. Use a rake to break up clumps of soil. Level site with a rake and clear away debris collected in the prongs. Don't walk on freshly dug soil. Instead, lay down wooden planks and walk over them.

COMPOST

Soil in flower beds is constantly being depleted of plant nutrients and is compacted by the action of weather and footprints. Eventually, this adversely affects the growth of plants. One of the best ways to combat loss of nutrients and maintain good soil texture is to add *compost*—the dark, fluffy material produced from decayed organic wastes.

I use compost as a mulch to prevent weed growth. It also conserves moisture and insulates soil. As it decomposes, compost adds organic matter to soil. This encourages earthworms, which further enrich the soil with their castings.

Garden and kitchen refuse is excellent as material for compost. Remains of kitchen peelings, lawn clippings and weeds are commonly used. Tough stems, leaves and hedge prunings should be shredded before adding to the compost heap. In addition to your own garden and kitchen scraps, large quantities of waste material can be obtained from outside sources. One of the best is animal manure from a stable or dairy.

A key to making a good compost is maintaining a balance between "green" material and "dead" material. Technically, this is a *carbon* (dead) to *nitrogen* (green) ratio. Under natural conditions, this ratio is approximately 12 to 1.

There is a simple way to attain this balance in your backyard compost pile. When you add a batch of grass clippings, fresh garden refuse or other green material, throw in a handful or two or sawdust—dead material. Some gardeners keep the sawdust in a can near the compost pile for ease of use.

The finished compost is especially useful as mulch. It will eventually decompose, improving the soil with its organic matter.

Leaf mold is one of the best soil amendments. Instead of throwing leaves away, make a simple container for them out of chicken wire. Use stakes for supports. Shred leaves with a lawn mower and they decompose faster. For more on composting, see text above.

FERTILIZER

Many annuals perform well with little fertilizer. Rock-garden favorites such as dianthus, alyssum, portulaca and African daisies grow in dry walls with minimal available nutrients. Other annuals are heavy feeders. They require a regular fertilizing schedule to encourage them to bloom abundantly and continually. These include delphiniums, begonias, dahlias, geraniums, pansies, petunias and sweet peas.

Fertilizers are available in *natural forms*, such as animal manures and compost. And they are available in *synthetic form*, made from chemicals. Both contain varying amounts of the three major plant nutrients: *nitrogen, phosphorus* and *potassium (potash)*, abbreviated to N-P-K.

The amount of nutrients in a package of fertilizer is always shown as a percentage of N-P-K, such as 5-10-10. This means the fertilizer is approximately 5% nitrogen, 10% phosphorus and 10% potassium. The remainder is filler, used as a distributing agent. As a general rule, flowering plants prefer a 1-2-2 ratio of plant nutrients, such as 5-10-10 or 10-20-20. Flowering annuals should not receive excessive nitrogen. Too much encourages foliage growth, sometimes at the expense of flower production.

Nitrogen is available in synthetic and natural forms. Synthetic nitrogen, nitrogen manufactured from chemicals, comes as either *fast release*—water soluble—or *slow release*—water insoluble. Fast release provides a quick effect, but soon drains from the soil. Fast-release nitrogen fertilizers can *burn* plants unless mixed into soil. Carnations and dianthus are particularly susceptible to nitrogen burn.

Slow release is more efficient. Burning does not occur because the fertilizer is almost water insoluble, so it releases into the soil slowly. One application per season is usually sufficient.

Read the product label to find out if your nitrogen is fast or slow release. Although nitrogen is the most important nutrient to have as slow release, because it can disappear so quickly, some fertilizers also control the release of phosphorus and potassium.

Natural nitrogen is available as decayed living matter such as animal manure and compost. Natural nitrogen is released slowly. If the material is thoroughly decomposed, there is no risk of burning.

Phosphorus—This is *the* most important nutrient for flowering annuals, because phosphorus specifically promotes flowering and subsequent seed production. It also encourages strong root development. The most common natural source of phosphorus is *bone meal*. Phosphoric acid and superphosphate are also used. Gardeners who win blue ribbons at flower shows for the most beautiful sweet peas, largest dahlias and tallest delphiniums usually have improved their soil with bone meal or other phosphorus source.

Potassium—The most common source of natural potassium is wood ashes. It is also included in general-purpose fertilizers. It is important for healthy annuals, acting like a vitamin tablet, promoting disease resistance and vigor.

Minor Elements—Soils kept in good condition by the addition of compost or other humus-rich products have sufficient quantities of elements such as calcium, iron and boron. These are needed by plants in small amounts.

Occasionally, some soils suffer deficiencies of certain minor elements.

The most common element to be deficient is iron. Iron deficiency shows itself as *chlorosis*. Leaves turn yellow, but veins remain green. This is a common problem in the Southwest. An excess of lime can also cause iron deficiency. It can usually be corrected by adding organic matter to soil. A faster method is to spray young leaves with iron in *chelated* form. Be sure to follow product label directions carefully.

NATURAL OR CHEMICAL FERTILIZER?

Natural fertilizers are composed of *organic* materials such as animal manure, bone meal and blood meal. Chemical fertilizers are made of *inorganic* or artificial materials. Each has advantages and disadvantages.

Chemical fertilizers are often termed *general-purpose fertilizers*. They are commonly available in garden centers. They increase soil fertility, but because they contain no organic matter, they do not improve the water and nutrient-holding capacity of the soil. This is discussed in detail on page 29.

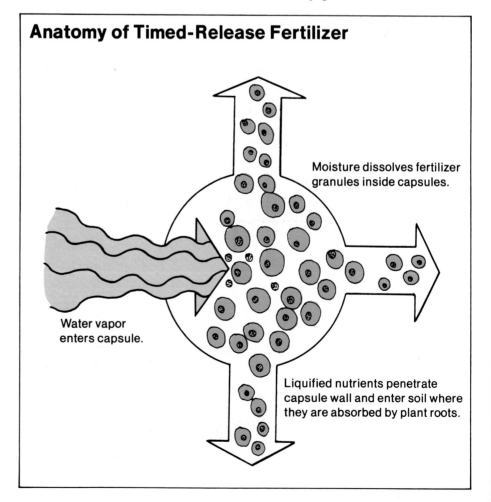

Anatomy of Timed-Release Fertilizer

Moisture dissolves fertilizer granules inside capsules.

Water vapor enters capsule.

Liquified nutrients penetrate capsule wall and enter soil where they are absorbed by plant roots.

Iron chlorosis on geranium leaf is identified by light-yellow color with darker-green veins. Correct by adjusting soil pH or add iron to soil.

Some natural fertilizers are high in nitrogen but low in phosphorus and potassium. For example, blood meal has an analysis of 13-2-1. Other natural fertilizers are available in convenient packages from garden centers. These generally rely on a mixture of blood meal, cottonseed meal and bone meal for their high nutrient content.

Animal manures are natural fertilizers. They are composed of varying degrees of nutrients. For example, poultry manure is usually higher in nitrogen than cow or horse manure. What the animal has been fed, age of manure and moisture content are all factors. Animal manures are sometimes slow to supply nutrients, and large quantities are needed to supply plants with adequate nutrient levels.

Don't put fresh manure directly in the garden—allow it to compost first. It can burn plants because of its high ammonia content. If you pick up manure from a stable or farm, look for manure from a year-old heap. If decomposed, it should have consistency of powdery soil.

Timed-Release Fertilizers—These are chemical fertilizers that release nutrients at a rate the plant can use efficiently. Many kinds are available. Some release only nitrogen at a slow rate and are identified as water-insoluble nitrogen. If you want a timed-release fertilizer that contains the three basic nutrients (N-P-K), check the label before you buy.

DRY OR LIQUID FERTILIZER?

Most flower fertilizers—chemical or organic—are sold in dry, granular form. They are sprinkled on soil according to rates given on the package before planting and raked into upper soil surface. Some of these dry granular fertilizers are *fast release.* They begin to work as soon as soil moisture dissolves them. To avoid burning, apply about 10 days prior to planting. These fast-acting fertilizers are quickly washed from soil and booster feeds may be necessary to maintain continual bloom.

Slow-release or *timed-release* fertilizers are also available in dry, granular form. They release plant nutrients slowly and can be added to soil at time of planting. Usually one application will keep plants healthy all season.

Liquid-feed fertilizers, also called *soluble* fertilizers, are sold in powder form or as liquid concentrate. Fertilizer is mixed with specified amount of water and applied to soil with watering can or sprayer. When applied according to label directions, there is little risk of fertilizer burn.

Some liquid fertilizers can be applied to leaf surfaces as a *foliar feed.* However, leaves are not as efficient as roots in absorbing nutrients. Foliar feeding is useful as a *booster,* applied at key times during the season.

BACTERIAL FERTILIZERS

Certain kinds of soil organisms are able to manufacture plant nutrients when present in soil. They work to restore exhausted soils to a naturally fertile condition. They feed plants, dissolve harmful salts, maintain an optimum soil pH and aerate soil.

These bacterial fertilizers have a low nutrient analysis—3-4-4 is typical. However, this is misleading. Once the microorganisms are added to the soil, they begin manufacturing nutrients much higher than the initial analysis stated on the label.

The most widely available bacterial fertilizer is Restore. Information is available from Judd Ringer Research, 6860 Flying Cloud Drive, Eden Prairie, MN 55344.

SAMPLE FERTILIZER SCHEDULE

You have several alternatives when it comes to providing your flower garden with nutrients. It is a good idea to experiment to see which method provides best results under your conditions.

Each form of fertilizer has advantages and disadvantages: *Timed-release fertilizers* are convenient and labor saving. They are more expensive than other fertilizers and require moisture before they begin to work. *Fast-release liquid fertilizers* provide nutrients to plants immediately but they require the use of a sprayer and frequent applications. *Fast-release granular fertilizers* are convenient and generally inexpensive. But they, too, require moisture before they can begin to work. They are washed from soil quickly. Applying booster applications of granular fertilizer is tedious. *Animal manure* and *compost* can provide nutrients as well as organic matter to the soil, but nutrient content is difficult to determine.

A combination of systems has worked best for me. The following is my fertilizer schedule for flowering annuals:

1. Add compost to soil in fall or winter to improve soil structure and provide basic nutrients. Or add compost to the soil in spring, prior to planting.
2. Apply granular, packaged general-purpose fertilizer such as 5-10-10 to the soil 7 to 10 days before planting. Brands of fertilizers vary, so read label directions for rate of application.
3. When plants begin to flower, apply booster feed in diluted liquid form. Spray on leaves and at the base of plants at twice-weekly intervals.

5

Seed Starting and Planting

Seeds of annuals come in a variety of shapes and sizes. For example, it takes 1,500,000 begonia seeds to equal 1 ounce. Seeds are so tiny they resemble dust particles. It seems impossible that something as beautiful as a begonia could grow from such tiny, insignificant specks. On the other side of the scale, an ounce of nasturtiums requires only about 175 seeds. They are as large as peas and easy to handle.

The many kinds of annuals represent a wide variety of methods for starting seeds and planting, with no single system suitable for all plants.

Some seeds, like begonias, need light to germinate. They should be *surface-sown*—barely pressed into the soil surface—and not covered. Nasturtiums, however, represent a large group of seeds that require total darkness for germination. They should be covered with soil to approximately three times their width.

Germination—the process of seeds sprouting roots and leaves—is stimulated by various conditions, depending on the requirements of individual varieties. All seeds need adequate *moisture,* suitable *temperature* and *air* (oxygen). Moisture is necessary to soften the seed coat and allow the *embryo*—the undeveloped plant—to grow. Correct temperature is necessary to break dormancy. Air is essential for seeds and seedlings to live. If the soil is poorly drained or compacted, seeds will die from suffocation.

SEEDS OR TRANSPLANT?
The tendency is to use transplants for most plantings of annuals. You can grow transplants from seeds or buy them from a garden center ready to plant. Even annuals that generally transplant poorly—zinnias for example—are being transplanted. Certain methods of growing transplants, such as peat pots and peat pellets, reduce root disturbance and transplant shock.

Large-area plantings devoted to naturalizing or ground covers are usually planted from seeds sown directly in place. In these instances, transplanting seedlings is too time-consuming or expensive.

Even though transplants are readily available from garden centers as bedding plants, there are many good reasons to start your own from seeds. Selection of bedding plants is limited, and most annuals are not offered for sale until plants are in bloom. This helps sell them more quickly. But blooming transplants generally do not perform as well and as long as plants that are transplanted "green," before flowering. See Transplanting Tips, page 44.

STANDARD OR HYBRID?
Annuals are available in *standard* and

Left: Seedlings of flowering annuals in greenhouse were started from seeds. Flats are divided into eight compartments each. When seedlings are large enough to handle, they are transferred to individual pots to grow to transplant size. Above: Geranium transplants in a "six-pack" are ready for planting.

hybrid forms. Hybrids cost more, or fewer seeds are included in each packet compared to standards. Standard varieties are sometimes called *open pollinated* because they are mass-produced through pollination by bees and wind. Hybrids require careful, *controlled pollination*—tedious hand pollination between selected parent plants. These plants are usually different species that are sexually compatible.

The word hybrid comes from the Latin word, *hybrida,* meaning the offspring of a wild boar and a domestic sow. A more familiar animal hybrid is the mule—a cross between a jackass, male donkey, and a mare—female horse. The mule is stronger and more useful than either parent. As with most hybrids, the mule is sterile and cannot reproduce itself. To create more mules the original cross must be repeated.

Seeds of plant hybrids are produced in a similar way. To make more seeds you must make the original cross. That's why you should not save seeds from hybrid flowers—the seeds will either be sterile or produce inferior plants.

If you have any doubts about the superiority of hybrids over standard varieties, visit a trial garden and compare performances. Hybrid wax begonias or triploid hybrid marigolds are good examples. A hybrid not only has more flowers per plant, it has stamina to bloom all season right up to fall frost.

The Making of a Hybrid—The main advantage of a hybrid is its vigor, a quality called *heterosis.* This results in increased size, improved disease resistance, earliness, heat or cold tolerance and other desirable characteristics.

Hybrid flowers are usually grown in greenhouses so that insects can be kept away from flowers. Insects may introduce pollen from other plants, which can ruin a hybrid cross. The sequence of photographs at right show the making of a *triploid* hybrid marigold—a plant made by crossing a French marigold, the male parent, with an American marigold, the female parent. A triploid has three sets of chromosomes and outstanding vigor.

Picture 1 shows the male parent, French marigold *Tagetes patula.* Pollen from this flower is crossed with

The Making of a Hybrid

1. Male parent, a French marigold, is crossed with female parent shown at right.

2. Female parent, an American marigold, is male-sterile and has only female parts. It cannot pollinate itself, which would ruin cross.

3. After cross, mature seeds form under petals. Seeds are harvested and cleaned before being packaged for sale.

4. Result of the cross is triploid hybrid 'Copper Canyon'. These hybrids are sterile and unable to set viable seeds, but plants bloom profusely.

the female parent. Picture 2 shows the female parent, American marigold *Tagetes erecta*. The flower has no outer petals because it is "male sterile." Possessing only female parts, it cannot pollinate itself to ruin the cross. In creating other hybrids, the male parts must be removed by hand. Occasionally, male-sterile flowers such as these are found as mutations, helping make the hybridizer's job much easier.

Picture 3 shows the mature seeds formed under the faded petals of the female parent. Seeds are harvested, dried and cleaned to remove chaff and placed into seed packets.

Picture 4 shows the resulting triploid hybrid variety 'Copper Canyon' in full flower. Triploid hybrids are sterile and unable to set viable seeds. They put all their energy into flower production, blooming early and continually until fall frost.

SEED PACKETS, PELLETS AND TAPES

New ways to plant seeds, such as seed pellets and seed tapes, are introduced frequently. But no one has come up with a more efficient system than the traditional seed packet.

Seed tapes are said to make thinning easier for small-seeded flowers like petunias and pansies. Tapes have seeds bound into transparent biodegradable material, pre-spaced at regular intervals. The material dissolves quickly after it comes into contact with moisture. Seed tapes are more expensive than conventional seed packets and you get fewer seeds. If germination is not high, you will end up with gaps in your plantings.

Pelleted seeds are the least gimmicky of the alternative seed-sowing systems. The pellet is a harmless clay coating around small seeds that makes them larger and easier to handle when planting. Coating dissolves on contact with moisture, and seeds germinate unhindered.

The biggest boon in recent years has been the introduction of foil packaging, creating a moisture-proof packet. Moisture deteriorates seeds quickly, and traditional paper packets offer little protection. Seeds lose viability quickly during periods of high humidity. Moisture-proof packets keep seeds in harvest-fresh condition until seal is broken.

When you buy seeds at the nursery or they arrive in the mail from a mail-order catalog, store them in a cool, dry place indoors until it is time to plant.

SEED RACK OR MAIL ORDER?

Flower seeds are readily available in seed racks at retail outlets, in nurseries, home centers and supermarkets. Or you can order them by mail through seed catalogs. Rack displays in local stores have the advantage of convenience. It's easy to visit your local store and make selections, using the color pictures and descriptions on the seed packet as a guide. But shopping the rack has its shortcomings. Selections are usually limited to only popular kinds of annuals, with an emphasis on standard, well-established varieties rather than hybrids. And if you delay making your purchases late in the season you may end up shopping from a picked-over rack.

Ordering by mail is more bother, and it takes time to receive your order. But you do have the advantage of a much larger selection, with many new varieties and hybrids. If you plan ahead, the delay in receiving your seeds should not make a difference to your planting schedule.

Some of the best flower-seed catalogs available to gardeners in the United States and Canada are listed on page 38. Some of these are European companies, but their catalog and seeds are available to you. You'll receive a special sheet giving instructions on how to order. These foreign catalogs generally offer large selections, with emphasis on certain classes of annuals that are not commonly found in North-American catalogs.

SAVING YOUR OWN SEEDS

Most flowering annuals will set seeds after flowering. Unless the plants are hybrids, seeds can be saved to produce beautiful flowering displays the following year. Seeds saved from *F-1 hybrids*—first generation hybrids—produce inferior results the second season.

If you want to save seeds, take some precautions to ensure success. To maintain viability, seeds should be kept *cool* and *dry*. Place seeds in packets in a wide-mouth jar that can be sealed with a tight-fitting lid. Put 2 heaping tablespoons of powdered milk in a paper envelope and place inside jar. Seal jar and store in vegetable bin of your refrigerator until you are ready to plant seeds. The powdered milk will absorb moisture from air inside jar, keeping seeds dry. This method should also be used to store seeds left over from purchased packets.

How long seeds last depends on seed type and storage conditions. High temperatures and high humidity deteriorate seeds rapidly. Delphinium seeds are naturally short-lived and germination is usually poor after only 1 year. However, sweet peas can stay viable for several years.

If you don't know the condition of stored seeds, it is a good idea to test their viability before you plant them. Select 10 seeds and lay them on a moist paper towel. Roll up towel and place inside a plastic bag in a warm location. The plastic bag prevents towel from drying out too quickly. After 10 to 14 days, count seeds that have germinated. If 2 out of 10 have sprouted, this indicates 20% germination rate—not good. If 5 out of 10 sprout, this shows 50% germination—acceptable. Keep the germination test results in mind when you sow seeds to compensate for the lower-than-normal germination rate.

Saving seeds from your own flowers for use the following season will not always produce as good a display as buying fresh seeds from the original seed company. Seedsmen maintain the purity of a strain by selecting special stock seed plants. These are usually plants that possess uniformity of height, color and flower size. If a mixture is involved it may contain a special balance of colors. Production fields are usually isolated to prevent cross-pollination from other strains. Also, seedsmen inspect their production fields before plants have a chance to set seeds. If *rogues*—those too tall, too short or wrong color—appear, they are pulled and destroyed.

If you grow a strain of annual where the resulting crop is uneven, the seedsman has probably done a poor job of "roguing." I have seen as much as 1/3 of a crop discarded to maintain quality. Hybrid seeds saved from a home-garden crop can quickly revert to their original wild forms if strict, quality-control methods are not followed.

Mail-Order Seed Catalogs

Agway Inc.
Box 4933
Syracuse, NY 13221
Color catalog with basic selection of annuals. Catalog free.

Applewood Seed Co.
Box 10761, Edgemont Station
Golden, CO 80401
Specialists in seeds for wildflower plantings. Catalog free.

W. Atlee Burpee
300 Park Ave.
Warminster, PA 18974
Extensive selection of annuals, many developed by the company's own plant-breeding program. Burpee also maintains trial gardens for testing and evaluating new varieties, including an All-America trial garden. Catalog free.

Comstock Ferre & Co.
263 Main St.
Wethersfield, CT 06109
Color catalog lists old and new annuals. Company also maintains trial gardens for testing and evaluating new varieties, including an All-America trial garden. Catalog free.

Dominion Seed House
115 Guelph St.
Georgetown, Ontario
Canada L7G 4A2
Good selection of annuals for Canada. Free full-color catalog available to Canadian gardeners only. Dominion maintains trial gardens for evaluating new varieties.

Farmer Seed & Nursery Co.
818 N.W. Fourth St.
Faribault, MN 55021
Good selection of flower seeds. Full-color catalog free.

Henry Field Seed & Nursery Co.
407 Sycamore St.
Shenandoah, IA 51602
Beautiful, full-color catalog offers an extensive listing of annuals. Catalog free.

Gurney Seed & Nursery Co.
Yankton, SD 57079
One of America's largest seed and nursery catalogs. Extensive list of annuals. Catalog free.

Jackson & Perkins
Box 1028
Medford, OR 97501
Beautiful, full-color catalog featuring good selection of annuals. Catalog free.

Joseph Harris Co.
Moreton Farm
Rochester, NY 14624
Excellent listing of annuals, many developed by the company's own breeders. Company maintains trial gardens for testing and evaluating new varieties, including an All-America trial garden. Full-color catalog is free.

The Charles Hart Seed Co.
Main & Hart Streets
Wethersfield, CT 06109
Good selection of annuals. Catalog free.

H.G. Hastings Co.
Box 4274
Atlanta, GA 30302
Assortment of annuals especially suited for Southern gardeners. Full-color catalog free.

Inter-State Nurseries
Hamburg, IA 51640
Full-color catalog features good selection of annuals. Catalog free.

J.W. Jung Seed Co.
Randolph, WI 53956
Full-color catalog features basic selection of annuals. Catalog free.

Johnny's Selected Seeds
Albion, ME 04910
Good selection of annuals for Northeast gardens.

Laval Seeds Inc.
3505 Boul St. Martin
Chomedey Laval
Quebec, Canada H7V 2T3
Quality seed house serving Canadian gardeners. Catalog free.

Orol Ledden & Sons
Center St.
Sewell, NJ 08080
Good selection. Catalog free.

Earl May Seed & Nursery Co.
Shenandoah, IA 51603
Full-color catalog featuring good selection of flowering annuals. Maintains trial gardens for testing and evaluating new varieties, including an All-America trial garden. Catalog free.

McLaughlins Seeds
Box 550
Mead, WA 99021
Flower-seed supplier serving mostly West-Coast gardeners. Catalog free.

Mellingers Inc.
North Lima, OH 44452
Good listing of annuals. Catalog free.

L. L. Olds Seed Co.
2901 Packers Ave.
Madison, WI 53707
Colorful catalog features good selection of quality annuals. Catalog free.

George W. Park Seed Inc.
Greenwood, SC 29647
Flower-seed specialists. Full-color catalog features extensive list of annuals. Company maintains trial gardens for evaluating new varieties, including an All-America trial garden. Catalog free.

W.H. Perron & Co. Ltd.
515 Labelle Blvd.
Chomedey Laval
Quebec, Canada H7V 2T3
Colorful catalog offers an excellent selection of annuals for Canadian gardens. Company maintains extensive trial gardens for evaluating new varieties, including an All-America trial garden. Catalog free.

Seedway Inc.
Hall, NY 14463
Formerly Robson's Seeds. Flowering annuals are especially selected for the Northeast. Full-color catalog free.

R.H. Shumway
628 Cedar St.
Rockford, IL 61101
Full-color catalog offers good selection of annuals, both newly developed and established. Catalog free.

Stokes Seeds Inc.
Box 548
Buffalo, NY 14240
This colorful catalog features an excellent selection of annuals, many that are difficult to obtain elsewhere. Company maintains trial gardens for testing new varieties, including an All-America trial garden. Catalog free. Canadian gardeners should write to: Box 10, St. Catharines, Ontario, Canada. L2R 6R6

Suttons Seeds
Hele Road
Torquay, Devon, England
Suttons does not have a mailing address in the United States or Canada, but they will supply free color catalog upon request. Company maintains trial gardens for evaluating new varieties.

T & T Seeds Ltd.
120 Lombard Ave.
Winnipeg, Manitoba, Canada R3B 3A9
Good selection of annuals for Canadian gardens. Catalog free.

Thompson & Morgan
Box 100
Farmingdale, NJ 07727
Full-color catalog claims to feature the most extensive listing of flower seeds in the world. Established company is headquartered in England, sold seeds to Charles Darwin. Catalog free.

Otis S. Twilley Seed Co.
Box 65
Trevose, PA 19047
Full-color catalog offering an excellent selection of flower seeds. Company maintains trial gardens for testing new varieties, including an All-America trial garden. Catalog free.

Wyatt-Quarles Seed Co.
331 S. Wilmington St.
Raleigh, NC 27602
Good selection of flower seeds for Southern gardeners. Catalog free.

STARTING WITH SEEDS—INDOORS AND OUTDOORS

When growing annuals from seeds, you have two options. Start seeds indoors to gain healthy transplants, or sow seeds directly in the garden. Sometimes you can do both with annuals such as marigolds, asters, zinnias and gloriosa daisies. These plants germinate outdoors readily when sown directly in the garden. And early flowering is possible if seeds are started indoors early in the season.

Sometimes there is a definite advantage to starting seeds indoors, or sowing them directly outdoors. For example, seeds of impatiens, begonias and lobelia are tiny and grow slowly in the seedling stage. They do best grown under controlled conditions indoors. Others, such as poppies, nigella and scarlet flax, don't do well when transplanted. They are best sown directly where you want plants to grow. Another group—polygonum, cornflowers and dahlberg daisies—tolerate crowding and transplanting is tedious. They, too, are best sown directly in the garden. Check the individual descriptions in the Gallery of Garden Annuals, pages 59 to 157.

SEED-STARTING BASICS
If you choose to start seeds indoors, be sure to provide the following conditions necessary for successful germination.

Regular Moisture—One of the biggest problems with growing seeds indoors is maintaining moisture. Seeds grown in small peat pots and soil blocks lose moisture rapidly. If germinating seeds or seedlings are allowed to become dry—even for only a few hours—they will probably wilt and die. Begonias, coleus, nigella, celosias, primulas and stocks are particularly sensitive to drying.

When watering seeds in seed trays, apply water in a fine mist from a mister. Or add water to a tray placed below the seed-starting medium. Pouring water directly on the soil surface disturbs seeds and hinders germination. To prevent rapid moisture loss, enclose trays or pots of newly planted seeds in a clear plastic bag. The bag slows evaporation and keeps the soil moist.

Scarifying—Some seeds have a tough seed coat and require moisture over a period of time to soften it so water can penetrate. *Scarifying* is a technique where the seed coat is chipped or sanded so moisture can penetrate more freely. Use a razor blade to nick a small portion of the seed coat, or use a nail file to cut into the hard coating. Scarifying is most often used on large-seeded annuals such as morning glories, hibiscus and sweet peas.

Another way to achieve water penetration for hard-coated seeds is to soak them in a glass of lukewarm water overnight. By morning, seeds should have swelled to twice their original size. If not, leave them to soak another day.

Best Temperature—Seeds require a predetermined, best temperature range in which to germinate. This temperature varies from annual to annual. Nemesias and schizanthus, for example, are sensitive to temperatures above 65F (17C). Coleus, impatiens and begonias are sensitive to temperatures below 70F (21C).

Pre-chilling—Some seeds germinate better by chilling them to break dormancy. Columbine, viola and delphiniums germinate more reliably if placed in the vegetable bin of a refrigerator for 3 weeks before planting.

Proper Light—Some seeds, usually large-seeded annuals such as sweet peas and morning glories, prefer total darkness in which to germinate. Seeds should be completely covered with soil. Seeds of most annuals, however, germinate better with exposure to light. These include mostly small-seeded varieties. For those annuals that require exposure to light, surface-sow seeds and gently press them into soil. Seeds should be anchored but above soil level. Larger seeds requiring light can be lightly covered with a fine layer of soil to anchor them.

Inadequate light after seeds germinate is a major reason for poor-quality transplants. Young seedlings often become spindly and "stretch" when not given sufficient light. Seedlings should be exposed to about 12 hours of sunlight each day.

Here is an example of materials you'll need to grow plants from seeds: peat pots, milk cartons, plastic trays, seeds, potting soil, peat pellets, fungicide and spray bottle.

If you grow transplants on a windowsill, raise pots to the level of the windowpane. Consider placing an aluminum-foil reflector on the dark side of seedlings so light will bounce back to increase illumination.

Where indoor lighting is poor, consider purchasing an artificial-light unit. Fluorescent lights are generally recommended. Fixtures and tubes can often be purchased in department and hardware stores. Many growers use a combination of *warm-white* and *cool-white* tubes, which supply plants with proper light rays for growth.

You can purchase plant-growth or wide-spectrum tubes, manufactured especially for growing plants. Mail-order catalogs usually offer them for sale.

Plant lights, which simulate daylight, can be set on timers to turn on and off automatically. Placing lights about 6 inches above seedlings helps keep them stocky and prevents stretching. Grown under artificial lights, plants need about 16 hours of light per day.

Disease Prevention—The biggest cause of poor germination is *damping-off* disease. It attacks seedlings at the soil surface, causing them to fall over and die. Damping-off is caused by a fungus present in unsterilized soil, dirty pots and unclean seeds. Overwatering, poor ventilation, poor light and high temperatures encourage the disease. It attacks seeds sown indoors and outdoors but is most destructive on indoor sowings. Germinating seeds are often killed before emerging through soil.

Prevent damping-off by using new or clean seed-starting pots and sterile potting soil. Spray surface of potting soil with a fungicide such as captan or benomyl before you plant.

MATERIALS FOR STARTING SEEDS INDOORS

No single seed-starting system suits all situations. Generally, indoor methods can be classified as *one-step* or *two-step*. A one-step method is best for large seeds such as nasturtiums and sweet peas. You simply plant a few seeds in a pot filled with potting soil. You can then thin seedlings to leave one healthy specimen. When seedling reaches sufficient size, you plant it directly in the garden.

With the two-step method, seeds are first sown in a tray or flat filled with potting soil. When large enough to handle, they are separated and transferred to individual pots—usually 2-1/2-inch size. They grow in these pots until they reach transplant size. Seeds of begonias, impatiens and coleus are best planted this way. Geraniums are sometimes transferred a third time to a larger pot—usually 4 inches in diameter—before seedlings are ready for transplanting.

Following are descriptions of popular materials and methods used to start seeds indoors. See photo, page 39.

Peat pots are small, round or square containers made of peat, an organic material. They are filled with potting soil, and seeds are planted in them. Plant roots are able to grow through the pot, which gradually decomposes after it is planted in soil. Transplanting is achieved without disturbing roots.

To prevent pot from restricting root growth after it is transplanted, gently remove pot bottom just before planting. This gives the root system greater freedom to grow into the soil. When planting these pots be sure top edge is set *below* soil surface, or it will act as a wick and draw moisture away from roots.

With small seeds it's better to use peat pots in a two-step operation. Start seeds in a tray, then transplant to the peat pot after they have sprouted and are large enough to handle.

Peat pellets are made of compressed peat that expands to seven times its volume when moisture is added. Peat pellets are a popular seed-starting product for large-seeded annuals. Two kinds are available.

Jiffy-7 peat pellets expand to 1-3/4 inches in diameter and 2-1/8 inches high. Netting holds the peat together, and there is a depression in the top of each pellet for seeds. At transplant time the entire pellet can be planted in the garden without bothering the seedling. It is a good idea to remove the netting before planting, or it may restrict plant growth.

Jiffy-9 does not have netting and is slightly smaller and less expensive. Peat is held together by an invisible binding agent. In my experience it is superior to the Jiffy-7 because roots have complete freedom to grow once the pellet has been planted.

Both types are excellent for starting large-seeded annuals in a one-step operation. They can also be used for small seeds. Asters, marigolds, pansies, petunias and zinnias are annuals that do well started in peat pellets.

Fiber blocks and cubes, like Jiffy pellets, have a depression in the top for seeds. They are light, clean and easy to use. Roots penetrate the block freely. After seedlings grow to transplant size, the whole block can be planted without root disturbance.

Cell packs are small planting trays sectioned into four or six compartments. You fill them with potting soil and plant medium and large seeds. Cell packs are also used for planting small-seeded annuals in a two-step method.

Peat, wood or plastic seed trays are used to start small, fine seeds such as begonias, petunias and coleus. The usual method is to fill planters with sterile potting soil. Make several furrows with a flat edge, then sow seeds thinly along furrows. Keep soil moist with a fine spray. When seedlings develop their first set of true leaves, transfer to individual containers.

Household containers that are normally thrown away every day are excellent alternatives to manufactured products. The quart-size paper milk carton is, in my estimation, one of the best transplant containers for large-seeded annuals. Because of the size of the container, the rootball will be several times larger at transplant time than the rootball started in a peat pot. Because the plant is well established when planted, it flowers earlier.

Use your imagination to seek out other seed-starting containers. Paper and styrofoam cups and the plastic bottoms of 1-liter soft drink containers work well. You can also use deep-dish plastic containers such as those used for holding dips, whipped butter and cheese spreads. These make excellent seed-starting trays.

Soil mixes are commonly used to fill peat pots, cell packs and other containers for seed starting. Regular garden topsoil is a poor growing medium for indoor-started seedlings. *Soilless mixes and substitutes* or *potting mixes*—combinations of sterile materials such as peat moss, vermiculite and perlite—are much better. They are lightweight, free from disease, and have better aeration and moisture retention than topsoil. Several ready-mixed brands are available from garden centers, including Jiffy Mix,

Starting Seeds Indoors

One-Step Method

1. Moisten peat pellets to expand them. Large seeds such as nasturtiums are best planted in peat pellets.

2. When pellets are fully expanded, plant one seed in each pellet. Push seed into depression in center of pellet. Pinch sides to cover seed.

3. A few weeks after planting—time varies from annual to annual—seedling is ready to plant. You can plant the peat pot with netting intact, but I prefer to remove it.

Two-Step Method

1. Materials needed for two-step method: plastic seed trays, bag of potting soil, labels, seeds, water and benomyl fungicide to prevent damping-off.

2. Throughly moisten potting soil before planting. This is easiest to do when soil is in bag. Squeeze bag so moisture is absorbed evenly into soil.

3. Fill seed trays with soil to about 1/2 inch from top of tray. If you have several trays, plant one annual or one variety in each tray.

4. Sow seeds on soil surface. Many seeds need light to germinate and can be pressed lightly into soil. See individual descriptions. Spray soil surface with benomyl.

5. Seedlings as they appear several days later. Be sure to provide seedlings with several hours of bright, indirect light after they emerge from soil.

6. Using a sharp pencil or similar object, lift seedlings from tray and transplant into larger container. Grow them in this container until they reach transplant size.

Pro-Mix, RediEarth, Super Soil and Starting Formula.

DIRECT SEEDING OUTDOORS

A common mistake many gardeners make is planting seeds too deep. As mentioned on page 39, most small and medium-size seeds of annuals need exposure to light to germinate. It is better to sow these on the soil surface and press gently to anchor them.

Before you plant seeds outdoors, determine which tolerate frost in the seedling stage and which are tender and susceptible to frost damage. Don't plant seeds of tender annuals until all danger of frost has passed.

When planting groups of annuals in a mixed bed or border, use a stick or tool handle to outline a planting section for each variety. Then scatter seeds thinly within each designated area.

Unless rain is predicted, water immediately after planting. Even drought-resistant annuals require plenty of moisture to germinate and grow from seedling stage.

If heavy rains threaten to cause erosion of the planting bed, cover seeded areas with a light layer of mulch such as straw, hay or pine needles. Mulching will also help retain soil moisture so the seed bed will not dry out as quickly.

After seedlings are established, thinning may be necessary. Some annuals such as alyssum, portulaca and California poppies tolerate crowding. Others such as marigolds and zinnias do best when thinned so each plant has adequate room to grow.

DIRECT-SEEDING TIPS

● Never walk on garden soil before or after planting. Heavy footprints compact soil and ruin a well-prepared seedbed. Use paths between rows or walk on planks.
● When fertilizing planting bed at time of planting, do not use high-nitrogen, fast-acting fertilizers. They may burn tender seedlings. After applying fertilizer, wait 7 to 10 days before planting. Or apply a timed-release fertilizer at time of planting. See page 33.
● A hand trowel is one of the best tools for creating seed furrows or planting holes. If you want a shallow, narrow furrow for small seeds, use the pointed tip of the trowel. To make a deep, wide furrow for larger seeds, press trowel in deeper, or dig out a

few scoops of soil to set transplants in place.
● Do not use the entire seed packet in one sowing. Save some seeds to fill in bare spots after the planting comes up, and to stagger flowering times. See page 11.
● Firm soil over planted seeds with your foot or back of a spade. Don't compress soil too much. Press just enough to eliminate air pockets.
● A strainer is handy for planting small seeds. To use, first spread seeds evenly on soil surface. Fill strainer with fine garden topsoil. Shake it over seeds until they are covered with about 1/4 inch of soil. Large stones, weed roots and other debris are left behind in strainer.

TRANSPLANTING

Plants grown indoors and transplanted to the garden should be handled with care. Treat them like eggs. Rough handling can shock plants, and they will grow poorly or die.

Hardening-off—Before moving transplants from a warm, comfortable indoor environment to the cool or windy outdoors, they should be *hardened-off*. This means to gradually acclimate them to their new home. Even cold-hardy plants such as sweet peas and dianthus should be given a gradual transition period from an indoor environment to the outdoors. Hardening-off is most important with tender plants such as impatiens, begonias and petunias.

Transplants should be planted when conditions are cool, such as on cloudy days or in late afternoon. After planting, do not let the soil dry out. You will probably have to water every day, maybe twice a day in warm weather. Place water directly on the soil around the root area. If sunlight is intense, protect seedlings with some sort of shade the first few days after planting.

A simple way to harden-off plants is to expose them to increasing amounts of cold or sunlight, depending on the weather. For example, place plants in the sun for an hour the first day, and gradually increase the exposure for about a week until plants can accept a full day of sun.

Water transplants before you plant them. Moisture helps the rootball ease out of the container or six-pack and lessens transplant shock. If the transplant is in a plastic pot, you may

need to run a knife around the rim between soil and pot. Rootball will then come free without disturbing roots. The more original potting soil you can plant, the better transplants will grow.

Placing transplants in a *cold frame* is the best way to get them adjusted to the outdoors. A cold frame is usually a wooden compartment set outdoors, sometimes partially below ground level. It has a covering of glass or plastic. The frame is left open during the day and closed at night. Normally transplants remain in a cold frame for 10 days. The best cold frames have an automatic vent opener that is activated by the sun. Information on solar-powered vent openers can be obtained by writing: Bramen Co. Inc., Box 70, Salem, MA 01970; or Dalen Products Inc., 201 Sherlake Drive, Knoxville, TN 37922.

If you don't want to invest in a cold frame, improvise with a wooden crate covered with a sheet of glass. Or place plants outdoors during the day and cover them with a sheet of plastic at night. Anchor sides with bricks or stones. Do not let the plastic touch plants.

BEDDING PLANTS

A garden center is a popular place to buy annuals. It's so easy to stop by at planting time and pick out your favorite ready-grown transplants, or *bedding plants.* Generally sold in "six-packs" or small containers, plants are often in bloom so it's easy to plant effective color schemes. The bedding-plant industry, which supplies garden centers with transplants, has been one of the fastest-growing segments in gardening.

After reading about a dazzling new hybrid flower in your local newspaper, don't expect to find it as a ready-grown transplant at your garden center. The bedding-plant industry prefers to satisfy the demand for established plants rather than create a demand for new varieties. Space at garden centers is limited. Usually the most popular, best-selling annuals are offered for sale.

Ten classes of annuals provide the majority of bedding-plant sales:

Geraniums	Scarlet sage
Petunias	Coleus
Marigolds	Ageratum
Impatiens	Celosia
Begonias	Zinnias

Planting a Garden

1. Select site in sunny, well-drained location. Lay out according to plan. Stakes and string are helpful for cutting gardens. See sample plans on pages 12 and 13.

2. Remove sod or weeds if present. Shake topsoil from roots. After removing sod, take soil sample for a soil test. See page 29.

3. Most garden soil requires addition of organic matter. Spread 3 to 6 inches of amendment over area to be planted.

4. Use a spade or power tiller to mix topsoil and amendment. Dig down about 12 inches.

5. Use a rake to level soil surface. Remove stones and pieces of weeds or grass roots. Watch for larvae of insect pests.

6. Scatter fertilizer over soil. Lime or sulfur may be required to adjust soil pH. Rake into top few inches of soil. Wait about 10 days before you sow seeds or set out transplants.

7. Use a hand fork or similar tool to loosen soil prior to planting.

8. Sprinkle seeds evenly in wide row. Most annuals germinate best when exposed to light. Read seed packet for instructions.

9. Thin seedlings to prevent overcrowding. For the earliest blooms, start seeds indoors or buy ready-to-plant transplants at your nursery.

With the exception of petunias, bedding-plant outlets usually do not offer more than four or five varieties in each class.

TRANSPLANTING TIPS

Be aware that the quality of plants can vary enormously. Following are some points to watch for:

• Buy stocky, compact plants that have healthy green color. Avoid tall, lanky specimens that have yellow leaves and appear to be stretched. Their spindly growth is a sign of stress—usually caused by crowding, inadequate light or infrequent watering. Never judge a plant by its height. Quality transplants are short with thick stems and have side branches close to the base.

• Ask nursery personnel if plants have been *hardened-off*—gradually acclimated from greenhouse to outdoors. If not, plants may sustain severe shock if transplanted immediately to your garden.

• Buy "green." Resist the temptation to buy plants already in flower. A young plant that hasn't blossomed generally puts on a better flowering display. This is especially true of zinnias, scarlet sage and celosias. Marigolds and petunias will flower longer and more profusely if transplanted before plants reach flowering stage.

• If you've decided on petunias, choose the small-flower *multifloras* over the large-flower *grandifloras*. The small ones live longer, produce more flowers and make a more colorful display. They also recover from rain more quickly.

• Examine the undersides of leaves for signs of pests. If you find colonies of aphids, mealy bugs or whiteflies, do not buy plants. Plants may die later of wilt disease even if you completely eradicate pests before transplanting.

'Orange Jubilee' marigold was transplanted while in full flower. Weeks later, growth is uneven, flowers are few and plant looks tired.

This 'Orange Jubilee' was transplanted while green. Weeks later, growth is sturdy, vigorous and flowers are plentiful. Plant has potential to bloom for several more weeks.

Flower garden in full bloom was planted with seeds sown directly in garden, and with seedlings transplanted from six-packs and small pots.

CLIMATES OF NORTH AMERICA

Almost three quarters of the United States has snow cover in winter and is subject to freezing temperatures. This region is influenced by a cold air mass that comes from the arctic through Canada. The cold air is funneled far south by two parallel mountain ranges—the Rockies in the west and the Appalachians in the east.

The second largest area of the United States is influenced by the Gulf of Mexico. Warm air in winter helps to hold back the arctic air mass coming down from the north. The area where the Gulf and the arctic play a weather "tug of war" in winter is the South.

Near the Gulf Coast and also along the Colorado River Basin, which receives warm air from the Gulf of California, frost occurs only from December thru February. This allows a long growing season for warm-weather plants and a mild, winter growing season for cool-weather plants. This area is generally referred to as the Gulf and Southwest.

California has the most diverse climate in the United States. Several different climates or significant climate differences can occur within short distances. The coastal area is influenced by warm air from the Pacific Ocean. Freezing weather occurs infrequently. The area south of Los Angeles is more equable and permits a year-round growing season.

Tropical Florida extends so far out into the Gulf Stream that frost is almost unknown. The area enjoys 365 days of good growing conditions, allowing even warm-season plants to be grown during winter. The tip of Texas around Brownsville, and the tip of Louisiana around New Orleans, experience a climate similar to tropical Florida. Warm-season plants can be grown year-round, although flowering may not occur until February and March.

Following is a more detailed description of each growing area:

The North—This is a vast area of the United States and the most heavily populated. It normally has snow cover in winter. Freezing air from the arctic brings frost in fall, producing a cold winter season with frost likely over a 6-month period.

Average last frost date for this section of the country is May 10. After this date, tender annuals can be planted. Hardy annuals are generally planted outdoors 3 to 4 weeks earlier.

The growing season for tender annuals in this area is roughly 150 days, although some areas of the extreme North have 100 days or less. Tender annuals such as zinnias, celosias and petunias are difficult to grow outdoors.

The area allows for two planting periods for cool-season plants—early spring for early summer flowers and midsummer for fall flowers. One planting of warm-season flowers generally remains colorful until frost. Gardeners in extreme northern and high-elevation locations should select special cool-season varieties of snapdragons, nasturtiums and lobelia to obtain best displays.

The climates of coastal Washington and Oregon have a frost-free growing season of up to 250 days. The climate closely resembles that of England. Last spring frosts generally occur in mid-March. Summer temperatures remain cool, creating excellent conditions for hardy annuals.

The South—In the South, the ground does not freeze, but heavy frosts are common. Prolonged cold spells can occur when the northern arctic air mass pushes back the warm Gulf air flow. Snowfall occurs some years, but it does not stay on the ground long. Spring planting can begin the previous fall and up to February for hardy annuals. The last spring frost is generally in late March, allowing tender annuals to be planted in April.

The South experiences long summers with a combination of high humidity and high temperatures. Some flowering annuals such as asters and snapdragons cease to flower under such conditions. It is good zinnia, marigold and petunia country, providing regular irrigation is supplied. For continual flowering, two plantings are best. Make one to begin flowering in early summer and another to flower in early fall. Summer heat and disease tend to quickly exhaust the first planting.

Drought is common and regular irrigation is essential.

The area is notorious for infestations of insect pests, notably armyworms, corn earworms, nematodes and mole crickets. An aggressive pest-control schedule is usually necessary.

The Deep South and Southwest—These areas are similar in that they have winter growing conditions for hardy annuals and an extremely long summer growing season for tender annuals. African daisies and poppies, particularly Iceland poppies, are planted in fall for winter and early spring flowers.

Although frost is prevalent, it generally occurs only in December to February. Hardy annuals generally shrug off the cold. Tender annuals are planted outdoors as early as February to take advantage of pleasant growing conditions in spring.

Summers are exceedingly hot and dry, allowing little except periwinkle, marigolds, zinnias and portulaca to survive the scorching heat.

Timing of plantings is critical. Cool-season plants must mature either in late fall and winter or early spring. The majority of warm-season plants must mature in early summer or fall. This usually necessitates two planting times for warm-season crops. Plant early and late in the season to maintain displays after midsummer heat has exhausted the early plantings

Northern California—This area has many small climates, called *micro-climates,* that are too complex to describe separately. The coastal region is generally influenced by the Pacific Ocean and cooling fogs that occur mostly in summer. The northern coastal region experiences moderate temperatures throughout the year and excellent conditions for growing cool-season plants year-round.

In the interior valleys summers are hot—excellent for tender annuals, especially zinnias, petunias and marigolds. Winters are mild. Hardy annuals are grown fall and winter.

Hardy annuals are usually planted October through March. April is the busiest month for planting tender annuals. Because the summer season is long, a second planting of warm-season annuals can be made in June for continual flowering displays.

Southern California—This part of California extends roughly south of Santa Barbara to San Diego, east to the Arizona border. Most of this area enjoys 260 frost-free days each year. Hardy annuals can be grown all winter.

In the lower sections of the Colorado Valley, a few, favored locations escape killing frosts 2 to 3 years at a time. Tender annuals can be grown unprotected all year, although flowering may be inhibited during January—the coolest month. The area immediately surrounding San Diego and other coastal areas is blessed with 365 growing days a year.

In southern California the busiest planting time for hardy annuals is September to October. The next planting time is March when warmer temperatures favor the growth of tender annuals.

Because of the long growing season, a second planting of tender annuals such as zinnias and petunias can be made in June and July to maintain continual flowering displays. This is especially true along the coast where the ocean influence keeps temperatures moderate.

Alaska—Except in coastal areas, Alaska is a difficult place to garden. Hardy annuals such as calendulas, sweet peas, larkspur and nasturtiums can be grown here. What Alaska lacks in growing season, it makes up in light duration. The extraordinary daylength—in midsummer the sun never sets—helps to produce flowers in record time. Displays of zinnias, petunias and celosias are possible, but usually only with the aid of a greenhouse or heated cold frame.

Hawaii—Hawaii is a gardener's paradise. Any annual can be grown in Hawaii, both hardy and tender types. Except in areas above 5,000 feet, the islands are completely frost-free. The temperature remains stable through the year at 78F (26C). Gardening is possible year-round for both cool- and warm-season flowers.

Canada—Hardy and tender annuals can be grown in most of Canada. Plantings should be timed so hardy annuals mature in early summer or late summer and fall. Tender annuals should bloom in midsummer.

Vancouver Island in western Canada is especially adapted for growing cool-season annuals. Certain tender annuals such as marigolds and begonias create exceptional midsummer displays.

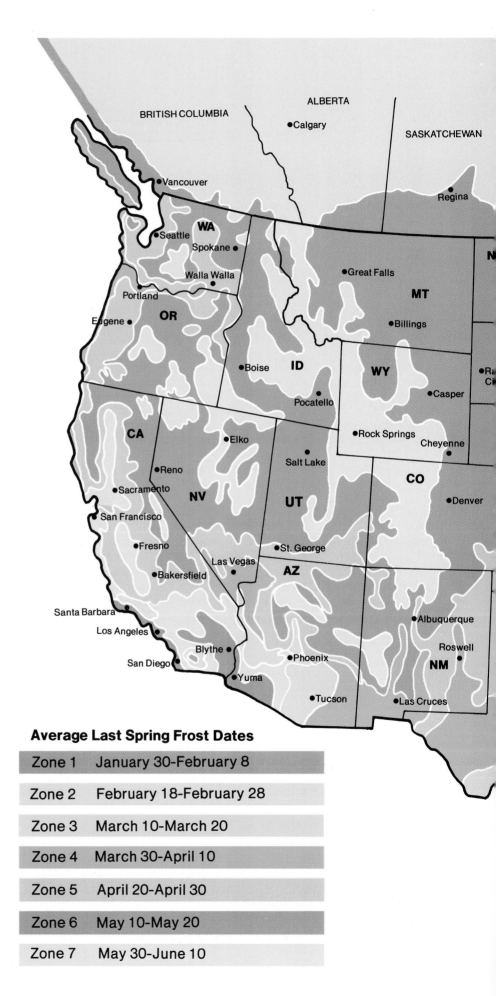

Average Last Spring Frost Dates

Zone 1	January 30-February 8
Zone 2	February 18-February 28
Zone 3	March 10-March 20
Zone 4	March 30-April 10
Zone 5	April 20-April 30
Zone 6	May 10-May 20
Zone 7	May 30-June 10

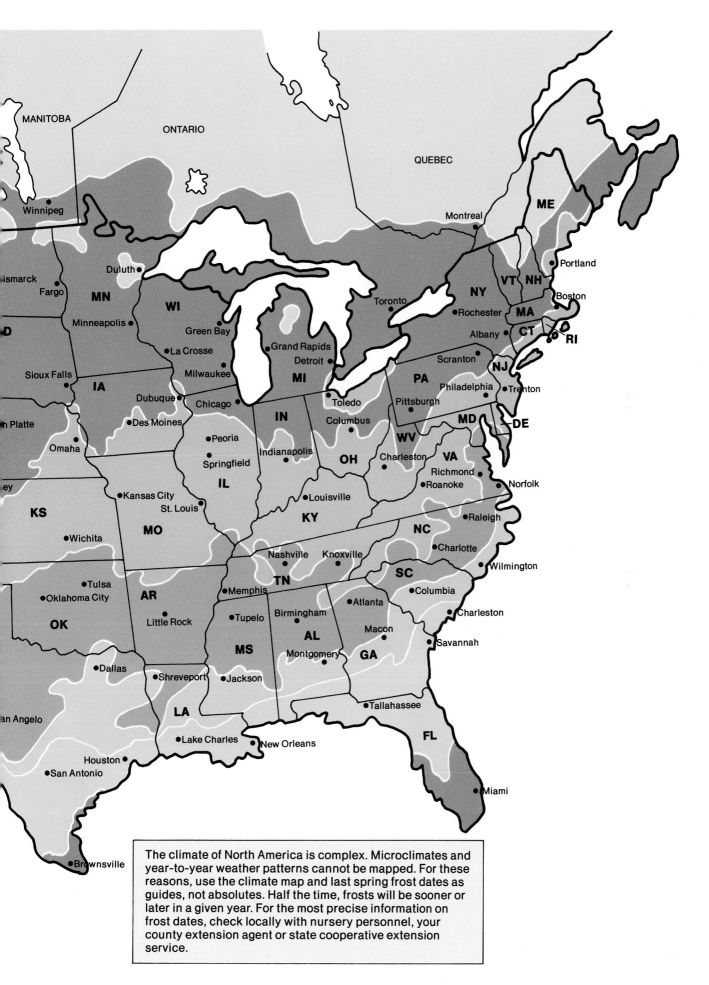

MANITOBA

ONTARIO

QUEBEC

Winnipeg

Montreal

ME

Duluth

ismarck

Fargo

MN

VT NH

Portland

NY

Boston

Toronto

Rochester

MA

Minneapolis

WI

Green Bay

Albany

CT

RI

D

Sioux Falls

La Crosse

Grand Rapids

Scranton

NJ

Milwaukee

Detroit

PA

Philadelphia

Trenton

IA

Dubuque

MI

Toledo

Pittsburgh

MD

DE

h Platte

Chicago

Columbus

Des Moines

IN

WV

Omaha

Peoria

Indianapolis

Charleston

Richmond

VA

Norfolk

Springfield

OH

Roanoke

ey

IL

St. Louis

Louisville

Raleigh

Kansas City

KY

NC

KS

MO

Charlotte

Wichita

Nashville

Knoxville

Wilmington

TN

SC

Tulsa

Columbia

Oklahoma City

AR

Memphis

Charleston

Little Rock

Tupelo

Birmingham

Atlanta

Macon

Savannah

OK

MS

AL

GA

Dallas

Shreveport

Jackson

Montgomery

an Angelo

LA

Tallahassee

Lake Charles

New Orleans

FL

Houston

San Antonio

Miami

Brownsville

The climate of North America is complex. Microclimates and year-to-year weather patterns cannot be mapped. For these reasons, use the climate map and last spring frost dates as guides, not absolutes. Half the time, frosts will be sooner or later in a given year. For the most precise information on frost dates, check locally with nursery personnel, your county extension agent or state cooperative extension service.

6

Caring for Annuals

Regular watering and weeding are the two most important maintenance chores after seeds or plants are in the soil. *Mulching*—putting a covering of material over the soil—helps conserve moisture and reduces the amount of weeding.

Another important part of caring for your garden is pest and disease control. Information on identifying and treating problem pests are discussed in the following pages.

WATERING
Water is the key to growth of all plants. In addition to supplying life-giving moisture, water dissolves nutrients so they can be absorbed by plant roots. Plants grow rapidly when moisture is plentiful, but become subject to both moisture and nutrient stress when water is scarce.

Water is also the key to seed germination. It softens the seed coat and swells the seed embryo to stimulate growth.

The most common mistake when watering flowers is failing to provide enough on a regular basis. Although many annuals are drought tolerant, surviving without water for extended periods, plants need water regularly to flower well.

Too much water can be detrimental. Constantly wet soil prevents air from reaching the root zone. If soil is wet for prolonged periods, it creates a stagnant condition that rots plant roots. Fungus diseases are more prevalent when foliage and soil is constantly wet.

Good soil drainage is essential. To improve a poorly drained site, you can install drainage tile to channel the water away. Or you can build a *raised bed*. A raised bed elevates the garden soil above the surrounding level so water drains freely. You may want to support the sides with railroad ties, lumber or stones.

WHEN TO WATER
Seeds and Transplants—When small seeds are planted directly in the garden, water every day if it doesn't rain. These seeds are planted close to the soil surface and are more susceptible to drying out than large-seeded annuals. Moisture is also important immediately following germination.

When transplants are set in the garden, water immediately and keep soil moist until plants are established. Transplanted seedlings often sustain root damage and need regular moisture for a couple of weeks to recover from transplant shock. If the temperature is warm when you set out your transplants, supply some kind of temporary shade until they become adapted.

Established Plants—As soon as a plant begins to wilt, it needs water immediately or it will die. Lack of moisture shows itself in different ways, depending on the plant and its sensitivity to moisture stress.

Do not wait until plants show symptoms of water need. Check the garden soil regularly—every day if temperatures are warm—and supply plants with water in their root zone. An easy way to check moisture content of garden soil is to grab a handful and squeeze it. If particles cling together,

Left: Tall-growing larkspurs are staked to keep them erect and to avoid wind damage. Bamboo poles are used for supports. Above: Pine-bark chips are among the most decorative mulches to use for flower beds.

soil has adequate moisture. If particles separate and feel dry, like sand, soil needs moisture.

A frequent question asked about watering is, "What time of day is best?" If possible, water in early morning. Watering at this time means less loss through evaporation and from wind.

MOISTURE-HOLDING CAPACITY OF SOIL

Different types of soil have varied capacities for holding moisture in the plant's root zone. Clay soils are prone to waterlogging. Sandy soils allow moisture to drain away too rapidly. The best kind of garden soil is a loam soil. Its composition is somewhere between sand and clay. A loam soil drains well, yet the spaces between soil particles retain water long enough to supply plant roots. For more information on soils, see page 30.

WAYS TO WATER

Irrigation methods that supply water in steady, regular amounts are desirable. Common methods for flowers are hand-held garden hoses, lawn sprinklers and drip-irrigation systems that apply moisture slowly for long periods directly to the root zone.

Hand irrigation is tedious and the least effective means of watering. It seems as if you are applying more water than you actually are. Usually only the top few inches of soil are getting moisture. If you have the time and patience to wet soil thoroughly to the root zone, hand irrigation is an acceptable way to water. Using an extension wand, which attaches to the end of the hose, makes hand watering easier and applies water in a rainlike spray.

Lawn sprinklers are an improvement over hand watering. They can be set in place to water as long as necessary, soaking the soil. But sprinklers can waste water through evaporation on hot days. In climates with humid summers they can promote disease. Fungus infestations such as powdery mildew and botrytis are encouraged if sprinkler systems soak foliage, creating a wet, humid environment around plants.

Drip irrigation is a system of hoses that lie across soil close to plant roots, either on top of soil or buried out of sight. Depending on design, drip hoses are usually attached to a garden hose, which is attached to an outdoor faucet. The drip hose oozes moisture through micropores along the hose wall, or drips moisture from *emitters*, tiny holes spaced at regular intervals along the hose. *Spaghetti* emitters have long, flexible tubes coming from a main hose. At the end of each flexible tube is a type of valve that drips moisture. Spaghetti emitters are probably best suited for watering individual plants in containers.

The biggest benefit of drip irrigation is that you can water the whole garden regularly by a single turn of the faucet. Plants receive regular moisture, and are not subjected to water stress. The basics of watering correctly still apply—putting sufficient amounts of water in the root zone.

Economically, drip-irrigation systems make sense. They save water due to less waste—as much as 30% compared to other methods. Because plants make continuous, rapid growth, they begin to flower early and flower profusely.

Drip irrigation is especially effective when installed under black plastic. This not only protects the hoses from damage, it reduces evaporation.

For a small area, it is sufficient to place drip hose up and down the rows with one end connected to a water spigot. With 1/2-inch diameter hose and emitters spaced 2 feet apart, and with average water pressure, water should be able to travel about 250 feet on level ground from your water spigot. This can be doubled to 500 feet if two hoses are connected to the spigot by a Y valve. For a drip system set-up such as this, see photos opposite and on page 52.

To irrigate large gardens, you may have to consider a more sophisticated set-up. Such a system might involve lateral hoses connected to a larger line, called a *header* line, fitted with a water-pressure regulator. Some systems can incorporate a special fertilizer unit that injects soluble fertilizer into water. Plants are fed automatically while they are being irrigated.

Water Correctly

The illustration at right shows what happens when a plant is given frequent, shallow waterings. Roots grow where there is water—in the upper soil surface. During periods of warm, windy weather or if an irrigation is missed, the plant is unable to absorb the water it needs. The plant at far right is given deep, regular waterings. The roots penetrate deeply into the soil so they have a greater reservoir of water and nutrients to draw upon.

Planting a Weed-Free Garden

Using black plastic for weed control and drip-irrigation hose for watering is an easy-care way to grow annuals. Weeding and watering chores are reduced considerably and plants flower continually.

To make a weed-free, drip-irrigated garden, dig a rectangular plot I7 feet wide by 30 feet long. Make 10 raised beds 2 feet wide by I5 feet long. Leave room for 1-foot-wide walkways between raised beds. Lay continuous length of drip-irrigation hose down middle of each bed. Hose should go from one row to the next. See photo, page 52.

Next, cover beds with lengths of 3-foot-wide strips of black plastic. Look for plastic that is 4 mils thick. Anchor edges with soil. Lay down straw between beds to reduce weed growth and to provide a mud-free walkway.

Space plants 12 inches apart in double rows through the black plastic. Cut an X in plastic for each transplant. Take care not to damage drip hose in middle of bed. Attach drip hose to outdoor faucet. Turn on faucet whenever garden needs watering.

Drip-irrigation hose, connections and instructions are available as a kit called *Derek Fell's Automatic Garden.* For more information, write International Irrigation Systems, 1555 Third Avenue, Niagara Falls, NY 14304.

If you don't have access to a well or water spigot, a gravity-feed system can be used. Place a water barrel several feet above the soil level and run a drip hose from its base.

Drip systems vary in cost and quality. To decide which system is best for you, look for advertisements in garden magazines. Send for their descriptive material and study it. Many retail garden centers carry drip-irrigation supplies that you can examine in the store.

Some drip-irrigation companies will help you design a system if you send them a plan of your garden with your order. Many have a specification sheet at the front of their supply catalog.

One of the least-expensive systems is Irrigro, consisting of white, plastic hose with tiny pores. The pores allow droplets of water to ooze through the sides. A source of Irrigro hose is International Irrigation Systems, 1555 Third Avenue, Niagara Falls, NY 14304.

Polyflex hose has emitters spaced at 18-inch or 24-inch intervals. Water drips from the emitters and saturates soil in a wide circle. For more information on Polyflex hose, write to Submatic Irrigation Systems, Box 246, Lubbock, TX 79408.

WEEDING

In a short time, unchecked weed growth can turn an attractive flower bed into a jungle. Weeds not only compete with your flowers for moisture and nutrients, they also block sunlight. It is easy to become discouraged when weeds claim your garden. The best way to combat them is to keep them from getting ahead.

When you do the initial soil preparation of your garden, remove all pieces of weed roots that you see. The smallest piece of plantain or dandelion root can grow into a full-size weed. Avoid walking on newly cultivated soil. The surface compaction helps many weed seeds to germinate.

A few minutes spent pulling young weeds at the end of each day is far more sensible than trying to catch up on a week of neglect. This is especially true in midsummer when weeds grow fast. If you kill weeds when they are immature, they will not have a chance to set seeds for a new crop. I use every good rain as a signal. I go outside immediately after the rain has ceased. Weeds are easy to pull while the

ground is wet and yielding.

Use a mulch between rows to reduce weed germination and growth. If installed correctly at the beginning of the gardening season, a mulch is the easiest way to control weeds.

Even when you use a mulch, some weeds are persistent enough to break through. Two tools are excellent for hand weeding—a hoe for weeding between plants and a hand fork for scratching out weeds. If you use one of these tools to remove weeds, try to cultivate the soil to a shallow depth—about 1-1/2 inches. Digging deeper tends to bring up a new crop of weed seeds that will germinate in the upper soil surface.

When using a hoe or hand cultivator, take care not to disturb roots of adjacent annuals. For example, dandelion roots are long and tapering. When pulled, they come up without disturbing adjacent soil area. Plantain roots spread. Yanking them out can unseat nearby plants.

Wear gloves when removing weeds by hand. Some cause skin irritations..

Try to remove weeds with roots intact. If the stem breaks above ground and the root remains in the soil, the weed will grow back.

Herbicidal Weedkillers—These are chemicals that are sprinkled or sprayed on flower beds prior to planting. They work by preventing the germination of weed seeds. There is usually a waiting period after applying them before you can plant. Follow label directions carefully.

MULCHING

A *mulch* is a covering over garden soil. It is a popular form of weed control and supplies many other important benefits.
- It reduces weed growth by cutting off light to germinating weed seeds. Weeds that germinate are easy to pull from a mulch.
- It conserves moisture by reducing surface evaporation.
- It modifies soil temperatures by cooling or warming soil. Organic mulches tend to cool soil. Plastic mulches tend to warm it.

Drops of water ooze slowly from tiny pores in drip-irrigation hose. Water is supplied slowly and directly to root zone of plants so there is less waste through evaporation. Various kinds of drip systems are available, including those with *emitters*—tiny valves—set at regular spaces along hose.

Author places drip hose in garden, which will supply plants with all water needs. Here hose is placed up and down a series of narrow raised beds, such as those shown on page 51.

- It reduces soil erosion and preserves good soil structure and nutrient levels.
- It reduces risk of disease by keeping foliage of annuals away from bare soil.

As mentioned, organic mulches such as wood chips and pine needles tend to cool soil. Inorganic mulches such as black plastic tend to warm soil. In areas with hot, dry summers, black plastic may overheat soil, but plastic can be covered with organic mulch for a weed-free garden. Drip irrigation works well in conjunction with black plastic to provide regular amounts of water, which also helps reduce soil temperature.

Black plastic is the best barrier against weeds. It is usually desirable to cover the plastic with a decorative organic mulch to maintain an attractive appearance. Some of the best decorative mulches include bark chips and ground bark, hay and straw, leaf mold, pine needles, coco bean hulls, licorice root and peat moss. These all have a natural appearance. They will eventually decompose to add their organic matter to the soil.

A disadvantage of mulches is that they can be great hiding places for snails and slugs. These pests are most prolific during rainy weather. If they are a problem, use a slug bait or pick them off plants with a gloved hand.

DEAD-HEADING
Removing dead flowers is called *dead-heading*. It is an important practice that should be followed regularly. Otherwise, annuals direct their energy into seed formation and stop flowering. Removing spent flowers before they form seeds maintains attractive floral displays. At the same time, this stimulates the plant into producing more flowers.

STAKING PLANTS
Certain types of tall-growing annuals may need staking to keep them erect. Larkspur, delphiniums, tall snapdragons and tall sunflowers have brittle stems that are easily damaged by wind. The best material for staking is bamboo stakes, which are readily available from garden and home-improvement centers. When tying stems to stakes it's best to use a twist-tie rather than string. String has a tendency to cut into stems. Twist-ties are easily looped into a figure-8. The stem goes through one loop and the stake occupies the other. This allows stake and stem to stand parallel.

Circular flower bed planted with wax begonias is kept free of weeds with an attractive mulch of pine bark. Area beyond garden is covered with decorative rock mulch.

Dead-heading means removing spent flower heads before they have a chance to set seeds, which drains the plant's energy. By removing spent flowers, plants are stimulated to produce more blooms.

PESTS AND DISEASES

Problems caused by pests and diseases among flowering annuals are not nearly as severe as with edible crops. After flowers pass the seedling stage, few serious problems occur.

The best pest and disease control is *prevention*. Keep your garden clean and do a major clean-up at the end of each season. Remove and destroy all garden debris.

Large animal pests such as stray dogs, deer, rabbits and groundhogs can be kept out by fencing your garden. Birds such as pheasants and quail like young transplants. It may be necessary to make portable cages from chicken wire and cover young plants until they pass the tender, succulent stage.

Before you implement a pest-control program, decide which pests and diseases present potential dangers. If you are new to an area or a beginning gardener, ask neighborhood gardeners, nursery personnel and county agents which pests and diseases are common.

CONTROLS: THE CHOICES

In deciding how to combat pests and diseases, you have two choices—*chemical controls* and *organic controls.* Most flower parts are not usually consumed by humans, so most gardeners do not mind using chemical controls. Many insecticides are specially formulated for use on ornamentals but are not approved for use on vegetables. There are some exceptions. Nasturtiums, for example, are sometimes used in salads. If you know you will be using flower parts for culinary use, avoid using chemical sprays altogether.

It's impractical and expensive to buy, store and use a multitude of insecticides—either organic or chemical. Most home gardeners prefer to use all-purpose controls that take care of most insects or most diseases. I recommend the use of a *pyrethrum-base* insecticide as an organic control for insects. It is a general-purpose, contact poison derived from a South-African daisy. It is short-lived, so it must be used at regular intervals and after every rain.

Pyrethrum is applied as a liquid spray or powder. It controls a wide

Gardener uses knapsack sprayer to apply herbicidal weedkiller in paths between rows of annuals.

range of insect pests, especially leaf hoppers, aphids and whiteflies. Pyrethrum leaves no poisonous residues in the soil.

Soaps can be used to control many pests, especially those with soft bodies, such as aphids and mealy bugs. A solution of liquid dishsoap—1 teaspoon to 1 gallon of water—can be used. Frequent applications are usually required. Because dishsoaps can vary greatly from one brand to another, it is a good idea to test-spray a few plants before spraying your entire planting.

Commercially available insecticidal soaps contain certain fatty acids that are known to be potent to pests. A commonly available brand is Safer Agro-Chem Insecticidal Soap.

An effective, all-purpose chemical control is *Orthene*. It is specially formulated for protecting ornamental plants and is not approved for edible kinds. Suitable alternatives to Orthene are Sevin or diazinon.

Certain insects—notably slugs, snails and Japanese beetles—can be so destructive they require *specific* controls. A Japanese beetle trap uses

a sex attractant to lure insects into a disposable bag. Slugs and snails can be killed with poisonous baits sprinkled among plants. Or use a mulch of cedar bark, which has been found effective in repelling slugs and snails from gardens.

Contact and Systemic—With both insect pests and fungus diseases you have a choice of using *contact* or *systemic* poisons.

A contact poison is sprayed or dusted directly on plants. Contact controls are washed off by rain. It is difficult to apply them under leaf surfaces and into densely foliaged areas.

Systemic controls are generally the most effective means of protection. A systemic is applied to the root zone. The plant absorbs it and distributes it to roots, leaves and stems. When a pest attacks the plant, the systemic goes to work and attacks the pest. Systemic controls protect plants for a longer period than contact controls. Bonide is a popular systemic insecticide effective against thrips, mites, aphids, whiteflies and other hard-to-control sucking insects.

DISEASES

Although annuals are relatively disease-free, certain plants are susceptible to particular diseases. Snapdragons and hollyhocks, for example, are prone to rust disease. Zinnias tend to be attacked by alternaria and powdery mildew. Asters are attacked by wilt and yellows disease.

Fortunately, plant breeders have been able to breed disease resistance into many of the more popular flower groups. Gardeners can now choose varieties of rust-resistant snapdragons, mildew-resistant zinnias, wilt-resistant asters and others.

Keeping your garden clean is an important part of disease prevention. Disease organisms will overwinter on dead leaves and stems, infecting your garden in spring and summer.

Air pollution is not a disease but produces diseaselike symptoms. It can cause unsightly blemishes on flowering annuals, with some classes more susceptible than others. Petunias—especially white and pale-pink grandifloras—are extremely sensitive to pollution. Resistant varieties are now being developed.

Avoid air-pollution damage by planting resistant varieties and locate flower beds away from roadsides and driveways.

Insect Pests

APHIDS are tiny, sucking insects that form large colonies on plant stems and leaf undersides. Colors are green, red, black or white. Aphids suck plant juices and produce a sticky substance called *honeydew,* formed by their excrement. Infested plants turn yellow, lose leaves and become stunted. Aphids are also carriers of disease.

Control: Effective chemical controls are malathion, diazinon or bonide. Organic controls include washing stems and leaves with insecticidal soap or spraying them with pyrethrum or nicotine sulfate. Ladybugs and lacewing larvae are natural enemies.

CUCUMBER BEETLES are 1/4 inch long, yellow-green with stripes or spots. They usually cluster around crowns of tender plants and among blossoms, chewing leaves, stems and flowers. They are carriers of disease.

Control: Apply Sevin or diazinon as a chemical control. Pyrethrum is an effective organic control.

COLORADO POTATO BEETLES are 3/8 inch long, yellow with black stripes. The equally destructive larvae are reddish, hump-backed and resemble grubs. They chew all tender plant parts.

Control: Sevin, diazinon and malathion are effective chemical controls. Pyrethrum is an effective organic insecticide.

CUTWORMS are black, brown or gray grubs, 1/2 inch to 1-1/2 inches long. They spend the day curled up in soil. They emerge at night to chew on plant stems at soil line, causing plants to fall over.

Control: The most common chemical control is a soil drench of diazinon applied in the early evening when grubs are most active. Transplants can also be protected by a paper or metal collar. Use bottomless paper cups slit along one side and wrap around plant stems. Bury tip of cup in soil.

JAPANESE BEETLES are 1/2 inch long, shiny, coppery brown with metallic-green shoulders. When disturbed, they fly off suddenly, emitting a whirring sound. Larvae resemble white cutworms. They overwinter in lawn. Adults eat leaves and flowers of many plants.

Control: Malathion and Sevin are effective chemical controls. The best organic control is a Japanese beetle trap using a sex hormone to attract male beetles.

LEAF HOPPERS are 1/8-inch-long, grasshopperlike insects, usually green. They sit on leaves then hop abruptly into the air. Leaf hoppers are especially troublesome in fall, sucking plant juices and transmitting disease such as aster yellows.

Control: Apply Sevin, diazinon or malathion as chemical controls. Dust plants with pyrethrum to control organically.

MEALY BUGS are white insects that cluster around tender plant parts, resembling bits of cotton. They suck juices from plants.

Control: Malathion is an effective chemical control. Washing stems with insecticidal soap or dabbing their bodies with rubbing alcohol are organic alternatives.

MITES are spiderlike pests only 1/50 inch long. They are yellow, green or red. They spin fine, silvery webs among leaves and stems. Mites suck plant juices, causing leaves to curl and wilt.

Control: The miticide dicofol is most effective. It must be administered early in the season. After mites are established they are difficult to eradicate. Diazinon and malathion sprays used regularly offer some control. The systemic insecticide, Bonide, is also effective. Spraying with water helps some. Ladybugs are natural predators of mites.

NEMATODES are microscopic worms that live in soil and attack plant roots, causing swellings called *galls.* Plants become stunted and turn yellow.

Aphids prefer to colonize vegetable plants, but will attack annuals, introducing diseases.

Cutworms were exposed while digging a flower bed for planting. Soil drenches containing diazinon are common means of control.

Mealy bugs will attack the tender stems of many flowering annuals. If infestations are minor, dislodge these pests with jets of water from the garden hose.

Control: Chemical controls such as soil drenches are generally ineffective. Soil fumigation using Vapam is best. Applied in liquid solution to soil, it releases a gas, destroying weed seeds and soil fungi in addition to nematodes. This is best done by a pest-control company. An organic control is French marigolds planted as a cover crop for 1 year. Studies have shown they help repel nematodes.

STEM BORERS are the caterpillar stage of a moth that lays its eggs at the base of plants. Larvae bore their way into stems. Borers are white, about 1 inch long. They leave holes and a sawdustlike material called *frass* where they enter plant. They are difficult to control because they are hidden inside stems. Plants wilt as larvae bore deeper.
Control: Some control is possible using malathion. The most effective control is endosulfan, trade name Thiodan. To control organically, use pyrethrum or rotenone. Garlic-pepper sprays help repel the egg-laying moth.

SLUGS AND SNAILS are similar pests. Snails have a shell they can retract into when threatened. Both are most active during wet weather and at night. They emerge from hiding places to chew tender plant parts.
Control: Slug bait sprinkled among plants is an effective chemical control. To control organically, use a mulch of cedar bark, which is repellent to slugs and snails. Or hand-pick them with gloved hand and destroy them.

THRIPS are tiny, threadlike, winged insects that suck plant juices. You can spot them on plants using a magnifying glass. They are pale yellow when immature, turning to a tan-brownish color as adults. Symptoms of their damage are white streaks on leaves and flowers. Edges of leaves sometimes turn brown.
Control: If these pests are discovered, spray with malathion solution every 5 to 7 days until signs of thrips and damage are no longer evident. Also spray soil surface around plant to kill *nymphs*—the immature stage of this pest. Remove spent blossoms regularly to prevent infestations.

WHITEFLIES are small, sucking insects with white bodies covered with powder. They fly up in a cloud like flakes of snow when disturbed.
Control: Diazinon and malathion are chemical controls. Also effective is the systemic Bonide. Washing stems with an insecticidal soap is an organic control. Ladybugs are natural predators of whiteflies.

Diseases

ALTERNARIA is a fungus disease that causes severe leaf spots and patches on a number of annuals, particularly zinnias and geraniums. Leaf spots and patches are usually light brown with a lighter-color center. Spots spread to cover leaves, which wither and die.
Control: Regular rainfall or frequent overhead irrigation such as from sprinklers helps spread the disease. Spray plants with wettable sulfur or copper-base fungicide. To control organically, pick off and destroy infected leaves. Do not save seeds from your own plants because they can spread infection the following season.

BOTRYTIS is a widespread fungus disease that attacks leaves, stems and flowers. It shows itself most noticeably in flower heads, especially those of geraniums. Center of flower becomes mushy and blackened. When the disease infects leaves and stems, plant tissue blackens and enlarges rapidly.
Control: Abundant rainfall or frequent overhead irrigation encourages spread of disease. Sprays of benomyl, zineb and captan are effective. Without these fungicides, control is difficult. Remove infected plants. Provide

Presence of mites on this hollyhock plant is indicated by curling leaf edges.

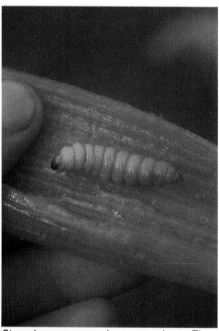

Stem borers come in many sizes. They attack numerous kinds of annuals, including zinnias and marigolds. This is squash-vine borer.

Botrytis disease on geranium plant is identified by mushy, black flower centers and brown patches on leaves.

space between plants for circulation.

DAMPING-OFF disease is most troublesome on seedlings grown indoors, but is a common cause of seedling death outdoors. Seedlings are attacked at soil line and fall over and die. The fungus is present in unsterilized soil, and can be transmitted by dirty pots. Tiny seedlings such as impatiens and begonias are particularly susceptible.

Control: Use only sterile potting soil and sterilize pots. The most effective control is to spray the soil surface with benomyl. Avoid waterlogged soil and provide seedlings with optimum light and temperature to help them resist the disease.

POWDERY MILDEW is a widespread fungus disease that thrives in wet weather and attacks a wide variety of flowering annuals. It is most prevalent on zinnias. Grayish-white, powdery patches appear on leaf surfaces, especially following periods of rainfall and high humidity. Plants turn brown, shrivel and die.

Control: Avoid irrigating with overhead sprinklers. Dust or spray plants with sulfur-base fungicides or dinocap, trade name Karathane. Benomyl is also effective in controlling the disease. As an organic control, grow mildew-resistant varieties. Clean the garden thoroughly in winter, destroying all infected plants.

RUST is a destructive fungus disease that commonly affects hollyhocks and snapdragons. It shows itself as orange or brown powdery pustules on leaves or stems—particularly the undersides. If infestations are severe, plants can die.

Control: Avoid overhead sprinkling. High humidity and periods of high rainfall promote the disease. Remove and destroy infected leaves as soon as they are noticed. Spray plants with sulfur, captan or zineb. Among certain flower classes, notably snapdragons, rust-resistant varieties can be planted. When pruning infected plant parts, disinfect shears after each cut by dipping in a solution of 50% bleach and water. Discard infected plant parts.

WILT is a name for numerous bacterial and fungus diseases that cause the plant to wilt. The most serious disease commonly called *wilt* is fusarium wilt. Its principal target is asters. Afflicted plants suddenly become limp, droop, turn brown and die. Sometimes part of plant will show symptoms. The plant may appear to recover briefly, but the entire plant usually dies.

Control: Plant wilt-resistant varieties. Spray soil with benomyl. Certain plants such as dahlias and cosmos are more susceptible to *bacterial* wilt. In these instances, the most effective prevention is to control insects, which are largely responsible for spreading the disease.

YELLOWS disease affects mostly asters, but also attacks marigolds, chrysanthemums and other flowering annuals. It is often called *aster yellows.* A microplasmalike organism is responsible for the disease, but leaf hoppers are the primary cause of its spread. First evidence is a yellowing of growing tips, especially around a flower bud. Stunted plants, deformed blooms and an abnormal number of side shoots are further symptoms. Affected plants do not generally wilt or die, but remain unsightly. See photo below.

Control: Destroy infected plants. Spray healthy plants with malathion to control leaf hoppers. Or spray with rotenone-pyrethrum organic insecticide.

Powdery mildew infests zinnia leaf. Zinnias resistant to this disease are available.

Rust disease on hollyhock shows orange-brown pustules that burst and spread spores.

Aster yellows attacked these marigolds. Deformed flowers and sickly yellow leaves identify this disease, which is often spread by leaf hoppers.

7

Gallery of Garden Annuals

The following encyclopedia includes more than 100 familiar and not-so-familiar flowering annuals. They are arranged alphabetically by common names used by the majority of North-American seedsmen. In some instances the botanical name is also the common name, such as *Delphinium* and *Impatiens.* If you are looking for an annual and its name is not listed in the description heading, refer to the Index on pages 158 to 160 for a cross-reference.

Each class of annual is shown in one or more photographs including several large "portraits." Many were grown in my own garden. When possible, a close-up and garden landscape scene are shown to present both *flower form* and *plant habit.*

HARDY OR TENDER
In the first paragraph of the descriptions, each annual is identified as *hardy* or *tender.* This is an important distinction. A hardy annual withstands some frost and can be planted several weeks before the last expected frost date in your area. A tender annual is susceptible to frost and should not be planted until all danger of frost has passed. For a guide to frost dates in your area, see the map on pages 46 and 47.

COOL SEASON OR WARM SEASON
In addition to classifying annuals as hardy and tender, many of the descriptions state whether the plant flowers best during cool or warm periods of the growing season. They are termed *cool season* or *warm season.* This is important in regions with warm summers. Cool-season annuals must be planted so they mature in the cool weather of early summer or fall. Some cool-weather annuals—nemesias, cinerarias, calceolarias and schizanthus—are not practical to grow in many regions of North America, except coastal areas and the Pacific Northwest. They need a long, cool, summer season to perform well. The midsummer heat common to most of North America burns them up.

HEIGHT AND SIZE
Where heights and sizes are supplied with descriptions, the standard is to state mature height at time of flowering. In conditions such as excessive rainfall and high soil fertility, dwarf varieties may grow much higher than usual. Conversely, if soil fertility is poor and regular moisture is not available, plants will not grow to their expected mature size.

VARIETY RECOMMENDATIONS
Descriptions give recommended varieties with reasons why they are superior. Realize that new varieties are continually being introduced. Be alert for new sizes, flower colors and improvements by visiting local arboretums and display gardens and by reading garden publications.

Left: Nasturtiums grown for seed production create a kaleidoscope of color. This field is located near Lompoc, California, flower-seed capital of the world. Above: Dark-purple rocket larkspur is striking in contrast to orange and yellow flowers in background.

When you're ready to plant, don't expect to find each annual or the recommended varieties as transplants at your local garden center. The bedding-plant industry that supplies local garden centers does 90% of its business in just five classes of annuals—petunias, impatiens, geraniums, marigolds and pansies. Within these classes, variety selection is limited. Local seed racks are also poor sources for recommended varieties. Seeds available are largely confined to old, established, standard varieties.

Recommended varieties are usually widely available from flower-seed catalogs. A list of mail-order sources is provided on page 38. By sending away for three or four catalogs—most are free—you should have no difficulty purchasing recommended varieties.

AWARD-WINNERS

When reading plant labels, scanning mail-order seed catalogs or searching seed racks, it is sometimes difficult to decide which varieties are best. Major classes such as petunias, marigolds and zinnias can be especially confusing.

Several award systems have been organized to help identify outstanding varieties. The three most important are the *All-America Selections, Fleuroselect*—the European seed trials—and the award system of the *Royal Horticultural Society* in England. In the following pages I have noted which varieties have won awards from these organizations.

All-America Selections was organized in 1932 by the American seed trade. Each year it makes awards of recognition to outstanding new varieties. New flowers are planted in test gardens located in every climatic region of the United States and Canada. Judges at each location evaluate the newcomers alongside plantings of existing, similar varieties, comparing performances. Judges are drawn equally from academic circles and the seed trade. They score points for each variety according to its performance in their test garden. The points are added. By averaging the scores, a committee decides the winners. Awards are Gold Medals, Silver Medals and Bronze Medals.

Winners are those that usually do well in most parts of North America. A network of display gardens allows the public to see current and recent award-winning varieties.

Fleuroselect is the European equivalent of All-America Selections. Founded in 1970, it also evaluates new varieties and makes awards of recognition based on plant performance. Trial gardens are located as far north as Finland and as far south as southern Italy.

A unique aspect of Fleuroselect is its recognition of "novelty" plants. Even if a new variety fails to win an award, the organization may feel it is different enough to rate recognition. Thus the plant is announced as a novelty.

The Royal Horticultural Society was founded in 1804. Its award system grants First-Class Certificates, Awards of Merit and Honorable Mentions for outstanding plants.

The RHS award system differs significantly from Fleuroselect and All-America Selections. Its testing system is open to *all* cultivated varieties, not just new ones. With few exceptions, only certain groups of plants are chosen for testing in a given year. All plants are tested in one location—at the society's headquar-

ters near Wisley (Surrey). If marigolds or scarlet sage are tested one year, they may not be tested again for another 20 years. Exceptions are sweet peas and delphiniums. They are so popular in England that the RHS tests them every year.

SEED FACTS

Under the heading *How To Grow,* information is given concerning seed germination. Care has been taken to give number of days to germination, as well as optimum temperature range and other factors that may influence germination. These would include exposure to light, need for darkness, pre-chilling, pre-soaking and other special factors. This information has been gained from my personal experience of growing from seeds every annual described here. It has also been verified with the *Journal of Seed Technology,* published by the Association of Official Seed Analysts, a group that establishes official seed germination standards for government and industry.

Many gardeners prefer to grow medium-size and large-seeded varieties from seeds, and buy nursery transplants of fine-seeded varieties. Fine seeds are more difficult to grow. Seeds need careful misting and close attention to light requirements. It also takes a long time for seedlings to reach transplant size.

All-America trial gardens like this are located in every climatic area of the United States. Entries are submitted by plant breeders from around the world, hoping to gain an All-America award.

AFRICAN DAISY
Dimorphotheca sinuata

These are tender annuals native to South Africa. Flowers are daisylike in white, yellow, salmon, pink and orange, with dark centers. Petals have a shimmering appearance, and close on cloudy days and at night. African daisies bloom mostly in spring. They bloom continually when nights are cool. Plants grow 4 to 12 inches high and spread 12 inches wide.

Recommended Varieties—In addition to a mixture usually listed as *Dimorphotheca aurantiaca* 'Mixed Colors', orange and white African daisies are available as separate colors.

How to Grow—Sow seeds directly in the garden after all danger of frost has passed. For earliest flowers, start seeds indoors 4 to 5 weeks before last frost date. Seeds germinate best with some light, so barely cover seeds with soil. Germination takes 10 to 14 days at 60F to 70F (16C to 21C) soil temperature. Sow in fall in cool greenhouse for spring flowers. Seeds are short-lived and do not store well.

Space plants 12 inches apart in full sun. Although they tolerate periods of drought, regular watering helps ensure continual bloom. Plants prefer loam or sandy soil. They flower best when night temperatures are 45F to 50F (7C to 10C).

Leaf hoppers can spread aster yellows disease. Control with Sevin chemical spray or pyrethrum organic spray. Leaves can become infected with powdery mildew disease. Control with copper fungicide.

Uses—Low beds, borders and as greenhouse plants in containers. Popular as flowering ground cover during spring months.

AGERATUM
Ageratum houstonianum

Also called *floss flower,* ageratums are tender annuals widely dispersed throughout the southern United States and Central and South America. Garden varieties are mostly dwarf, compact plants growing 6 to 12 inches high, spreading 9 to 12 inches wide. The powderpuff blooms are borne in tight clusters, creating a fluffy appearance in shades of blue, pink and white. Plants bloom continually from early summer to fall frost.

Recommended Varieties—Hybridizing has greatly improved the display qualities of ageratum. 'Midget Blue', 5 inches high, and 'Blue Mink', 10 inches high, are widely available. 'Summer Snow' hybrid, 5 inches high, is a popular white variety.

How to Grow—Sow seeds directly in the garden after all danger of frost has passed. Better results are obtained by starting seeds indoors 6 to 8 weeks before last frost date. Seeds are tiny and require light to germinate. Press them into the soil surface to anchor them. Seeds germinate in 7 to 10 days at 70F to 85F (21C to 27C).

Space plants 6 to 9 inches apart in a sunny location, although they will tolerate light shade. Soil should be fertile, high in organic material and well drained. Water plants regularly to maintain regular bloom.

Where powdery mildew disease is a problem, avoid wetting foliage. If mildew does occur, control with fungicides. Slugs and snails are attracted to young plants. Control by using slug bait.

African daisies show the beautiful color range that makes these tender annuals popular as a ground cover.

'Blue Mink' ageratum creates a carpet of fluffy blue flowers. Flowers in foreground are lobelia. Those in background are American marigolds.

Agrostemma is grown mostly for cutting.

Uses—Excellent edging plant for beds and borders. Try it as companion plant in window boxes and tubs. Tall kinds are useful for cutting.

AGROSTEMMA
Agrostemma milas

This hardy annual is native to the Mediterranean, where it appears as a weed in grain fields. Plants grow 3 feet high, bearing grasslike leaves and 2-inch, rose-pink flowers resembling miniature hibiscus blossoms. Black spots form stripes leading to the center of each flower.

Caution: Seeds are poisonous if eaten.

Recommended Varieties—'Milas' is a cultivar of *Agrostemma githago* and generally the only variety offered.

How to Grow—Plants grow quickly from seeds. They are usually sown directly in the garden and covered lightly with soil. Because plants tolerate mild frosts, seeds may be sown outdoors several weeks before last frost date. Plants tolerate crowding. Broadcast evenly on cultivated soil. They usually require no thinning. Seeds germinate in 5 to 10 days at 55F to 70F (13C to 21C) soil temperature.

Agrostemma tolerates a wide range of soil conditions, including poor soil and periods of dry weather. Sow seeds at 2- to 3-week intervals until mid-summer for a succession of blooms.

Uses—Adapted to cutting gardens and mixed borders. Flowers are striking in arrangements.

ALYSSUM
Lobularia maritima

This low-growing, hardy annual from the Mediterranean covers itself with clusters of tiny, fragrant flowers. Plants grow 3 to 6 inches high and spread 12 inches wide. White is the most popular color, but light pink, deep pink and purple are available.

Recommended Varieties—'Carpet of Snow' is the most widely grown white variety. 'Wonderland', deep pink, won a Fleuroselect award for its improvement over light-pink 'Rosie O'Day'. 'Royal Carpet' is deep purple with a white eye.

How to Grow—Alyssum tolerates mild frosts. Sow seeds directly in the garden several weeks before last frost date. Scatter seeds on the soil surface. They require light to germinate. For earlier flowers, start seeds indoors 4 weeks before planting outdoors. Press seeds into the seed-starting medium just deep enough to anchor them. Germination takes 8 to 15 days at 60F to 70F (15C to 21C) soil temperature.

Although alyssum is usually planted as separate colors, mixtures are available. Because flowers appear soon after seeds germinate, it's possible to start a mixture indoors. Grow plants to flowering stage and separate colors into groups of white, pink and purple. Transplant the colors in sections to create a color pattern.

Flowers are most profuse during cool weather. Plants prefer full sun and tolerate a wide range of soil conditions, as long as drainage is good. Space plants 12 inches apart.

Uses—Popular for edging beds and borders. Use to create fast-growing, temporary ground cover among

'Carpet of Snow' alyssum drapes gracefully from strawberry pot.

paving stones, in rock gardens and along dry walls. As a novelty, try planting alyssum in a pattern on a slope or bank to spell out a number or name. It also cascades nicely from hanging baskets or window boxes.

AMARANTHUS
Amaranthus tricolor

This tender annual is grown mostly for its colorful crown of leaves. Plants grow to 4 feet high and spread 2 wide. Leaf colors include red, yellow, orange, chocolate and lime-green. Some varieties have several combinations of these colors. Native to India.

A related species, *Amaranthus caudatus,* produces long, drooping, blood-red flowers in clusters. It is commonly called *love-lies-bleeding.* Plants grow to 2 feet high and spread 2 feet wide.

Recommended Varieties—'Joseph's Coat', 3 feet high, is sometimes listed as 'Perfecta'. It displays three distinct colors in its crown of lance-shape leaves—bright red, yellow and green. 'Illumination', 3 feet high, has broad, rose-red leaves tinged gold. 'Early Splendor', 3 feet high, has narrow, deep-red leaves at the top and dark, chocolate leaves below.

How to Grow—Amaranthus does not transplant well. Sow seeds directly in the garden after all danger of frost has passed. Lightly cover seeds with soil because exposure to light aids germination. Seeds will germinate in about 8 to 10 days at 70F to 85F (21C to 30C) soil temperature.

Plant 2 feet apart in full sun. Plants tolerate poor soil, heat and drought. Leaves of both species, especially *Amaranthus tricolor,* are edible, and may attract chewing insects such as Japanese beetles. Control pests with traps or Sevin chemical spray. Young plants may need protection from slugs and snails. Use slug bait or hand-pick from plants and destroy. If conditions are excessively wet or if drainage is poor, root rot may occur, causing plants to collapse.

Uses—*Amaranthus tricolor* works well as tall background next to walls and fences, and as a highlight in island beds. *Amaranthus caudatus* is used mostly in borders of mixed annuals and for summer bedding.

ANCHUSA
Anchusa capensis

Anchusa is strictly a hardy biennial that was discovered in South America. Dwarf varieties are available that can be grown as annuals. Commonly called *summer forget-me-nots,* they have blue, forget-me-not flowers that bloom in summer when nights are cool. Plants grow 10 to 18 inches high and spread about 10 inches wide.

Recommended Varieties—'Blue Angel', 10 inches high, and 'Blue Bird', 18 inches high, are annual types. Plants are compact and mounding.

How to Grow—Sow seeds outdoors several weeks before the last frost date. Cover seeds with 1/4 inch of fine soil. For earlier flowers, start seeds indoors 6 to 8 weeks before planting outdoors in early spring. Germination occurs in 6 to 16 days at 60F (16C).

Plant in full sun in fertile, well-drained soil. Space plants 8 to 10 inches apart. Keep soil moist. If plants stop blooming during summer heat, shear to within 6

Amaranthus caudatus, love-lies-bleeding, has rusty-red seed panicles that add color in late summer and fall.

Anchusa is also called *summer forget-me-not* because of its similarity to forget-me-not flowers.

Arctotis flowers come in wide range of colors, which makes them popular for cutting.

inches of the soil line. This will encourage new flowers when cool weather returns in late summer or fall.

Plants are generally free of pests and diseases except for occasional problems with powdery mildew. Control by spraying with benomyl.

Uses—Beds and borders as an edging.

ARCTOTIS
Arctotis stoechadifolia

South Africa—particularly the region known as *Namaqualand*—is rich in wildflowers. Most rainfall occurs in spring, prompting entire coastal meadows and inland desert regions to erupt into a mass of color. Hundreds of varieties compete for attention while the brief rains allow them to flower. Most are tender annuals and members of the daisy family. They include *Mesembryanthemum, Osteospermum, Gerbera, Gazania, Drosanthemum, Venidium* and *Arctotis*. Arctotis, also called *African lilac-daisy,* produces the largest flowers—up to 4 inches across. Flowers are daisylike with shimmering petals that close at night and in cloudy weather. They bloom in early summer when nights are cool. Colors include white, yellow, pink, red and orange. Plants grow 12 to 15 inches high and spread 12 inches wide.

Recommended Varieties—'Giant Mixed Colors' is a beautiful mixture with the largest flowers.

How to Grow—Sow seeds directly in the garden after all danger of frost has passed. Or start indoors 6 to 8 weeks before last frost date. Germination takes 6 to 18 days at 60F to 70F (16C to 21C) soil temperature. Seeds are sensitive to temperatures above 70F (21C).

Space plants 12 inches apart in full sun. Plants grow in almost any soil. Arctotis tolerate drought but must have cool nights to flower. They do well in coastal areas. Remove faded flowers regularly for continual bloom. Pinch the main shoot to encourage side branching. Botrytis and gray mold may cause rotting during wet weather. Benomyl and captan are fungicides that can be used to help control gray mold.

Uses—Beds, borders and as cut flowers.

Arctotis growing in seed-production field in Lompoc, California.

ASTER, CHINA
Callistephus chinensis

China asters are magnificent, tender annuals native to China. They would be more popular in North America if plants were not so susceptible to several common diseases. Plants grow 6 inches to 3 feet high, depending on variety, spreading 12 to 15 inches wide. The fluffy, mostly double, chrysanthemum-type flowers can measure up to 7 inches across. Color range is extensive, including white, yellow, pink, red and blue. Under cool conditions, plants flower continually from summer to fall frost.

Recommended Varieties—'Giant Perfection', mixed colors, 2 feet high, grows upright as narrow bunches of loosely double, 4-inch flowers. Long stems are excellent for cutting. 'Powderpuff Super Bouquet', mixed colors, 2 feet high, has double flowers with creamy yellow centers. The entire plant can be cut and presented as an instant bouquet. Dwarf varieties are suitable as bedding plants. 'Dwarf Queen' strain is especially attractive, growing 10 to 12 inches high in a mound shape. Large double flowers come in red, white, blue and pink.

How to Grow—Asters do not transplant well. Sow seeds directly in the garden after all danger of frost has passed. Cover with 1/4 inch of fine soil. For earliest flowers, start seeds indoors in peat pots 6 weeks before last frost date. Avoid root disturbance as much as possible when transplanting or plants may wilt. Germination takes 4 to 10 days at 60F to 70F (16C to 21C) soil temperature. Space dwarf varieties 6 inches apart. Space tall varieties 12 to 18 inches apart.

Avoid planting China asters in the same location where asters grew previously. This reduces risk of wilt disease. Rotate planting site each year. Plant in full sun, in loose, fertile, well-drained soil. Keep soil moist.

The two most serious problems with asters are fusarium wilt and aster yellows. Fusarium wilt is caused by a fungus. Young seedlings stricken with the disease topple over suddenly and die. Older specimens that are afflicted may remain stunted or become lopsided. Yellowing of leaves and collapse of the entire plant may follow. Sometimes the disease does not show itself until plants are ready to bloom. To control, grow only wilt-resistant varieties.

Aster yellows disease is caused by a microorganism that attacks several other plants but is especially destructive to asters. The microorganism responsible is spread by leaf hoppers. Controlling these insect pests reduces risk of infection. Sevin chemical spray or pyrethrum organic spray are effective against leaf hoppers. Pull up and destroy plants known to be affected with aster yellows to prevent its spread.

Uses—Tall kinds are excellent for cutting and create beautiful flower arrangements. China asters are widely grown in greenhouses to provide cut flowers during winter months. Dwarf varieties are commonly used as edging for beds and borders.

Scarlet 'Powderpuff Super Bouquet' China aster.

China Aster: Flowering Heights

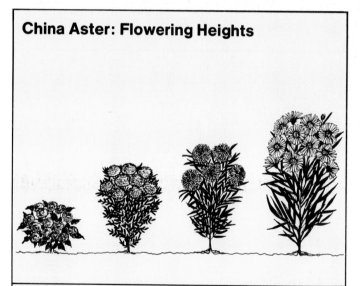

1 foot	1-1/2 feet	2 feet	2-1/2 feet
'Color Carpet'	'Early Charm'	'Crego'	'American Beauty'
'Dwarf Border'	'Pompon'	'Duchess'	'American Branching'
'Dwarf Queen'		'Early Bird'	'California Giant'
'Dwarf Spider'		'Fluffy Ruffles'	'Ostrich Plume'
'Mini-Lady'		'Giant Perfection'	'Super Giants'
'Mumsters'		'Perfection'	'Totem Poles'
'Pinocchio'		'Princess'	
'Red Mount'		'Powderpuff Super	
'Star Flowered'		Bouquet'	
		'Unicum'	

'Tom Thumb' balsam is often used as bedding plant.

'Dark Opal' ornamental basil contrasts well with yellow Dahlberg daisies.

BALSAM
Impatiens balsamina

These tender annuals grow as upright, bushy plants studded with double flowers up to 2 inches across. Flowers have a waxy texture and resemble miniature camellias. Colors include white, yellow, pink, red and purple with some bicolors. Plants grow 1 to 3 feet high and spread 1 to 2 feet wide. They flower continually from summer to fall frost. Native to India and other parts of tropical Asia.

Recommended Varieties—'Tom Thumb', mixed colors, is an extra-dwarf variety that grows 12 inches high. Flowers are held well above foliage rather than partially hidden among stems and leaves like taller varieties. 'Royal', mixed colors, is a camellia-flower type, with maximum height of 2 feet.

How to Grow—Seeds can be sown directly in the garden after all danger of frost has passed. Better to start seeds indoors 6 to 8 weeks before last frost date. Cover seeds lightly because light aids germination. Seeds germinate in 8 days at 70F to 85F (21C to 30C) soil temperature.

Space plants 12 inches apart in full sun or partial shade. They prefer a loose, fertile, well-drained soil high in organic matter. Balsam tolerates high heat if soil is kept moist.

Chewing insects such as cucumber beetles can spread wilt disease. Control with Sevin chemical spray or pyrethrum organic spray. Inspect plant tips soon after planting for signs of aphid colonies. Wash off with insecticidal soap.

Uses—An old-fashion favorite for beds and borders.

BASIL, ORNAMENTAL
Ocimum basilicum

Two kinds of ornamental basil are popular in home gardens. The most widely used is purple-leaved basil, which grows 1-1/2 to 2 feet high. Increasing in popularity is miniature green basil, which grows 8 to 12 inches high. It forms a neat, green mound of small leaves. Flowers are tiny and white. Both are tender annuals and native to the Mediterranean.

Recommended Varieties—'Dark Opal', the purple-leaved variety, won an All-America award for its shining, purple-bronze foliage. 'Green Bouquet' is a dwarf, bushy plant useful for edging beds and borders. Flavor of leaves is same as the popular herb, sweet basil.

How to Grow—Sow seeds outdoors after all danger of frost has passed. Or start seeds indoors 6 to 8 weeks before last frost date. Germination takes 14 days at 70F to 85F (21C to 30C) soil temperature.

Space miniature varieties 8 inches apart. Space tall types 18 inches apart. Plant in full sun in fertile, well-drained soil amended with plenty of organic matter. Keep soil moist.

Plants are generally disease-free. Slugs and snails will strip plants overnight unless controlled. Japanese beetles are also attracted to basil. Spray with Sevin or use special traps.

Uses—Tall, purple-leaved basil is commonly used as a background plant in beds and borders to contrast with light-color flowers such as white petunias and yellow marigolds. Miniature kinds are used for edging beds and borders, and in pots and window boxes.

BEGONIA, WAX
Begonia semperflorens

The late Ernst Benary, a master plant breeder who produced the first begonia hybrids, was showing me around his company's test garden, at Hanover-Munden, West Germany. Standard varieties of wax begonias were planted directly alongside his newest hybrids. "Look at my beautiful begonias," he exclaimed. "No other flower has benefited more from hybridizing." He was right. The standard varieties looked pale compared to his hybrids, which were smothered in blooms and uniform in growth habit. Even though hybridizing has produced astonishing improvements in other flower classes—notably petunias and marigolds—nothing shows it more dramatically than begonias.

Wax begonias are tender annuals descended from species native to Central and South America. They flower continually from early summer until fall frost. The term *wax* refers to the texture of the leaves, which are fleshy, smooth and shiny. Most are green or bronze. Although wax begonias are commonly grown for their non-stop flowering displays, the leaves are decorative. Flowers are small but masses of blooms create a dense, colorful display. Colors include rose, pink, red and white, plus bicolors. Plants grow 6 to 12 inches high and spread 6 to 12 inches wide, depending on variety.

Recommended Varieties—Wax begonias are available in three sizes: dwarf—growing 6 to 8 inches high; intermediate—8 to 10 inches high; and tall—10 to 12 inches high. They are also classified as *green leaved, bronze leaved* and *variegated.* Flower form can be single or double. Dwarf, green-leaved, single-flower varieties are the most popular as bedding plants. The best of the green-leaved hybrids are 'Viva', white; 'Linda', deep rose; and 'Scarletta', scarlet. For bronze foliage look for 'Whisky', white; 'Gin', deep pink; and 'Vodka', scarlet. They were introduced by Ernst Benary. He also produced 'Cocktail', an excellent mixture. Plants grow 6 to 8 inches high and are excellent bedding plants.

Intermediate varieties include 'Glamour' hybrids, which produce large flowers up to 2 inches across. Colors include pink, rose, red, white and an unusual combination called *picotee.* With picotee flowers, inner parts of petals are white, shading to pink at the edges. Leaves are green. Plants remain bushy and compact, growing to 10 inches high. 'Venus' is an especially bright rose-pink. It is also valued for its early flowers. See photo, page 68.

The 'Danicas' are the best tall cultivars, growing 12 inches or more high. Flowers are huge—up to 2-1/2 inches across. Use plants individually in tubs or create a low, flowering background hedge.

'Calla Queen', 12 inches high, is strictly for indoor culture. It has green leaves. Pink flowers are flecked with white.

How to Grow—Wax begonias are one of the most difficult annuals to grow from seeds. Seeds are like specks of dust. It takes up to 2 million to make an ounce! Germination is relatively slow, requiring 14 to 20 days at 70F to 85F (21C to 30C) soil temperature. Subsequent growth in the seedling stage is also slow, requiring 12 weeks to produce transplants.

Seeds need light to germinate and should be pressed into the soil surface just enough to anchor them. Plant-

'Vodka' wax begonia is growing in a border of mixed annuals, including purple-leaf ornamental pepper, yellow coleus, rose-pink zinnias and pale-pink spider plants.

'Glamour Rose' wax begonia is valued as container subject. In background are red geraniums and blue browallia.

Close-up of 'Venus' wax begonia.

ing mix of peat, perlite and vermiculite is ideal. Plant seeds in trays or flats. Moisture is essential to germinate the seeds. If soil surface dries, germinating seeds will die. To maintain high humidity and to prevent drying out, enclose the seed tray in a clear, plastic bag. Seeds also require bright light. If natural light is not available, fluorescent lights may be necessary. When seedlings are large enough to handle, transfer to individual pots. The root system of a seedling begonia is extremely small. Provide with regular moisture—preferably by misting—to grow to transplant size.

Feed seedlings with diluted liquid fertilizer once a week until they reach transplant size.

Hybrid varieties can be planted in full sun or partial shade. Standard varieties usually perform well only in partial shade. Space dwarfs 8 inches apart. Space taller varieties 12 inches apart. Green-leaved varieties planted in shade sometimes turn bronze. Young plants are highly sensitive to cold. Harden-off transplants for 10 days before planting outdoors. Plant outdoors after all danger of frost has passed.

The most important requirement for a stunning floral display is good soil. If your soil is not a rich loam, amend with lots of organic matter, especially peat moss, garden compost or leaf mold. This helps cool the soil and retains moisture without creating a waterlogged condition, which will cause stem rot. Begonias are shallow-rooted plants and benefit from frequent watering and booster feedings of diluted liquid fertilizer.

To propagate begonias from stem cuttings, cut stems in sections 4 to 5 inches long. Immerse in water. Add some activated charcoal to keep water from becoming stagnant. When stem produces roots, plant in container with potting soil.

Wax begonias are troubled by few insect pests but are susceptible to a number of diseases. To prevent damping-off of seedlings, spray seed trays with captan or benomyl. Bacterial leaf spot may appear as small, round, brown spots on leaves. It is usually caused by overcrowding of plants. Infected plant parts should be discarded. Botrytis blight shows itself as a brownish-gray mold on leaves. It can be controlled with benomyl. Powdery mildew, a white, dusty coating on leaves, is a fungus disease that can also be controlled by spraying with benomyl. Crown and stem rot can be avoided by using sterilized soil for seed starting or propagation. Give plants enough space to maintain good air circulation.

Uses—Excellent for mass plantings in beds and borders. Exceptional for window boxes, tubs and as container plants for greenhouse and home.

Wax begonias make spectacular hanging baskets.

BELLS OF IRELAND
Moluccella laevis

Green flowers are rare. Bells of Ireland—native to Asia—is one of the best. A tender annual, plant produces tall flower spikes studded with green, cup-shape *bracts,* modified leaves that look similar to flowers. The actual tiny, white flowers are located within these bracts. Plants grow 2 to 3 feet high and spread 1 foot wide. Flowers appear in midsummer and bloom until frost.

Recommended Varieties—Not sold by variety name.

How to Grow—Seeds have a hard coat that slows germination unless the soil is warm and moist. Sow them directly in the garden after all danger of frost has passed. Or start seeds indoors 8 weeks before last frost date. Germination takes 7 to 21 days at 70F to 85F (21C to 30C) soil temperature. Soaking seeds overnight in lukewarm water helps speed germination.

Plants tolerate crowding but do best spaced about 9 inches apart. Plant in full sun or light shade. Bells of Ireland tolerate poor soils if drainage is good. They grow best if soil is kept moist. The more frequently flower stems are picked, the more flowers the plant produces. Plant reseeds itself readily and new plants may appear as volunteers in subsequent years. Generally free of pests and diseases.

Uses—Cutting for fresh or dried-flower arrangements.

BLUE-LACE FLOWER
Trachymene coerulea

Blue-lace flower resembles Queen-Anne's lace, but blooms are mainly blue. This native Australian wildflower is a tender annual. Flowers last a few weeks during early summer. Plants grow upright to 2 feet high and spread 1 foot wide.

Recommended Varieties—Not normally sold by variety name.

How to Grow—Sow seeds outdoors after all danger of frost has passed. Transplanting from seeds started indoors is difficult because plants dislike root disturbance. Germination takes 15 to 20 days at 70F (21C) soil temperature.

Plants tolerate crowding but grow best spaced 9 to 12 inches apart. Give them full sun and light, well-drained, fertile soil. Generally free of pests and diseases.

Uses—Grown mostly for cutting.

BRACHYCOME
Brachycome iberidifolia

This tender annual creates a beautiful mound of daisy-like flowers. Flowers are 1-1/2 inches across, and come in blue, rose-pink, white and violet, with contrasting dark centers. Although the blooming period is mostly confined to a 3-week period during summer, the display is spectacular. Flowering height is 10 to 18 inches with a spread of 12 to 14 inches. Succession plantings spaced 3 weeks apart will ensure continual bloom. Brachycome is also known as *Swan River daisy,* referring to the region of Australia where it grows wild.

Recommended Varieties—Not normally sold by variety name, although five separate species are known to be in cultivation.

Flower spike of bells of Ireland.

Blue-lace flower shows its cluster of beautiful blue flowers.

Brachycome can flower so profusely that blooms completely hide foliage.

How to Grow—Seeds can be sown directly in the garden after all danger of frost has passed. For earlier blooms, start seeds indoors 6 weeks before last frost date. Germination takes 12 days at 60F to 70F (16C to 21C). Seeds are sensitive to temperatures above 70F (21C).

Space plants 12 inches apart in full sun, preferably in a loose or sandy soil. Keep soil moist and fertile. Brachycome prefer cool night temperatures to grow well. Plants are generally free of pests and diseases.

Uses—Plant in beds and borders for massed displays. Also attractive in rock gardens and for cutting. Sometimes grown as flowering container plants in a cool greenhouse during winter.

BROWALLIA
Browallia speciosa

Plant breeder Claude Hope of Linda Vista Seed Farms, Costa Rica, introduced this beautiful, tender annual into general cultivation. It was found growing wild in the rain forests of Central America. The first specimens that were collected could be kept alive only by constant misting. After years of selection, more robust plants were created. He was able to introduce them as greenhouse plants for pots and hanging baskets, then as bedding plants for outdoor display. Modern varieties cover themselves in blooms and flower all summer until fall frost. Principal colors are blue and white. Individual flowers measure up to 2 inches across and resemble small petunias. Plants grow 12 to 18 inches high and spread 10 to 18 inches wide.

Recommended Varieties—'Blue Bells Improved', 14 inches high, is good for hanging baskets as well as in beds and borders. 'Silver Bells' is a beautiful, pure-white companion to 'Blue Bells'. 'Jingle Bells' is an excellent mixture of white and blue shades.

How to Grow—For outdoor plants, start seeds indoors 8 weeks before the last frost date. Germination takes about 6 to 14 days at 70F to 85F (21C to 30C) soil temperature. Do not cover seeds with soil because they need light to germinate. Press into soil surface just enough to anchor them. Water by misting. For flowering indoors under greenhouse conditions, seeds can be sown year-round.

Space plants 12 inches apart in sun or partial shade. Plants tolerate full sun if soil can be kept cool by frequent watering. Otherwise, plant in partial shade. Soil should be fertile and rich in organic matter such as peat moss. Cuttings can be taken from established plants for use in the house or greenhouse. Plants grown indoors need bright light but not direct sunlight.

Tomato wilt diseases can infect browallia, so keep them away from tomato plants. Root aphids and leaf hoppers are potential insect pests. Control root aphids with diazinon chemical spray or organic garlic spray applied as a soil drench. Sevin chemical spray and pyrethrum organic sprays control leaf hoppers.

Uses—Beds and borders where a long-lasting blue accent is desired. Popular as hanging baskets and flowering container plants.

'Blue Bells' browallia make spectacular hanging baskets.

CALCEOLARIA
Calceolaria crenatiflora

Calceolaria are also known as *pocketbook plants* because of their curious, pouch-shape flowers. They are challenging to grow. Plants are sometimes listed as *grandiflora* or *multiflora* types. This is to distinguish between large-flower hybrids—*grandifloras*—that have flowers up to 2-1/2 inches across, and small-flower hybrids—*multifloras*—which produce a greater number of blooms. Multifloras are most often grown as flowering container plants for indoor display.

Colors of the grandifloras and multifloras include red, rose-pink, orange and yellow. Many have freckles or spots. Plants grow 6 to 18 inches high, depending on variety, spreading up to 12 inches wide. All are tender annuals native to Chile.

Calceolaria rugosa is a similar species with yellow flowers. They are more adaptable to outdoor bedding in cool, sunny locations.

Recommended Varieties—'Anytime' hybrids bloom early, flowering when plants are just 5 inches high—4 or 5 months after planting seeds. Calceolarias are usually started in September to take advantage of cool winter weather. 'Anytime' hybrids can be grown any time of the year except during periods of extreme high heat. A dwarf *rugosa* hybrid, 'Sunshine', 12 inches high, is excellent for outdoor beds and borders in cool locations. Each plant produces hundreds of bright-yellow flowers that are especially appealing in window boxes.

How to Grow—Start seeds of the regular multifloras and grandifloras indoors 7 months before projected flowering date. When seedlings are large enough to handle, pot each in a 2-1/2-inch peat pot. Later, transplant into 5-inch pots for flowering. Seeds are small and require exposure to light for germination. Press seeds into the soil surface just deep enough to anchor them. Germination takes 8 to 18 days at 60F (16C) soil temperature. Grow in a cool location—48F to 50F (9C to 10C)—out of direct sun. When *Calceolaria rugosa* is used outdoors, start seeds 10 to 12 weeks before last frost date. Plant after all danger of frost has passed. When flowering stops, cut back to half of plant height and they will flower again.

Plants grown under glass require bright light with shade from direct sunlight. Mist potting soil to keep it moist but do not overwater. Use sterile seed-starting materials and spray surface with benomyl to control fungus diseases. Provide good drainage and air circulation to avoid stem rot and root rot. Infestations of whiteflies can be a serious problem indoors and in greenhouses. Control with malathion chemical spray or pyrethrum organic spray.

Uses—Grandiflora and multiflora hybrids of *Calceolaria crenatiflora* are commonly used indoors as flowering plants in containers. They can be used outdoors in sheltered locations for beds and borders during cool, sunny, spring weather. *C. rugosa* is popular as an outdoor bedding plant, particularly in cool, coastal areas in California and the Pacific Northwest.

'Anytime' calceolaria flowers earlier than most other varieties.

'Pacific Beauty' calendula shows the basic color range available. See page 72.

CALENDULA
Calendula officinalis

This is a hardy annual growing 1 to 2 feet high, spreading 1 to 2 feet wide. Another common name is pot marigold. Flowers are usually yellow, orange and apricot. Most are double, 3 to 4 inches across, closely resembling chrysanthemums. Plants bloom from spring to fall during cool weather. Leaves have a pleasant, spicy fragrance. Native to the Mediterranean.

Recommended Varieties—'Pacific Beauty', 2 feet high, mixed colors, is the most popular for bedding and cutting. 'Gypsy Festival', 1 foot high, is a free-flowering dwarf mixture with contrasting dark centers. 'Mandarin', 2 feet high, is a vigorous orange hybrid.

How to Grow—Easy to grow from seeds sown directly in the garden. Plant seeds 4 to 6 weeks before your last frost date in spring. Seeds germinate in 4 to 10 days at 70F (21C). Cover with 1/4 inch of soil and thin plants to stand 12 to 15 inches apart. In mild areas sow seeds in August through September for blooms at Christmas. In areas with snow cover during winter, seeds can be sown in September. Plants will make strong growth then remain dormant during cold weather to bloom early in the spring. Plants prefer full sun and tolerate poor soil if drainage is good. Irrigate during dry spells.

Young plants are susceptible to damage from slugs and snails. Leaves are susceptible to mildew.

Uses—Excellent for beds and borders. Good for cutting. Popular as a container plant during winter in a cool greenhouse.

Calendula is commonly used by herbalists. The slightly bitter leaves and flowers are added to salads. In addition, a dye can be made from the flowers.

'Mandarin' calendula is a vigorous grower and bloomer.

CALIFORNIA POPPY

Eschscholzia californica

California poppy is the state flower of California, where they are native. If conditions are correct for germination and growth, the wild species present a spectacular sight in spring, carpeting hillsides and meadows with shimmering orange petals. Among cultivated varieties, flower colors include pink, red, white and yellow. In addition to single-flower types, double varieties are available; some have fluted petals. Individual flowers measure up to 3 inches across. Plants are hardy, growing 12 inches high, spreading 12 inches wide. They flower for several weeks during cool weather.

Recommended Varieties—'Monarch Art Shades' produce large, semidouble flowers in a rich assortment of colors. It received an Award of Merit from the Royal Horticultural Society. 'Ballerina' is a more recent introduction. It has fluted or crinkled petals, which enhance the shimmering effect.

How to Grow—In the North, sow seeds outdoors in early spring for early summer flowers. In the South, West and other locations with mild winters, sow seeds in fall for early spring flowers. Cover seeds lightly with soil. Germination takes 4 to 10 days at 60F (16C) soil temperature. Seedlings are difficult to transplant.

Plant in full sun in sandy, alkaline soil. After plants are past the seedling stage, they tolerate dry conditions but require cool nights to flower freely. Flowers close up on cloudy days. Plants tolerate crowding and are ideal for naturalizing on dry banks and in open meadows. For garden displays, space plants 6 to 8 inches apart. California poppies are easy to grow and generally free of pests and diseases.

Uses—Excellent for beds, borders and rock gardens. Commonly included in wildflower mixtures.

CALLIOPSIS

Coreopsis tinctoria

This hardy annual is widely distributed throughout North America. It produces masses of daisylike flowers in summer. Colors are mostly yellow, orange and crimson, plus many bicolors. Height ranges from 8 to 36 inches high, spreading 8 to 12 inches wide, depending on variety.

Recommended Varieties—Few choices are available. Varieties generally listed are 'Dwarf Mixed Colors', 8 to 12 inches high; and 'Tall Mixed Colors', 3 feet high. Dwarfs are preferred for garden displays.

How to Grow—Sow seeds outdoors where plants are to bloom after all danger of frost has passed. Seeds prefer darkness to germinate, so cover with 1/4 inch of soil. Or start seeds indoors 6 weeks before last frost date. Germination takes 8 days at 70F (21C) soil temperature.

Plant in full sun. Tolerant of poor soil. Space dwarf varieties 6 inches apart. Space tall varieties 12 inches apart. Generally not troubled by pests or diseases. Plants tolerate dry conditions after they pass seedling stage.

Uses—Dwarf types are adapted to beds and borders. Tall types are often grown for cutting and for naturalizing in meadows.

California poppy makes an excellent, temporary ground cover.

Calliopsis 'Tall Mixed Colors' works well as wildflower planting.

Canary creeper resembles a bird in flight.

CANARY CREEPER
Tropaeolum peregrinum

This tender annual from the Andes is closely related to nasturtiums. It is also called *canary bird vine.* Small, 1-inch, yellow flowers resemble the wings of a bird in flight. Vines grow to 8 feet long and spread 1 foot wide. Foliage is finely cut and highly ornamental, resembling tiny fig leaves. Blooms are continual during cool, sunny weather.

Recommended Varieties—Not normally sold by variety name.

How to Grow—Seeds may be sown directly outdoors after all danger of frost has passed. Or start seeds indoors in individual peat pots 4 to 6 weeks before last frost date. Germination takes 14 days at 70F (21C) soil temperature.

Space plants 12 inches apart in full sun or partial shade. Soil should be high in organic matter. Keep plant cool and moist by applying an organic mulch such as peat moss or compost around root area. Plants may stop flowering during warm weather but resume bloom in fall.

Uses—Grow as a flowering vine to decorate walls, fences and trellises.

CANDYTUFT
Iberis umbellata

The popular, hardy perennial candytuft, *Iberis sempervirens,* is grown mostly in rock gardens. The hardy, annual form of candytuft, *I. umbellata,* is more compact and low growing, flowering in early summer. Plants cover themselves for several weeks with a dense mass of flowers in white, pink, purple and crimson. Plants grow to 12 inches high and spread 12 inches wide. Native to Spain.

Recommended Varieties—'Dwarf Fairy Mixed Colors' is a popular home-garden variety.

How To Grow—Sow seeds directly in the garden as soon as soil warms in spring. Cover with 1/4 inch of fine soil. In the South, West and other areas with mild winters, sow seeds in fall for early spring flowers. Or start seeds indoors 6 to 8 weeks before planting outdoors. Germination takes 5 to 14 days at 60F (16C) soil temperature.

Plants tolerate crowding but do best spaced 6 inches apart, creating a solid carpet of color. Provide with full sun and plant in almost any soil. Plants tolerate dry conditions after they become established. Shear plants that become tall and untidy to encourage new growth and more blooms. Most flowering occurs in early summer and fall, declining in hot weather. Powdery mildew disease occasionally attacks plants grown in wet, humid conditions. Control with sprays of benomyl.

Uses—Edging next to beds and borders. Plant in drifts in rock gardens. Dried flowers form intricate seed heads valued by flower arrangers.

Assortment of annual candytuft shows basic flower colors available.

CANTERBURY BELLS

Campanula medium

Although Canterbury bells are hardy *biennials,* requiring 2 years to flower, modern cultivated varieties can be grown as hardy annuals. They will flower the first year in early summer while nights remain cool. Canterbury bells are popular in England and Scandinavian countries. But in the United States, they have a reputation of being difficult to grow. They are more often seen as a container plant in cool greenhouses. Outdoors, plants have a tendency to fall apart unless staked. Tall stems are packed with large, bell-shape flowers. Common colors are blue, white and pink. Plants grow to 3 feet high and spread 1 foot wide. Native to Europe.

Recommended Varieties—'Cup and Saucer Mixed Colors', 2-1/2 feet high, is the most widely grown variety.

How to Grow—To have flowers the first year, start seeds indoors 10 weeks before time to plant outdoors. Germination takes 6 to 12 days at 70F (21C) soil temperature. Exposure to light aids germination, so barely cover seeds with soil. Transplant to garden in early spring for extra-early flowers. Seeds can be sown in cold frames in August to produce husky plants for overwintering.

Plants tolerate light shade but prefer full sun. Provide with fertile soil amended with plenty of organic matter. Set plants 12 inches apart and stake to prevent damage from wind and rain.

Canterbury bells are susceptible to a number of pests and diseases. Control slugs and snails with snail bait. Spray aphids and onion thrips with malathion. Control powdery mildew disease with benomyl. Aster yellows disease cannot be controlled. Destroy infected plants to avoid infection of healthy plants.

Uses—Mixed beds and borders. Grown as container plant during winter in cool greenhouse.

Canterbury bells are biennials, but can be grown as annuals to flower the first year.

CARNATION

Dianthus caryophyllus

Carnations are semihardy perennials usually grown as hardy annuals. Flowers of most varieties are heavily fragrant and widely grown in Europe for use in cosmetics. Significant improvements in hybridizing have been made in recent years. Formerly, most carnations were tall, ungainly plants grown by florists for cutting. New dwarf varieties remain compact at 12 inches high. Flowers are double, up to 3 inches across, in white, yellow, pink, red and violet, plus bicolors. Plants flower continually through summer. Recent hybrids are also heat resistant. Native to the Mediterranean.

Recommended Varieties—'Chabaud's Giant', 1-1/2 to 2 feet high, is the most popular tall variety. They are excellent for cutting because of their wide color range and long, strong stems. 'Juliet' hybrid won an All-America award for its dwarf, compact habit, 12 inches high, and its ability to bloom in hot weather. Large, fully double red flowers are fragrant. 'Knight' series of hybrids is similar to 'Juliet'. A range of flower colors is available. Plants are excellent for bedding and containers. 'Scarlet Luminette', 22 inches high, also won an All-America award. Plants are heat resistant,

Carnations are available in a range of colors. A bonus is their pleasant fragrance.

'Scarlet Luminette' carnation won an All-America award for its earliness and vigor.

vigorous and good for cutting. Flowers are red.

How to Grow—Seeds can be sown directly in the garden but it is better to start seeds indoors 10 weeks before last frost date. Germination takes 8 days at 65F to 70F (19C to 21C) soil temperature.

Space plants 12 inches apart in a sunny location. Soil should be sandy, porous and well drained. Keep soil moist. A cool climate such as coastal California and the Pacific Northwest is best for outdoor plantings. New hybrids have good heat resistance if soil is kept moist. Tall kinds may need staking.

Outdoor plantings are generally free of pests and diseases. Greenhouse-grown plants are susceptible to a number of plant diseases, including alternaria, botrytis and rust.

Uses—Grow tall varieties for cutting. Grow dwarf varieties for beds and borders. All are popular if grown in containers in cool greenhouses during winter.

CASTOR BEAN PLANT
Ricinus communis

Gigantic, deeply lobed leaves of the castor bean plant create a beautiful highlight in beds and borders. In parts of the United States that are free of frost—especially Florida—plants have naturalized and thrive as perennial weeds. Elsewhere, they are grown as tender annuals. In a single season, plants can reach 10 feet high and spread 6 feet wide. Flowers are usually white and inconspicuous. They are located under large, green or bronze leaves that can grow to 2 feet long. Native to tropical Africa.

Caution: All parts of this plant are potentially poisonous.

Recommended Varieties—Usually not sold by variety name, although 'Red Spire', red stems and bronze leaves, and 'Zanzibarensis', bright-green leaves, are sometimes available.

How to Grow—Sow seeds directly in the garden after all danger of frost has passed. Cover seeds with 1 inch of soil. Or start seeds indoors 6 weeks before last frost date. Germination takes 7 to 14 days at 70F to 85F (21C to 30C) soil temperature.

Space plants 4 to 6 feet apart in full sun. Although they tolerate poor soil and dry conditions, a fertile, moist soil promotes spectacular growth. Generally free of pests and diseases.

Uses—Use sparingly as a background or a highlight in mixed beds and borders. Striking as decorative highlight planted in tubs on deck or patio. Seeds can be used in making decorative necklaces but are highly poisonous.

Huge leaves of the castor bean give plant a tropical appearance.

'Jewel Box' crested celosia is compact and low growing.

Celosia: Flowering Heights

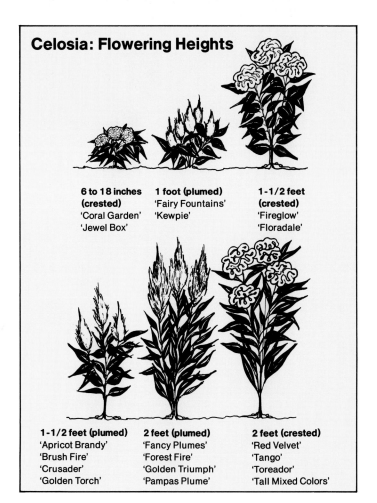

6 to 18 inches (crested)	1 foot (plumed)	1-1/2 feet (crested)
'Coral Garden'	'Fairy Fountains'	'Fireglow'
'Jewel Box'	'Kewpie'	'Floradale'

1-1/2 feet (plumed)	2 feet (plumed)	2 feet (crested)
'Apricot Brandy'	'Fancy Plumes'	'Red Velvet'
'Brush Fire'	'Forest Fire'	'Tango'
'Crusader'	'Golden Triumph'	'Toreador'
'Golden Torch'	'Pampas Plume'	'Tall Mixed Colors'

CELOSIA
Celosia cristata and *Celosia plumosa*

There are two kinds of celosia. Both are tender annuals native to Asia. *Celosia cristata* is the crested type known as *cockscomb*. Flowers of crested varieties resemble a clump of coral. *C. plumosa* has plume-shape flowers that are loose and feathery. Both have spear-shape leaves that are green or bronze. Flowers range from yellow through shades of orange and pink to red and deep crimson. Plants range in size from 6 inches to 2-1/2 feet high, depending on variety. Flowers appear in early summer. If flowers are *dead-headed*—removed as soon as they pass their prime—flowers will appear until fall frost.

Recommended Varieties—Among crested and plumed celosias, dwarf, intermediate and tall kinds are available. Dwarf and intermediate varieties are usually preferred by home gardeners.

Crested celosias: 'Jewel Box', 6 inches high, is offered as a mixture of beautiful colors. They are excellent for edging beds and borders. 'Fireglow', 18 inches high, won an All-America award for its velvety, cardinal-red, globular blooms. Combs are heavy, measuring 6 to 8 inches across. They are supported by long, strong stems that are excellent for cutting and drying.

In the taller class, 'Toreador', 18 to 20 inches high, grows massive, spectacular, bright-red combs that measure 12 inches across. Winner of an All-America award.

Plumed celosias: In the dwarf types, 'Fairy Fountains' grows to 12 inches high. Uniform, compact plants produce a large number of flower plumes. These make excellent mass plantings in beds.

For intermediate height and stems long enough to cut for flower arrangements, grow 'Red Fox', 19 inches high. It was a winner of an All-America award. It features brilliant-red plumes and bright-green foliage. Or grow 'Apricot Brandy', 16 inches high, which introduces a sensational new color to celosias—apricot-orange.

For taller height—useful as a background—consider 'Forest Fire Improved' 2-1/2 feet high. In addition to handsome, dark-bronze foliage, the scarlet plumes are dazzling. The old 'Forest Fire' flowered a little too late, so the plant breeder produced an earlier flowering strain. Be sure to buy the 'Improved' strain.

How to Grow—Sow seeds directly in the garden after all danger of frost has passed. Plants resent any kind of root disturbance or check in growth. If they experience reduced growth during the juvenile stage, flowering is inhibited. Light is required for germination. Cover seeds with just enough soil to anchor them. Celosia can be transplanted if grown in peat pots. Start seeds indoors 4 to 5 weeks before time to plant outdoors. Germination takes 8 to 14 days at 70F to 85F (21C to 30C) soil temperature. Keep planting medium moist.

Plant in full sun and provide with moist, fertile soil amended with plenty of organic material. Leaf spots caused by fungus diseases are common during wet weather. Control by spraying with a general-purpose fungicide such as zineb.

Uses—Excellent display plants for beds and borders. Flower heads are easily dried to make beautiful, long-lasting, dried-flower arrangements.

'Fairy Fountains' celosia.

CHINESE FORGET-ME-NOT
Cynoglossum amabile

This easy-to-grow hardy annual closely resembles the forget-me-not. Flowers are blue and white, produced continually from early summer to fall frost. Plants grow 18 to 24 inches high and spread 12 inches wide. They self-sow readily. Native to Asia.

Recommended Varieties—'Firmament' is an All-America award winner with blue flowers.

How to Grow—Although seeds may be sown outdoors as soon as the soil can be worked in spring, you can have flowers earlier by starting seeds indoors. Sow 6 to 8 weeks before time to plant outdoors. Do not cover seeds completely because exposure to light aids germination. Seeds germinate in 4 to 10 days at 70F to 85F (21C to 30C) soil temperature.

Space plants 6 to 12 inches apart in full sun. They grow well in moist or dry conditions, in cool or warm climates. Moderate watering and feeding occasionally with diluted liquid fertilizer will keep plants blooming.

Tobacco mosaic disease can cause mottling of leaves and stunted growth. Discard infected plants to prevent infecting healthy plants.

Uses—Beds, borders, edging and rock gardens. Stems can be cut to make dainty flower arrangements.

Chinese forget-me-not is variable in color, ranging from deep blue to pale blue and white.

CHINESE LANTERN
Physalis alkekengi

Although Chinese lanterns are actually tender perennials, they are usually grown as tender annuals. They flower the first year when started from seeds, producing beautiful, reddish-orange seed cases that resemble Chinese lanterns. Plants grow to 15 inches high, spreading 18 inches wide. Native to Asia.

Recommended Varieties—Not normally sold by variety name. The largest-flowering plants are sometimes sold as 'Gigantea'.

How to Grow—Start seeds 8 weeks before last frost date. Plant after all danger of frost has passed. Barely cover seeds with soil because exposure to light aids germination. Seeds germinate in 12 to 24 days at 70F to 85F (21C to 30C) soil temperature.

Space plants 1-1/2 to 2 feet apart in full sun. Plants tolerate poor soil. Keep soil moist. Generally free of pests and diseases.

Uses—Plants are usually pulled out of the ground by the roots when the seed cases—lanterns—have turned color. Hang them in bunches and dry to make colorful dried-flower arrangements.

Decorative seed cases of Chinese lanterns are popular for use in dried arrangements.

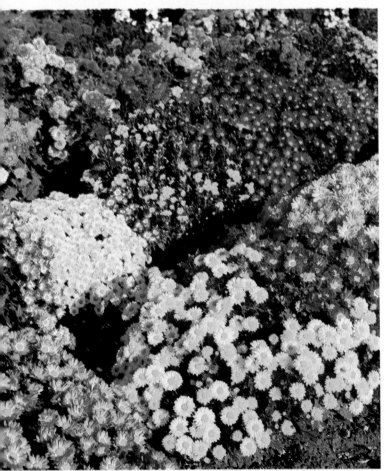

'Golden Dream' annual chrysanthemum is a magnificent, yellow cushion mum.

CHRYSANTHEMUM — CUSHION MUM
Chrysanthemum morifolium

A number of species of perennial chrysanthemums are popularly known as *cushion mums*. They can be grown as hardy annuals from seeds to bloom the first year. Plants grow as compact mounds 1 to 2 feet high, spreading 1-1/2 to 2 feet wide. They are densely covered with beautiful, daisylike flowers. Colors include white, yellow, gold, bronze, rose-pink and lavender. Flowering is governed by day length. As summer turns to fall and day length shortens, buds begin to open. Plants finish the fall season in a rush of color unrivaled by other flowering plants.

Recommended Varieties—Almost all annual types of cushion mums grown from seeds have been developed by T. Sakata & Company, a Japanese plant breeder. Their premier mixture is the class 'Autumn Glory'. Plants are well shaped, growing in mounds 12 inches high and 20 inches wide. The 2-1/2-inch, single and semidouble flowers cover the entire plant, completely hiding the foliage. 'Golden Dream', a golden-yellow hybrid in the 'Autumn Glory' class, creates a carpet of color when planted in a mass.

Ferry-Morse Seed Co., an American plant breeder, has developed the 'Applause' series of cushion mums. They are not as sensitive to day length. Plants are compact, 12 to 15 inches high, with 2-inch flowers.

How to Grow—Plants are slow growing and take a long time to flower. Start seeds indoors 10 weeks before last frost date. Germination takes 14 to 20 days at 60F to 70F (16C to 21C) soil temperature. Cover seeds with 1/4 inch of fine soil. At time of transplanting, pinch off the growing tip to encourage plants to branch sideways. Pinch plants again in early summer and in midsummer to maintain the cushion growth habit.

Plant in loose, fertile soil, preferably enriched with organic matter. Space plants 12 inches apart in full sun. Keep soil moist and feed occasionally with liquid plant food.

Cushion mums are susceptible to a number of diseases, notably wilt, powdery mildew, rust and aster yellows. See controls for these on pages 54 to 57. A common insect pest is mealy bug. Wash them off plants with an insecticidal soap.

Uses—Valuable for fall plantings in beds, borders and containers, when other flowering annuals are declining.

'Autumn Glory' annual chrysanthemum has cushion growth habit. It is available in a wide range of colors.

CHRYSANTHEMUM— PAINTED DAISY
Chrysanthemum carinatum and other species

The genus *Chrysanthemum* encompasses a number of flowering annuals. Many of them are familiar to home gardeners as feverfew and Shasta daisy. These plants are described under those names in this book. Several other chrysanthemums are often listed in seed catalogs under the heading Annual Chrysanthemums. These are *Chrysanthemum carinatum*, painted daisy; *C. coronarium*, crown daisy; and *C. paludosum*, miniature marguerite. A group of perennial chrysanthemums, *C. morifolium*, bloom the first year if seeds are sown early in the season. They are described under Chrysanthemum—Cushion Mum, opposite page.

Painted daisy, *Chrysanthemum carinatum*, is the most popular of the three aforementioned. It is a hardy annual that grows to 3 feet high and spreads 2 feet wide. Plants produce lots of large, beautiful, single flowers. Flowers are ringed with several bands of color, mostly in combinations of red, white and yellow. Native to Morocco.

Recommended Varieties—'Rainbow Mixed Colors' is a popular painted daisy. *Chrysanthemum coronarium* and *C. paludosum* are not sold by variety name. *C. coronarium* is often included in Western wildflower mixtures. It naturalizes freely in meadows and waysides.

How to Grow—Sow seeds outdoors after soil has warmed in spring. Or start seeds indoors 6 to 8 weeks before time to plant outdoors. Germination takes 5 to 10 days at 60F to 70F (16C to 21C) soil temperature. Cover seeds with 1/4 inch of soil.

Plants require full sun and thrive even in poor soils. They do not do well where summers are hot. They are good performers in coastal California, the Pacific Northwest and coastal areas of Canada and Maine.

Uses—Commonly used for mixed beds and borders. Popular in cutting gardens and for naturalizing in wildflower meadows. *Chrysanthemum coronarium* can be used for the same purposes. *C. paludosum* makes a good low-growing plant for edging beds and borders.

CIGAR PLANT
Cuphea ignea

Also called *firecracker plant,* this tender annual first became popular as a flowering house plant. Planted outdoors, it flowers continually from midsummer to fall frost. Although flowers are small there are lots of them. Tubular in shape, they are red with a black band at the tip, resembling the ash of a lit cigar. Plants grow to 12 inches high and spread 12 inches wide. Native to Mexico.

Recommended Varieties—Not normally sold by variety name.

How to Grow—Seeds may be sown directly in the garden after all danger of frost has passed. For best results, start seeds indoors 6 to 8 weeks before last frost date. Germination takes 8 to 10 days at 70F to 85F (21C to 39C) soil temperature. Seeds need light to germinate, so lightly press seeds into soil mix.

Space plants 12 inches apart in full sun or partial

Chrysanthemum paludosum shows its dainty white flowers.

Cigar plant makes an interesting specimen for a hanging basket.

Cineraria is popular for bedding displays in areas where summers remain cool.

shade. Soil should be loose, fertile and well drained. Keep soil moist and feed occasionally with a liquid fertilizer to maintain bloom.

Uses—Cigar plants are colorful in beds, borders and planters—especially hanging baskets. Indoors, plants can be grown in pots and hanging baskets.

CINERARIA
Senecio hybridus

It is a pity these beautiful, daisylike plants have such strict requirements for cool conditions. Except for coastal California, the Pacific Northwest and isolated high-elevation areas, they do not do well outdoors. They are usually grown in cool greenhouses during winter as magnificent container plants. Although they are tender perennials in the wild, cineraria are best treated as tender annuals. The 2-1/2-inch single flowers are clustered at the top of the plant, creating a perfect mound of color. Colors include blue, red, pink and white—many of these with contrasting rings around a dark eye. Plants grow 12 inches high and spread 12 inches wide. Native to the Mediterranean.

Recommended Varieties—Numerous European plant breeders have developed different strains of cinerarias. Those classified as 'Hybrid Grandiflora' generally produce the best floral displays.

How to Grow—Start seeds indoors, allowing 5 to 6 months before flowering. Plants are usually started from seeds August to October to flower midwinter through April. Scatter seeds on soil surface—light aids germination. Seedlings will emerge in about 10 to 14 days at 70F to 80F (21C to 27C) soil temperature. Interestingly, small seedlings that germinate late usually have the best flower color. Transplant seedlings to 2-1/2-inch peat pots, then to 5-inch pots for flowering.

Plants prefer full sun but tolerate light shade. Soil should be loose, fertile and high in organic matter. Peat moss, compost or leaf mold are recommended. It is necessary to provide plants with a cool environment—55F to 60F (13C to 16C). Keep soil moist and feed occasionally with a liquid fertilizer.

Cinerarias are relatively free of pests and diseases. Two virus diseases—mosaic and streak—can cause unsightly leaves. Curling, wilting, yellowing and death of leaves are symptoms. Both diseases are inherent in the seeds, so purchase seeds from reliable sources. Aphids and thrips can also transmit these diseases. Malathion chemical spray is the most common control for these insects. Washing plants with insecticidal soap is the recommended organic control.

Uses—Usually grown as flowering container plants in cool greenhouses during winter. In areas with mild winters or cool summers, cinerarias are sometimes used as short-lived bedding plants outdoors. They are particularly successful used in this manner in the San Francisco Bay area.

Cinerarias growing as pot plants in a cool greenhouse.

CLARKIA
Clarkia unguiculata

The name clarkia is sometimes used to describe the annual godetias—*Clarkia amoena*. Both are species of hardy annuals in the same family and are native to California. In cultivation, clarkias are more erect, carrying 2-inch, double flowers clustered on tall stems. Clarkias grow 3 feet high and spread 2 feet wide. They are best planted in clumps, massed together in a corner of the cutting garden or in a mixed border of annuals. Colors include white, red, orange, pink and purple. Their flowers appear in early summer and last several weeks.

Recommended Varieties— Seedsmen in the United States rarely offer clarkias, but several varieties are available from British mail-order seed houses. See listing, page 38. 'Royal Bouquet Mixed Colors' is a good mixture.

How to Grow—Clarkias do not transplant well. Sow seeds directly in the garden after soil has warmed in spring. Seeds germinate in 7 days at 60F (16C) soil temperature.

Space plants 6 to 12 inches apart in full sun. Plants tolerate poor soils. Keep soil moist during hot, dry spells. In mild-winter areas such as coastal California and the Pacific Northwest, clarkias can be planted outdoors in fall. Scatter seeds on the soil surface. Plants will bloom early the next spring. Generally free of pests and diseases.

Uses—Cutting in mixed annual borders.

Clarkias are grown for cut flowers.

CLEOME
Cleome hasslerana

This tall-growing, tender annual flowers continually from midsummer to fall frost. Also known as *spider flower,* ball-shape flower heads 6 to 7 inches across produce a succession of long seed pods. They radiate from the tall stem like the legs of a spider. Colors include white, pink, rose and purple. Plants begin flowering at 3 feet and may ultimately reach 6 feet high. Native to Central America.

Recommended Varieties—'Queen Mixed Colors' contain a balance of the most popular colors. Separate colors are also available, including 'Helen Campbell, white; and 'Rose Queen', a lovely, deep rose-pink.

How to Grow—Sow seeds directly in the garden after all danger of frost has passed. Or start seeds indoors 4 to 6 weeks before last frost date. Germination takes 5 to 14 days at 68F to 85F (20C to 30C) soil temperature. Light aids germination, so barely press seeds into soil.

Space plants 1-1/2 feet apart in full sun. Soil should be fertile and well drained, preferably amended with plenty of organic matter. Plants tolerate dry conditions. Rarely troubled by pests or diseases.

Uses—Background or as centerpiece for beds and borders because of their height. Flowers are also popular for cutting to create large arrangements.

Cleome, or spider plant, works well as tall background plant for beds and borders.

'Scarlet Wizard' coleus.

COLEUS
Coleus blumei

Few plants remain colorful and last as long both indoors as a container plant and outdoors in the garden. Impatiens and wax begonias are in this category, but these plants are grown for their attractive flowers. It takes time to bring them into bloom unless you purchase mature plants. The exotic foliage of coleus is responsible for its colorful display rather than its flowers. The brilliance of a coleus leaf can outshine the most colorful flowering plant. Leaves develop color soon after seeds germinate, intensifying in color as they mature.

Wild, native coleus plants are drab compared to modern cultivated varieties. It is largely the plant breeder who has been responsible for producing the brilliant, paint-box coleus that is commonly available. Careful selection among wild types and perpetuating random mutations have developed a broad range of colors and leaf shapes. In some instances, a leaf will show four distinct colors: bronze, red, yellow and green. Leaf shape can vary from long and slender to broad and arching. Some have scalloped edges like an oak leaf. Others are delicately fringed.

Although classified as a tender annual in seed catalogs, coleus is actually a perennial. If greenhouse conditions can be provided during winter, you can grow coleus all year. If flower spikes are removed and lower leaves are pruned as they deteriorate, coleus can be trained as a *standard*. A standard has a long, slender, woody trunk with crown of leaves at top.

Used as a outdoor plant, coleus is best grown as an annual. Plants reach 1 to 2 feet high, spreading 2 feet wide. Flowers are usually blue and unattractive. It is best to pinch them out in bud stage to save the plant's energy.

Recommended Varieties—Selection of varieties used to be limited. Until recently, many catalogs offered only the 'Rainbow' series. 'Rainbow' have broad, arching leaves and come in bold colors. In spite of their handsome looks and recognizable name, they have some limitations. Mature height of plants is variable. A bushy, compact plant can be created only by rigorous pinching of the lead shoots. This prevents it from going to seed and promotes branching.

In my experience, 'Rainbow' are best grown as separate colors. The most colorful are 'Pagoda', yellow leaves with red freckles; and 'Salmon Lace', rosy red leaves with an intricate, green-lace pattern toward edges.

The 'Wizard' series is more colorful and uniform in height than 'Rainbows'. Most important, plants are prolific at producing side branches, and do not require pinching to encourage bushy growth. This ability to produce side shoots without pinching is called *basal branching*. It is a characteristic that has become one of the most sought-after qualities in annuals for outdoor bedding, pots and hanging baskets.

'Rose Wizard' has bright, rosy-pink leaf center edged with cream-green borders. Large, heart-shape leaves resemble those of 'Rainbow', but are more closely set along stems. This avoids a leggy appearance. Other coleus in the 'Wizard' series include 'Pink', 'Scarlet', 'Velvet', 'Pineapple' and a colorful mixture.

A recently developed class of coleus—'Fijis'—is ex-

'Carefree' coleus mixed colors have bands of contrasting colors, creating a dramatic effect.

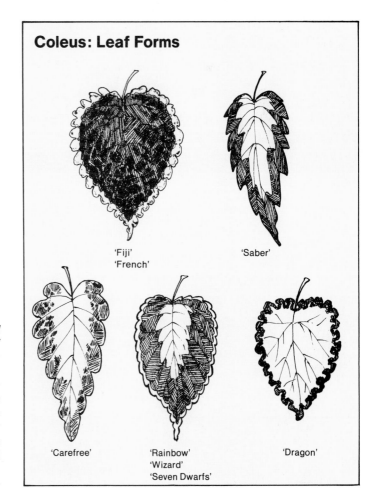

Coleus: Leaf Forms

'Fiji'
'French'

'Saber'

'Carefree'

'Rainbow'
'Wizard'
'Seven Dwarfs'

'Dragon'

'Fiji Red' coleus used as a hanging basket above planting of red geraniums.

pected to replace the old 'Fringed Leaf' class, sometimes sold as 'French Lace'. Fringed leaf edge is a highly attractive feature in coleus. Before the introduction of 'Fijis', this feature was variable and the seed supply was unreliable. You would be fortunate if 50% of plants grew true to description. 'Fijis' are 100% fringed and colors are more dramatic than other coleus. The fringed effect is also more pronounced and the heights more uniform. They make superb container plants and hanging baskets.

The best of the colors is 'Fiji Red'. Broad, arching leaves are brilliant red, with a darker zone around leaf veins. Contrasting yellow edge accentuates fringed area around leaf. Other separate colors among 'Fijis' include 'Pastel', 'Rose', 'Pink', 'Scarlet', 'Jade' and 'Velvet'. A mixture is available that contains all these colors.

In addition to the broad, arching, heart-shape leaves characteristic of 'Rainbows', 'Wizards' and 'Fijis', other interesting leaf shapes have been developed. Coleus in the 'Saber' series have long, slender, serrated leaves that cascade. 'Sabers' are slow to flower and have natural, basal-branching habit so plants do not need pinching. Each plant grows as a bushy mound of leaves. In addition to being good bedding plants, 'Sabers' are excellent as hanging baskets. Nine separate colors are available, plus a mixture. Outstanding are 'Saber Jade', ivory-white with bright-green border, and 'Saber Scarlet', bright red with yellow edge.

'Carefree' coleus have scalloped leaf edges, similar to an oak leaf. A contrasting band of color follows the scallop shape for a dramatic effect.

How to Grow—Start seeds indoors 10 weeks before last frost date. Plant after all danger of frost has passed. Seeds are tiny and need light to germinate. Press them into soil surface just enough to anchor them. Germination takes 12 days at 70F to 85F (21C to 30C) soil temperature. Lower temperatures inhibit germination.

The most difficult task in starting coleus from seeds is preventing the soil from drying out. To maintain moisture, plant seeds in seed tray filled with peat-based potting soil. Mist surface thoroughly and enclose entire tray in plastic bag to slow evaporation. Water with a mister. Water applied from a watering can or other device disturbs seeds or uproots the delicate seedlings.

Set plants 10 to 12 inches apart in full sun or partial shade. Plants in open beds do best if plenty of organic material has been mixed into soil. Soil should be fertile. Feed plants occasionally during growing season with liquid plant food.

With most varieties it is necessary to pinch out the lead shoot to encourage side branches to develop. Without pinching, plants tend to get leggy. Pinch off flower spikes that develop except those of 'Wizard'. Plants are naturally self-branching and grow best without pinching.

The most serious coleus pests are slugs and snails. They can devour transplants overnight. Control them with slug bait. Mosaic is a virus disease that causes mottling, ring spots and blotches on leaves. Discard diseased specimens to prevent infecting other plants.

Uses—Excellent for massed planting in beds and borders. Dwarf types are good for edging. Cascading types make exquisite hanging baskets. All are suitable for window boxes, tubs and other containers.

'Fiji' coleus have fringed leaf edges, making them striking in border plantings such as this.

COLUMBINE
Aquilegia hybrida

Columbines are generally regarded as hardy perennials. Several varieties can be grown as hardy annuals, flowering the first year from seeds started early indoors. Annual columbines have graceful foliage and produce masses of intricate flowers called *granny's bonnets.* Flowers grow to 3 inches across with prominent spurs in white, yellow, red, blue, lavender, pink and some bicolors. They bloom for several weeks in early summer. Plants grow 2 to 3 feet high and spread 2 feet wide. Native to North America.

Recommended Varieties—'McKana Giants' are unique because of their large flower size, long spurs and wide color range. They were the first annual columbine mixture, introduced by Burpee Seeds in 1955 after receiving an All-America award. The original breeding material for 'McKana Giants' came from a home gardener, Mr. J. P. McKana.

How to Grow—Seeds may be surface-sown outdoors in spring as soon as the soil can be worked. Seedlings are hardy and able to tolerate frosts. For earliest flowers, start seeds indoors 8 to 10 weeks before time to plant outdoors. Press seeds into soil surface because seeds need light to germinate. Germination takes 7 to 21 days at 65F to 85F (19C to 30C) soil temperature. Pre-chilling seeds in the refrigerator at 40F (5C) for 3 weeks before planting aids germination.

Space plants 12 inches apart in full sun or partial shade. Plant in soil enriched with organic matter. Keep soil moist. After flowering, water and feed with diluted liquid fertilizer. Plants will survive summer heat and continue to grow and flower as perennials. For early spring flowers, sow seeds outdoors in late summer and protect seedlings with mulch through winter.

Aphids sometimes colonize tender stems. Spray with malathion chemical insecticide. Spray with insecticidal soap for organic control. Borers can cause plants to wilt. Sevin chemical spray or pyrethrum organic spray are effective controls.

Uses—Plant in clumps in mixed beds, borders and rock gardens. Flowers have long stems for cutting and make magnificent fresh-flower arrangements.

CORNFLOWER
Centaurea cyanus

Few flowering annuals can match the intensity of blue available among cornflowers, also called *bachelor's buttons.* In addition to deep blue, the circular, ruffled, tufted flowers come in red, pink, white, mauve and mahogany. Cornflowers generally grow to 3 feet high, spreading 1 foot wide. Some dwarf types have been developed that grow just 15 inches high. Plants are hardy annuals and flower freely from early summer to fall frost. Native to Europe.

Recommended Varieties—'Blue Diadem', 2 feet high, has the largest flowers, up to 2-1/2 inches across. 'Polka Dot', 15 inches high, is a good dwarf mixture. 'Jubilee Gem', 12 inches high, makes an attractive bedding plant where summers are cool.

How to Grow—Sow seeds directly in the garden because seedlings do not transplant well. Plants tolerate mild frosts so you can sow seeds outdoors as soon as soil warms in spring. Cover seeds with 1/4 inch of fine

Single flower of 'McKana Giants' columbine shows its intricate petal pattern.

'Polka Dot' cornflower mixed colors are displayed against background of alyssum.

Main assortment of colors available in 'Sensation' cosmos mixture.

soil. Germination takes 4 to 8 days at 60F (16C) soil temperature. In mild-winter areas, seeds can be sown in fall for early spring flowers.

Although cornflowers tolerate crowding, plants do best spaced 12 inches apart. Sunlight and cool temperatures encourage largest blooms and longest flowering displays. Plants tolerate poor soils. Self-seeding is common, but volunteers usually have smaller flowers than original plants. Cornflowers are normally free of pests and diseases. Check stems occasionally for aphids or mealy bugs. Control with sprays of Sevin or wash with insecticidal soap.

Uses—Mixed beds and borders. Excellent for cutting gardens because they make beautiful fresh-flower arrangements.

COSMOS
Cosmos bipinnatus and *Cosmos sulphureus*

Two kinds of cosmos are popular among home gardeners. *Cosmos bipinnatus* produces large, single, daisylike flowers up to 4 inches across in white, pink and red. *C. sulphureus* produces flowers up to 2 inches across in yellow, orange and orange-red. Both are tender annuals, flowering from early summer to fall frost. Tall kinds can grow to 5 feet high, spreading 2 to 3 feet wide. Dwarf varieties reach 1 to 2 feet high, spreading 1 foot wide. Native to Mexico.

Recommended Varieties—Among *Cosmos bipinnatus*, 'Sensation Mixed Colors' produces white, pink and red 5-inch flowers. Plants grow to 4 feet high. 'Anemone-Flowered', also sold as 'Double-Crested', has ruffled, crested centers and is a good choice for flower arrangers.

Among *Cosmos sulphureus*, 'Diablo', to 4 feet high, won an All-America award for its deep, orange-red flowers. It is far superior to 'Sunset', with lighter orange flowers. Among those with tall, yellow flowers the best is 'Lemon Twist', 2-1/2 feet high. A breakthrough is 'Sunny Gold', 12 inches high, a dwarf variety that covers itself in masses of 1-1/2-inch, semidouble, golden-yellow flowers.

How to Grow—Sow seeds directly in the garden after all danger of frost has passed. Barely cover seeds with soil because exposure to light aids germination. Or start seeds indoors 5 to 6 weeks before last frost date. Germination takes 3 to 8 days at 70F to 85F (21C to 30C) soil temperature.

Although cosmos tolerate crowding, it is best to space plants 12 inches apart in full sun. They tolerate poor soils and deep, infrequent watering. In general, cosmos are heat resistant, easy to grow and relatively free of pests and diseases.

Uses—Tall kinds are often planted in mixed beds and borders. Flowers can be used for cutting. Dwarf kinds are planted for edging and summer bedding.

'Yellow Twist' cosmos is a heat-resistant variety.

CYPRESS VINE

Quamoclit pennata

This fast-growing vine is a tender annual closely related to morning glory. It produces fine, feathery foliage and lots of small, white and red flowers. Although each flower lasts only one day, vines bloom continually from early summer to fall frost. Plant reaches an ultimate height of 25 feet in one season, spreading 1 to 2 feet wide. Native to South America.

Recommended Varieties—Not normally sold by variety name.

How to Grow—Sow seeds outdoors after all danger of frost has passed. Or start seeds indoors 6 to 8 weeks before last frost date. Plant seeds 1/4 inch deep in individual peat pots to minimize root disturbance when you transplant. Germination takes 5 to 10 days at 70F to 85F (21C to 30C) soil temperature.

Space plants 12 inches apart in full sun. Provide a trellis for support. Plants tolerate poor soil and high heat. Keep soil moist. Several beetle pests are known to bother plants. Spray with Sevin chemical insecticide or pyrethrum organic insecticide.

Uses—Great as temporary flowering screen to cover fences and bare walls.

DAHLBERG DAISY

Dyssodia tenuiloba

The dahlberg daisy is a tender annual. Plants grow just 4 to 6 inches high, spreading 12 inches wide. They are covered with small, bright-yellow, daisylike flowers from early summer to fall frost. Native to Texas and Mexico.

Recommended Varieties—Not normally sold by variety name.

How to Grow—Seeds may be surface-sown directly outdoors after all danger of frost has passed. Or start seeds 6 to 8 weeks before last frost date. Germination takes 10 days at 60F to 80F (16C to 27C) soil temperature.

Plants will tolerate crowding but it's best to space them 9 to 12 inches apart. Plant in full sun. Plants grow well even in poor soil and are tolerant of heat and drought. They require watering only after soil has dried out. Generally free of pests and diseases.

Uses—Few flowering annuals can outshine or outlast this low-growing plant for edging beds and borders. Good as a temporary ground cover.

Cypress vine is related to morning glories. This shows the main color range available.

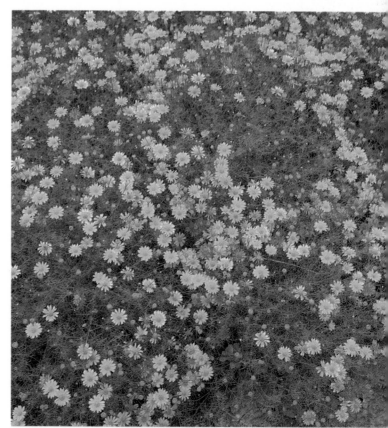

Dahlberg daisy makes a long-lasting, eye-catching ground cover.

Unwin-type dahlia, green foliage, is planted in bed of mixed annuals.

DAHLIA
Dahlia hybrida

The American Dahlia Society officially recognizes 12 dahlia classifications according to flower form. They range in size from small, ball-shape, pompon types to huge dinner-plate dahlias that measure up to 12 inches across. Dahlias are native to Mexico. Most modern cultivated varieties are grown from *tuberous roots,* a fleshy root connected to a stem. Tuberous roots must be connected to a stem with a bud or they will not grow.

Seed-grown types are tender perennials but are best treated as tender annuals. They include tall varieties that grow 3 to 4 feet high and dwarf varieties that grow 12 to 15 inches high.

Dwarf varieties are commonly grown from seeds as annuals. They are everblooming from early summer to fall frost. Another name for them is *bedding dahlias.* Some have bright-green leaves. A few have bronze leaves. Flower colors include white, yellow, orange, purple, pink, red and some bicolors.

Recommended Varieties—Among green-leaved varieties of bedding dahlias, the best is 'Rigoletto', 12 to 15 inches high. Winner of a Fleuroselect award, it remains neat and compact, producing a beautiful mixture of clear colors. Double flowers come early in the season and remain in bloom for several weeks. Among bronze-leaved varieties 'Redskin' is outstanding. Winner of an All-America award for its highly ornamental foliage, it produces a high percentage of double flowers. Rich selection of colors is available, some of them in two tones.

How to Grow—Sow seeds directly in the garden after all danger of frost has passed. For earliest blooms, start seeds indoors 8 weeks before last frost date. Cover seeds with 1/4 inch of soil. Keep soil moist. Germination takes 4 to 15 days at 60F (16C) soil temperature.

Space plants 12 inches apart in full sun. Dahlias are heavy feeders and have high moisture requirements. However, soils with excessive nitrogen may cause plants to produce too much leafy growth at the expense of flowers. Loose, loam soil high in organic material suits them best. Superior floral displays occur during cool, sunny weather. They will flower satisfactorily in warm-summer areas if watered regularly. Tall kinds generally require staking because stems are brittle.

Leaves are susceptible to attack from chewing pests. Slugs and snails can be serious problems when plants are in seedling stage. Protect with slug bait or remove these pests by hand. Japanese beetles may attack flower petals. Control with Sevin chemical spray or use traps. Aphids can be controlled with nicotine sulfate organic spray or Sevin or malathion chemical sprays. Spider mites weave fine webs among foliage, causing leaves to brown and curl of leaves. A miticide such as dicofol can help control them. Bacterial wilt can cause plants to die suddenly. Botrytis blight and powdery mildew are controlled by benomyl.

Uses—Tall kinds are usually grown in mixed beds and borders. Popular as a cut flower. Dwarf kinds are excellent as mass displays for bedding. Also good for window boxes, tubs and planters.

Principal colors of 'Redskin' dahlia. Foliage of this variety is bronze.

DELPHINIUM
Delphinium elatum

Delphiniums are actually hardy perennials. True annual kinds are known as *larkspur*. However, some perennial strains can be treated as annuals to bloom the first year from seeds sown indoors. Delphiniums tolerate mild frosts but are sensitive to freezing.

Plants produce tall flower spikes up to 6 feet high and spread 2 feet wide. Colors include white, blue, purple and pink. Individual florets measure up to 2-1/2 inches across. At the center of each floret is a ring of smaller petals known as a *bee*. These decorative bees are usually white or black in contrast to the floret. Native to Siberia.

In addition to tall species—*Delphinium elatum*—seedsmen offer *D. belladonna*. Plants are bushy, growing up to 2-1/2 feet high, producing a loose cluster of flowers. Both species generally flower for several weeks during cool weather in early summer or fall.

Recommended Varieties—'Pacific Giants', 6 feet high, are the most popular tall type. They are available in a mixture in a beautiful assortment of colors. 'Blue Fountains', 3 feet high, is a good, earlier-flowering mixture classified as a dwarf. 'Blue Heaven', 3 feet high, is a selection of 'Blue Fountains'. It produces flowers that are sky-blue with a white bee—the most appealing color combination in delphiniums.

How to Grow—Delphinium seeds do not stay viable long after harvest. Fresh seeds are essential for good germination. Seeds are often harvested and packaged before they can be *vernalized*—winter chilled. To ensure that dormancy is broken, store seeds in the refrigerator for 24 hours before planting. Germination takes 8 to 18 days at 70F to 85F (21C to 30C) soil temperature.

Space plants 1-1/2 to 2 feet apart in full sun. Plant in fertile loam or fertile, sandy soil with plenty of organic matter mixed in. Keep soil moist and feed every 2 weeks with diluted liquid fertilizer. Delphiniums flower spectacularly during cool, sunny weather, but expire rapidly when summer days turn hot and humid.

Where summers are hot and winters are severe, tall types should be started in a cold frame or greenhouse in September of the year prior to flowering. Protect plants in cold frames until spring and transplant when the soil warms. Plant will flower in early summer. Some dwarf varieties such as 'Blue Fountains' can be started indoors 10 to 12 weeks before planting outdoors. They are transplanted in early spring to bloom in early summer. Similarly, 'Connecticut Yankees' can be started from seeds 10 weeks before time to plant outdoors to produce flowers the first year.

Slugs and snails are pests of delphiniums. Control with slug bait or pick by hand. Thrips are another common pest. Control by using a systemic insecticide such as Di-Syston. The most common plant disease affecting delphiniums is aster yellows, also known as *stunt* and *witch's brooms*. Symptoms are yellowing of new growth. It can be spread by leaf hoppers. Control leaf hoppers with sprays of Sevin or malathion. Pyrethrum is an organic alternative.

Uses—Tall delphiniums are best used as a background in mixed flower beds and borders. Dwarf kinds are best as bedding plants. Both are valued for cutting to make fresh-flower arrangements.

'Summer Skies' delphinium displays huge, light-blue flower spikes and dark "bees" at petal centers.

'Pacific Giant' delphinium mixed colors are valued as cut flowers and for flower arrangements.

DIANTHUS
Dianthus chinensis

Few other annuals have undergone more dramatic changes through plant breeding in recent years than dianthus. It began in 1962 when 'Bravo' won an All-America award. 'Bravo' surprised the seed industry with its unusually high sales. It was the first scarlet-red dianthus in its class, representing the same degree of breeding achievement among annuals as the black tulip among bulbs. A rare mutation, it was found growing wild in Japan. Using 'Bravo' as a parent plant, breeders were able to develop a wide selection of new varieties.

Dianthus are hardy annuals native to China. Plants are mostly bushy and compact, growing to about 12 inches high and spreading 12 inches wide. Clusters of fragrant, 1-inch flowers bloom non-stop in cool-summer areas from early summer to fall frost. Colors include white, red, pink, purple and bicolors.

Recommended Varieties—The original 'Bravo' that started the dianthus breeding program is still available. But it has been superceded by 'Queen of Hearts' hybrid, 10 inches high, a free-flowering scarlet-red. Hybrid mixtures are now quite popular, especially 'Magic Charms', which won an All-America award. 'Magic Charms' comes in a rich range of colors. It has a compact growth habit and flowers early—12 weeks from seeds. 'Baby Doll' is a non-hybrid that produces the largest flowers—up to 2-1/2 inches across. Plants grow 8 inches high and flower profusely for several weeks during cool weather. Among special colors available, 'Snowfire' hybrid, 8 inches high, is remarkable. The 1-1/2-inch white flowers are fringed with cherry-red centers.

How to Grow—For earliest blooms, start seeds 8 weeks before time to plant outdoors. Plants that are hardened-off will tolerate mild frosts, so they can be planted outdoors several weeks before the last frost date. Germination takes 7 days at 70F (21C) soil temperature. Handle seeds carefully because they are easily damaged.

Space plants 6 to 12 inches apart in full sun. Plants tolerate poor soils and dry conditions, making them suitable for planting in dry walls and rock gardens. They bloom best during cool periods. If plants stop blooming in midsummer because of high heat, tops can be sheared. They will usually flower again when cool weather returns.

Dianthus are sensitive to damage from high-nitrogen ammonia-base fertilizers and animal manures. To avoid tip burn on leaves, use diluted liquid fertilizer. Stem rot, caused by overwatering, is another occasional problem.

Uses—Compact varieties are used for mass plantings in beds, borders, edging and containers. Tall varieties are excellent for cutting. Both types are popular for rock gardens.

'Coral Charm' dianthus has interesting petals with fringed edges.

'Magic Charms' dianthus mixed colors planted in a flower bed.

DUSTY MILLER

Centaurea cineraria and *Pyrethrum ptarmicaeflorum*

Several plants are valued for their long-lasting silvery foliage. The two most widely grown are *Centaurea cineraria* from the Mediterranean and *Pyrethrum ptarmicaeflorum* from the Canary Islands. Although they are tender perennials in mild climates, both are best grown as tender annuals. Plants grow 6 to 10 inches high and spread 8 inches wide. Both have heavily serrated leaves.

Recommended Varieties—Two varieties—'Silver Lace', *Pyrethrum ptarmicaeflorum,* and 'Silverdust', *Centaurea cineraria*—are the most popular. Leaves of 'Silver Lace', 10 inches long, are finely cut. Formerly grown from cuttings, germination of seeds is usually substandard—only about 50%. Leaves of 'Silverdust', 8 inches long, are similar to 'Silver Lace' but not as finely cut.

How to Grow—Start seeds indoors 10 weeks before last frost date. Germination takes 7 to 21 days at 60F to 70F (16C to 21C) soil temperature. *Pyrethrum ptarmicaeflorum* is slower growing and generally requires 4 extra weeks from seeds to transplant stage.

Space plants 8 inches apart in full sun in fertile loam soil. Keep soil moist and remove any flower buds that develop. Flowers generally look weedy and spoil the neat, silvery effect. Plants are generally free of pests and diseases.

Uses—Beds and borders as an edging. Also used as a color divider between groups of brightly colored annuals and in containers of mixed annuals.

'Silver Dust' dusty miller has an interesting, decorative leaf pattern.

FELICIA

Felicia bergeriana

Commonly called *kingfisher daisy,* this tender annual produces profuse numbers of dainty, sky-blue, daisy-like flowers with bright-yellow centers. Plants grow 6 to 8 inches high and spread 8 inches wide. They flower continually from early summer to fall frost in cool, coastal areas. Flowers remain closed on cloudy days. Native to South Africa.

Recommended Varieties—Not normally sold by variety name. Perennial species *Felicia amelloides* is sometimes sold as blue marguerites. Flowers are larger than *F. bergeriana,* and plants grow to 3 feet high. *F. amelloides* and is grown as an annual in cool-summer areas.

How to Grow—In coastal California, seeds are sown directly in the garden when soil temperatures exceed 55F (13C). Or start seeds indoors 6 weeks before time to plant outdoors. Germination takes 10 days.

Plants prefer full sun and sandy soil. Water only after soil has dried out. Felicias flower prolifically during cool, sunny periods. Plants tolerate crowding but are best spaced 6 inches apart. Generally free of pests and diseases.

Uses—Edging beds and borders, in rock gardens and dry walls. Popular as container plant grown in cool greenhouses during winter for flowers in early spring.

Felicia, also known as *kingfisher daisy,* covers dry wall in coastal California.

Feverfew, *Chrysanthemum parthenium*, is popular for edging and for cutting.

Scarlet flax is often included in wildflower mixtures because it naturalizes easily.

Most forget-me-nots are biennial, but 'Blue Bird' can be grown as an annual.

FEVERFEW
Chrysanthemum parthonium

Sometimes listed by seedsmen as matricaria, this hardy perennial from Europe and Asia is best grown as a hardy annual. Cultivated varieties have mostly white flowers with yellow tinting at the center. Small, 1-inch, double flowers appear in clusters. Leaves are fragrant. Plants grow to 2 feet high and spread 1 foot wide. Native to Europe and Asia.

Recommended Varieties—Tall kinds are usually sold as 'Double White'. Dwarf 'White Stars' grows 6 inches high, creating a neat, mounded plant useful for edging.

How to Grow—Sow seeds outdoors in early spring as soon as soil can be worked. Scatter seeds on soil surface because they need light to germinate. Or start seeds indoors 8 weeks before time to plant outdoors. Germination takes 15 days at 70F (21C) soil temperature.

Space plants 12 inches apart in full sun. Plants tolerate poor soils and are drought resistant. Water during dry periods. Relatively free of pests and diseases.

Uses—Cutting and accent in mixed beds and borders. Plants naturalize freely. Feverfew seeds are often included in wildflower mixtures where it is adapted.

FLAX, SCARLET
Linum grandiflorum

Scarlet flax is a hardy annual. Intense crimson flowers 1-1/2 inches across are produced in abundance during early summer. Plants grow 15 to 18 inches high and spread 5 to 6 inches wide. Leaves are narrow, pointed and grasslike. Native to Algeria.

Recommended Varieties—Not normally sold by variety name.

How to Grow—Plants tolerate mild frosts. Sow seeds directly in the garden several weeks before the last frost date in spring. For earlier blooms, start seeds 6 weeks before time to plant outdoors. Germination takes 5 to 12 days at 60F to 70F (16C to 21C) soil temperature.

Space plants 6 inches apart in full sun. They will tolerate crowding. Plants adapt to a wide range of soil conditions—even poor soil. Keep soil moist during dry spells. Generally free of pests and diseases.

Uses—Grow as clumps in mixed beds and borders. Plant in pots for spring flowers indoors.

FORGET-ME-NOT
Myosotis sylvatica

Forget-me-nots are usually considered *biennials,* plants that require two seasons to flower. But some varieties can be treated as hardy annuals to flower the first year if seeds are started early in the season. Low-growing, mound-shape plants are covered with dainty blue, white or pink flowers. Plants grow 12 inches high and spread 12 inches wide. Flowering generally lasts for several weeks in spring or early summer. Native to Europe and Asia.

Recommended Varieties—'Blue Bird' is one of the best to grow as an annual.

How to Grow—For earliest blooms, start seeds indoors 6 to 8 weeks before last frost date. Germination takes 5 to 12 days at 70F (21C) soil temperature.

Forget-me-nots do best in cool, moist location in sun or partial shade. Mix plenty of organic matter into soil. Although plants tolerate crowding, spacing 6 to 8 inches apart is preferred.

Uses—Good for edging beds and borders. Plants are also valued as a dense ground cover around water and bog gardens where they will naturalize freely.

FOUR O'CLOCK
Mirabilis jalapa

In frost-free areas, four o'clocks are strictly perennials. Otherwise, they are best grown as tender annuals. The genus name *Mirabilis* means miraculous, and refers to the number of different flower colors that appear on a single plant. They are everblooming from summer until fall frost. Flowers are so variable as to their petal colors and patterns, no two are identical. Flowers remain closed during most of the day, opening in midafternoon. If weather is cloudy, they remain open all day. Colors include white, red, pink, yellow and purple, plus intricate bicolor and tricolor combinations.

Plants are bushy, freely branching from the base. They grow 2 to 3 feet high, spreading 2 feet wide. Native to Peru.

Recommended Varieties—'Jingles', 2-1/2 feet high, is an excellent mixture. It is compact and uniform with a close branching habit.

How to Grow—Sow seeds outdoors after all danger of frost has passed. Or start seeds indoors 4 to 6 weeks before last frost date. Cover seeds with 1/2 inch of fine soil. Germination takes 12 days at 70F to 85F (21C to 30C) soil temperature.

Space plants 1 to 2 feet apart in full sun or partial shade. Plants grow well in poor soils, resist heat, high humidity and air pollution. Generally free of pests and diseases.

Uses—Accent in mixed beds and borders.

FOXGLOVE
Digitalis purpurea

Most foxgloves are biennials, requiring two seasons to produce flowers. 'Foxy' is an exception. It can be grown as a hardy annual if seeds are started early in the season and transplanted. Foxgloves produce tall flower spikes studded with funnel-shape blooms. Blooms have exotic spots and freckles as a means of attracting bees for pollination. Individual flowers resemble the fingers of a glove. Colors include white, yellow, red, purple and pink. Plants grow 3 to 4 feet high and spread 1 foot wide. Native to Europe.

Caution: Seeds are poisonous if eaten.

Recommended Varieties—Developed by a California plant breeder, 'Foxy' won an All-America award for its ability to flower within 5 months of sowing seeds. Plants have a natural branching habit and may produce up to nine flower spikes.

How to Grow—Sow seeds outdoors in spring as soon as soil can be worked. For earliest blooms, start seeds indoors 8 to 10 weeks before time to plant outdoors. Seeds are tiny and require light to germinate. Germination takes 7 days at 70F to 85F (21C to 30C) soil temperature.

Space plants 12 inches apart in full sun or partial

Main color range of four o'clocks. Such color variation often occurs on a single plant.

'Foxy' foxglove won an All-America award for its tendency to perform as an annual, flowering from seed the first year.

Gaillardias are heat-resistant plants popular for cutting.

shade. Soil should be fertile and enriched with plenty of organic matter. Keep soil moist.

Mealy bugs, Japanese beetles and other chewing insects are occasional problems. Control with Sevin chemical spray or pyrethrum, an organic spray. Destroy plants infected with virus diseases such as mosaic and curly top. Fungus diseases include anthracnose leaf spots and wilt. Control by spraying with a copper-base fungicide.

Uses—Mostly grown as background plants in beds or borders. Also a favorite of woodland gardens, where it often naturalizes.

GAILLARDIA
Gaillardia pulchella

Both annual and perennial kinds of gaillardias are native to the United States. They are widely dispersed throughout the central and western states, thriving in the sandy soils prevalent to these regions. Plants are sensitive to frost. Among tender annual types, there are single and double forms to choose from. Flowers are daisylike, mostly red and yellow, with dark, contrasting centers. Plants grow to 3 feet high and spread 1 to 1-1/2 feet wide. Most flowering occurs in summer.

Recommended Varieties—'Gaiety Mixed Colors', 2 feet high, grows beautiful, 2-1/2-inch, fully double, ball-shape flowers in red, rose, yellow, orange and maroon.

How to Grow—Sow seeds directly in the garden after all danger of frost has passed. Because light is needed for germination, sow seeds on soil surface. Or start seeds indoors 6 weeks before last frost date. Germination takes 4 to 10 days at 70F to 85F (21C to 30C) soil temperature.

Space plants 12 inches apart in full sun. Plants tolerate heat, drought and poor soil, but prefer light, sandy soils. Pick faded flowers regularly to ensure continual bloom. Relatively free of pests and diseases.

Uses—Mass planting in beds and borders. Also good for cutting and for naturalizing in open meadows and sunny slopes.

GAZANIA
Gazania rigens

This tender perennial is commonly grown as an annual. It has received a lot of attention from plant breeders in recent years. Efforts have been made to develop special colors and to eliminate the tendency of flowers to close during cloudy weather. Flowers measure 3 to 5 inches across. Colors include yellow, gold, orange, cream, white, pink, red and maroon. Some have green or black zones and dark centers. Plants grow 8 to 12 inches high and spread 12 inches wide. They flower continually during summer. Leaves of many varieties are attractive gray-green, providing contrast to plants with deep-green foliage. Native to South Africa.

Recommended Varieties—Few separate colors are available. 'Mini Star Yellow', 8 inches high, is one of the best. Also outstanding is 'Golden Marguerita', 10 inches high, and 'Red Hybrids', also 10 inches. Because of the rainbow color effect when gazanias are planted in a mass, mixtures are popular. Among those

Gazanias are resistant to drought and heat after plants become established.

with the largest flowers—measuring up to 5 inches across—are 'Sundance' hybrids.

How to Grow—Sow seeds outdoors after all danger of frost has passed. Cover seeds with 1/4 inch of fine soil. Or start seeds indoors 6 weeks before last frost date. Germination takes 4 to 12 days at 60F (16C) soil temperature. Seeds are usually surrounded by a dense mass of fibers or fluff. Separate carefully before planting.

Space plants 12 inches apart in full sun. They prefer light, sandy soils and tolerate poor soils. Gazanias are heat and drought tolerant, troubled by few pests and diseases. Avoid overwatering, which can promote root rot and powdery mildew.

Uses—Plant in beds and borders. Also good for rock gardens, dry walls and sunny slopes.

GERANIUM

Pelargonium hortorum

Geraniums are believed to be the most popular flowering plants in the United States. It is estimated that 40 million ready-to-bloom plants are purchased each year for outdoor gardens and indoor decorations. Millions more are grown by home gardeners from seeds of hybrid varieties that can bloom within 14 weeks from sowing.

Some geraniums bloom so prolifically they will flower 12 months of the year. Old plants beginning to decline often have cuttings taken from them to produce a new generation.

Grown as indoor flowering plants, geraniums are second in popularity only to African violets. As outdoor bedding plants, they are second only to petunias.

There isn't a single month of the year when you can't grow flowering geraniums. Outdoors, varieties bloom non-stop until fall frosts. Indoors, varieties may flower any time of year. Colors include white, pink, rose, red, crimson, orange and bicolors, usually with a contrasting eye. Some geraniums have a dark leaf zone, considered an ornamental feature. Others have plain leaves. Even among geraniums classified as *zonal,* the intensity of the leaf zone may vary. Plants grow 10 to 18 inches high and spread 12 inches wide.

Geraniums are tender perennials best grown as annuals, derived from crosses between species native to South Africa.

Recommended Varieties—New kinds of geraniums appear every year. It is difficult to keep pace with them. Among the best are the 'Sprinter' series, 17 inches high, available in deep red, salmon, scarlet and white, plus a mixture. Compact plants are shorter than standard varieties and bloom profusely.

'Sprinters' have plain leaves. For zoned foliage try the 'Ringo' series, developed in Holland. Nine varieties are available. They are a little earlier than 'Sprinters'. My favorite is 'Ringo Heidi', a rose-salmon bicolor with a white eye.

An interesting form are the 'Stardust' geraniums, named 'Startel' in England, where they originated. Petals are *quilled,* and leaves are attractively zoned. 'Stardust' blooms in 18 weeks from seeds. They create an unusual display in the garden as bedding plants or in containers.

How to Grow—Start seeds indoors 10 to 12 weeks before last frost date. Plant after all danger of frost has

Geranium 'Playboy Cherry Scarlet' makes an eye-catching planting for beds and borders.

Geraniums are being grown for evaluation at seed farm near Santa Paula, California.

'Smash Hit' geranium creates a beautiful mass display.

'Tiffany' geranium, shown at peak bloom.

passed. Germination takes 7 to 15 days at 70F to 85F (21C to 30C) soil temperature. Germination is sometimes erratic. Soaking seeds for 48 hours on a moist paper towel may improve your success. Plant 1/4 inch deep in loose, sterile potting soil in seed trays. When seedlings are large enough to handle, transfer to 4-inch pots and grow to transplant size. Keep soil moist and feed every 2 weeks with diluted liquid plant fertilizer.

Space 12 inches apart in full sun. Soil should be fertile loam, preferably with plenty of organic matter mixed in. Geraniums produce the best floral displays when watered regularly. As flowers fade, pick them frequently to encourage continual bloom. During periods of heavy rainfall, seed-grown geraniums are prone to *shattering*. This is when petals are stripped off and the floral display is temporarily delayed. Generally, seed geraniums flower longer than those grown from cuttings.

Outdoor-grown geraniums usually drop their leaves when potted in containers and brought directly indoors. To grow outdoor geraniums indoors through winter, cut back stems severely after potting. Keep soil on the dry side until February. Fertilize, water thoroughly and provide bright, indirect sunlight. Plants will produce more leaves and become bushy for spring planting and flowering.

It is generally more successful to take cuttings of outdoor geraniums in fall before frost. Select the best of these cuttings to produce fresh, new plants for indoor flowering. Use a sharp knife or razor blade to remove 3 to 5 inches of healthy stem with leaves growing closely together. Plant in rooting medium such as potting soil or vermiculite. As soon as cuttings anchor themselves with a healthy root system, usually after 8 weeks, transfer to individual pots. Plant in soil mixture that contains 2 parts sterilized garden topsoil and 1 part peat moss.

Geraniums are subject to a number of diseases caused by fungi, viruses and unfavorable conditions. These diseases are less likely to affect geraniums grown from seeds as compared to cutting-grown geraniums.

Stem rot is common when plants are overwatered or too crowded. A fungus disease called *botrytis,* or gray mold, can be identified as grayish spots on leaves. Fungicides such as benomyl and captan control this disease. Seriously infected plants should be discarded to prevent spread of infection. Careful watering, keeping plants clean of dead vegetation and adequate ventilation helps prevent botrytis. Leaf drop is usually caused by an uncomfortable environment—one that is overly hot, dry, stuffy, dark or wet.

Yellowing of leaves is a common occurrence. A disorder known as *chlorosis* is usually a sign of nutrient deficiency or improper soil pH. Or you may need to apply fertilizer or certain trace elements. See photo, page 33. Control spider mites with sprays of dicofol. Control aphids with sprays of malathion.

Uses—Massed plantings in beds and borders. They also do well as container plants in tubs, urns and window boxes. Indoors, geraniums make excellent container plants—especially during winter and early spring.

HISTORY OF HYBRID SEED GERANIUMS

In 1958, Dick Craig, an undergraduate student at Penn State University, made a plant breeding breakthrough with bedding geraniums—*Pelargonium hortorum*.

It was generally believed that geraniums would not grow true to color from seeds. In other words, seeds from a pink geranium might just as easily produce a white or red variety. Seedsmen that sold geranium seeds sold them as mixtures. And because geraniums could be grown so easily from cuttings in less time, there was no point in wasting valuable breeding time on seed geraniums.

In addition, geranium seeds were difficult to germinate, having a hard seed coat. Germination was not only erratic, the flowering time was late.

Dick Craig, now an associate professor of plant breeding at Penn State University, says he was too innocent to realize these obstacles. He began his project by ordering 'Floradale Fancy Mixed', a popular mixture of seed geraniums, straight out of the Burpee seed catalog. He *scarified* the seeds, a treatment whereby the seed coat is made pervious to moisture. To his delight he discovered among the plants some that would grow true to color. The best of these was a bright red he later perfected and called 'Nittany Lion'.

'Nittany Lion' was entered in the All-America Selections, the national seed trials, but failed to win an award. The majority of judges felt that the new geranium was of little value to home gardeners when cutting geraniums were so easy to grow.

Ferry Morse, a California-based seed company, was more optimistic. They backed the Penn State variety by growing a commercial seed crop and offering it for sale world-wide. It was an instant hit in Europe, and suddenly the advantages of seed geraniums were being realized.

The scarifying technique shortened the blooming time by making germination faster and more reliable. The resulting plants bloomed longer than cutting-grown geraniums, didn't carry disease and seeds were less costly than cuttings.

Several commercial seed breeders used 'Nittany Lion' as a parent to create special hybrids, which shortened the blooming time even more. The first of these was 'New Era', introduced by Joseph Harris Company. These were almost immediately overshadowed by the 'Carefree' class, introduced a year later. Two separate colors in the class—pink and red—scooped up All-America awards. A commercial breeder, Pan American Seed Company, introduced 'Carefree'. Each year Pan American and other breeders have worked to shorten the blooming time even more.

From 18 weeks to flowering, the time period was reduced to 16 weeks with 'Sprinter'. A number of recently developed varieties bloom within 14 weeks. The objective of plant breeders is to develop a geranium that will bloom within 10 weeks after being planted from seed.

'Carefree Fickle Rose' geranium has white centers that seem to make the flowers sparkle.

"Juggy" Sharma, plant breeder for Pan American Seed, displays an assortment of early flowering geraniums that can be grown from seed.

'Mardi Gras' gerbera is a special early flowering strain. Yellow is just one of many colors in the mixture.

GERBERA
Gerbera jamesoni

Gerbera is also known as *Transvaal daisy* for the region of South Africa where it grows wild. This tender perennial is usually grown as a tender annual. Large, daisy-like blooms measure up to 5 inches across. They appear on long, strong stems above a rosette of leaves that grow close to the ground. Colors include yellow, orange, white, pink, red and salmon. Flowers appear continually during summer. Plants grow 15 inches high and spread 12 inches wide.

Recommended Varieties—'Florist's Strain' is a popular mixture. 'Mardi Gras' flowers weeks earlier. Both produce single flowers. No variety will produce 100% double flowers, but 'Fantasia' produces up to 75% double, crested flowers.

How to Grow—For flowers outdoors, start seeds indoors 10 weeks before last frost date. Plant after all danger of frost has passed. Barely cover seeds with soil because they need light to germinate. Sow only fresh seeds, because they do not store well. Seeds germinate in 5 to 10 days at 70F to 85F (21C to 30C) soil temperature.

To bring plant to flower indoors, they will need 14 to 18 weeks of continuous growth. Germinate seeds in flats or seed trays and transfer to individual 6-inch pots when large enough to handle. Fill pots with a mixture of 1/3 sand, 1/3 peat or leaf mold and 1/3 sterile topsoil. Feed every 2 weeks with a diluted liquid fertilizer. Maintain night temperatures as close as possible to 50F to 55F (10C to 13C).

Space plants 12 inches apart in full sun in fertile loam soil. Water during dry spells. Gerberas tolerate daytime heat and prefer cool nights. Without cool nights, flowering will stop.

Control slugs and snails by using slug bait or pick them off by hand. Mites can be a serious problem indoors. Spray with dicofol or wash plants with an insecticidal soap.

Uses—Usually grown as cut flowers in a cool greenhouse. Popular for beds and borders.

GILIA
Gilia tricolor

Commonly known as *bird's eyes,* this California wildflower is a hardy annual that requires cool, sunny conditions to grow well. Flowers are small, borne in clusters. They are white with pink tips to the petals and have black centers. Plants grow to 2 feet high and spread 6 inches wide. Flowers appear for several weeks in early summer.

Recommended Varieties—Not sold by variety name.

How to Grow—Sow seeds directly in the garden as soon as soil has warmed in spring. Germination takes 8 days at 60F (16C) soil temperature. Seeds are sensitive to temperatures above 70F (21C).

Space plants 6 inches apart in full sun. Plants tolerate a wide range of soil conditions—even poor soils—but prefer loam or sandy soil. Water regularly during dry spells. Plants cannot tolerate heat or drought and do best in cool regions such as coastal California and the Pacific Northwest. Generally free of pests and diseases.

Uses—Usually grown in beds and borders of mixed annuals and in wildflower plantings.

Gilia, or bird's eyes, is a California wildflower that grows best in cool, sunny conditions.

GLOBE AMARANTH

Gomphrena globosa

Globe amaranth are bushy and spreading, producing masses of 1-inch, cloverlike flowers with a papery texture. Colors include white, yellow, orange, pink and purple. Plants grow 6 to 30 inches high, depending on variety, spreading up to 2 feet wide. Tender annual native to India.

Recommended Varieties—Tall types are generally not sold by name but are offered as mixtures. A superior dwarf, 'Buddy', 6 to 8 inches high, produces rich purple flowers. *Gomphrena haageana aurea,* to 2 feet high, is valued by flower arrangers for its deep reddish-orange, cone-shape flowers.

How to Grow—Surface-sow seeds outdoors after danger of frost has passed. Or start seeds indoors 6 weeks before last frost date. Seeds need light to germinate. Germination takes 14 days at 70F to 85F (21C to 30C) soil temperature.

Space dwarfs 6 inches apart. Space tall types 12 inches apart in full sun. Plants tolerate poor soils, heat and drought. Generally free of pests and diseases.

Uses—Grown for cutting to create dried-flower arrangements. Popular for beds and borders.

GLORIOSA DAISY

Rudbeckia hirta

Gloriosa daisies were developed from wild black-eyed Susans, or *Rudbeckias,* common throughout the waysides of North America. Gloriosa daisies are hardy perennials but are easy to grow as hardy annuals if seeds are sown early in the season. There are single- and double-flower kinds, with flowers measuring up to 5 inches across. Colors are mostly yellow and orange. Some have contrasting mahogany and bronze zones toward the flower center, with a contrasting eye—usually dark brown or bright green. Flowers appear continually during summer. Plants grow 2 to 3 feet high and spread 2 feet wide.

Recommended Varieties—The first gloriosa daisy was 'Single Mixed', introduced by Burpee Seeds in 1957. It is still considered a superior selection. After the success of 'Single Mixed', Burpee produced 'Double Gold', rich, golden-yellow double with brown eyes. It won an All-America award. This was followed by 'Pinwheel', mahogany and gold bicolor, and 'Irish Eyes', golden yellow with contrasting green eye. All are tall types growing 3 feet high. Dwarf kinds are also available that are especially adapted to mass plantings.

How to Grow—Sow seeds over soil surface outdoors in spring as soon as soil can be worked. For earlier blooms, start seeds indoors 8 weeks before time to plant outdoors. Germination takes 5 to 10 days at 65F to 75F (19C to 24C) soil temperature.

Plant 12 inches apart in full sun. Gloriosa daisies are tough, low-maintenance plants that tolerate poor soils, freezing temperatures and dry spells. They do best in fertile loam soil with regular water. Slugs and snails will eat young plants. Control with slug bait or pick by hand.

Uses—Appealing when massed in beds and borders. Also good for cutting to create beautiful indoor flower arrangements.

Globe amaranth creates a long-lasting border. Flowers are popular for use in dried-flower arrangements.

Planting of gloriosa daisies provides a mixture of colors in midsummer.

'Dwarf Mixed Colors' godetia create a carpet of color in early summer wherever cool sunny conditions exist.

Ornamental grasses are popular for use in flower arrangements.

GODETIA
Clarkia amoena

Godetia is also called *satin flower* because of the way the petals shimmer. In cool, sunny conditions, the mound-shape plants cover themselves for several weeks in early summer with dazzling, cup-shape flowers. Colors are white and shades of pink, red and purple, plus bicolors. Plants are hardy annuals and grow to 1 to 2 feet high, spreading 1 foot wide. Native to California.

Recommended Varieties—Generally sold as 'Tall Mixed Colors', 2 feet high, and 'Dwarf Mixed Colors', 1 foot high. Dwarf varieties are more popular for garden displays. Single and double-flower types are available. Single-flower kinds produce the most colorful display.

How to Grow—Plants do not transplant well so it is best to sow seeds directly in the garden. Barely cover them with soil because light is necessary for germination. In mild-winter areas, sow seeds in fall for early spring bloom. Germination takes 8 days at 60F (16C) soil temperature.

Space plants 12 inches apart in full sun. Light, sandy, well-drained soil is preferred. Keep soil moist. Godetias are popular in coastal California and the Pacific Northwest, where their requirement for cool nights can be supplied. Generally free of pests and diseases.

Uses—Beds, borders, rock gardens and for naturalizing in open meadows.

GRASSES
Pennisetum setaceum and other genera

Ornamental grasses are usually sold as mixtures. Those sold separately include *Pennisetum setaceum,* fountain grass; *Briza maxima,* quaking grass; and *Coix lacryma jobi,* Job's tears. Some are grown for their beautiful flower plumes or seed heads. Others are grown for their ornamental leaves. Plants grow 2 to 4 feet high, depending on species. They are distributed throughout the world and grown as tender annuals in most regions.

Recommended Varieties—The most beautiful annual ornamental grass is *Pennisetum setaceum,* fountain grass. Plants produce masses of graceful, arching leaves and pink, silky plumes. They can be cut and used in dried arrangements. In frost-free locations, it grows as a long-lasting perennial. 'Mixed Kinds' offers a good assortment of popular species.

How to Grow—Ornamental grasses are sold mostly as mixtures. It's best to broadcast seeds outdoors in a special area of the garden after danger of frost has passed. Or start seeds indoors 6 weeks before last frost date. Germination takes 7 to 16 days at 70F to 85F (21C to 30C) soil temperature.

Space plants 12 inches apart in full sun. Fertile, sandy soils are recommended. Water regularly during dry spells. Spreading, vigorous types such as fountain grass should be thinned to stand 2 feet apart. Plants are generally free of pests and diseases.

Uses—Cutting to create beautiful dried arrangements. Attractive in the landscape as background or feature planting.

GYPSOPHILA

Gypsophila elegans

The botanical name for this tender annual—*Gypsophila*—means love of chalk. This refers to its liking for limestone soils, which are alkaline. Plants produce a cloud of small, white or pink flowers on what seem to be leafless plants—the foliage is so thin. Plants grow to 2 feet high and spread 2 feet wide. Native to eastern Europe.

Recommended Varieties—'Covent Garden' is the most widely grown white-flower type. 'Rosea' is beautiful rose-pink.

How to Grow—Sow seeds directly in the garden after all danger of frost has passed. Barely cover seeds with soil because light aids germination. For earlier flowers, start seeds indoors 4 to 5 weeks before last frost date. Germination takes 10 days at 70F (21C) soil temperature.

Space plants 1-1/2 feet apart in full sun. Plants prefer poor soils. They dislike soils that are heavily clay, acid or overly moist. Plants are drought tolerant once established. On the Pacific Coast, sowings can be made in June for October and November bloom. Plants are generally free of pests and diseases.

Uses—Widely used as accent plant in mixed beds and borders, and for cutting to make flower arrangements. Flowers can be dried for use in dried arrangements. Because of its tolerance to drought, gypsophila is adapted to rock gardens.

'Covent Garden' gypsophila is popular among flower arrangers.

HELIOTROPE

Heliotropium arborescens

Although strictly perennials in Peru where they grow wild, heliotrope is best grown as a tender annual. Plants produce clusters of tiny, fragrant, violet-blue flowers. Mature size is 12 to 18 inches high, spreading 12 to 15 inches wide.

Recommended Varieties—'Marine', 18 inches high, has deep violet-blue flowers and handsome, dark-green foliage.

How to Grow—Start seeds indoors 6 to 8 weeks before last frost date. Barely press seeds into soil because light aids germination. Seeds germinate in 7 to 21 days at 70F to 85F (21C to 30C) soil temperature.

Space plants 12 inches apart in full sun. Soil should be fertile and well drained. Water freely during dry spells.

Outdoors, heliotrope is troubled by few pests or diseases. Indoors as a greenhouse plant it is susceptible to attack from spider mites, aphids, mealy bugs and whiteflies. Kelthane controls mites. Malathion controls the others. Washing plants with an insecticidal soap is an effective organic remedy.

Uses—Popular as an accent plant in mixed beds and borders and in containers. Grown in cutting gardens and as a flowering plant indoors. In Europe, perfume is distilled from the fragrant flowers.

'Marine' heliotrope has fragrant flowers.

'Mixed Colors' helipterum grows in cutting garden.

HELIPTERUM
Acroclinium roseum

Helipterum is from Australia. Plants are hardy annuals, similar to strawflower, *Helichrysum.* They differ in that their colors are predominately soft pastels, including white, rose, pink and carmine. Papery petals are pointed and have a satinlike sheen. Plants grow 1-1/2 to 2 feet high and spread 1 foot wide. Flowers last several weeks in summer.

Recommended Varieties—Normally sold only as a mixture. However, plant may be sold as acroclinium or rhodanthe.

How to Grow—Sow seeds directly in the garden after all danger of frost has passed. Or start indoors 6 to 8 weeks before last frost date. Germination takes 10 to 18 days at 70F to 85F (21C to 30C) soil temperature.

Space plants 12 inches apart in full sun. Plants tolerate poor soils and require water only during dry spells. Generally free of pests and diseases.

Uses—Usually grown for cutting and to create dried-flower arrangements.

HIBISCUS
Hibiscus moscheutos

This hibiscus, commonly known as *rose mallow* and *swamp mallow,* is a tender perennial. Certain cultivated varieties can be grown as tender annuals. They will flower the first year from seeds started indoors early in the season. Flowering occurs in midsummer and continues until frost. Individual blooms measure up to 10 inches across in white, red and pink. Plants grow 5 feet high and spread 4 feet wide. Native to the southern United States.

Recommended Varieties—'Southern Belle' won an All-America award for its large flowers and earliness.

How to Grow—Seeds have hard coats. Soak them overnight in lukewarm water before sowing. Notching seed coat with a nail file allows moisture to penetrate for faster germination. Sow seeds 1 inch deep in individual peat pots 8 weeks before last frost date. Plant after all danger of frost has passed. Germination takes 7 to 21 days at 70F to 85F (21C to 30C) soil temperature.

Space seedlings 3 to 4 feet apart in full sun. Plants prefer loam or sandy soil high in organic matter. Although plants tolerate high heat and humidity, they require regular amounts of water. If you live in an area where frost kills top growth in fall, cover roots with 6 inches of straw or shredded leaves. Plants may survive winter to re-grow and flower the following season.

Protect young seedlings from slugs and snails by using slug bait. Or hand-pick the pests in early morning.

Uses—Good background or lawn centerpiece. One plant flowering in a circular bed creates a spectacular highlight.

'Southern Belle' hibiscus is available in white and red. Flowers measure a full 10 inches across.

HOLLYHOCK
Alcea rosea

Sown early in the season, hollyhocks will flower the first year. Botanically they are hardy perennials, and usually come up each year. They are tall-growing plants with large blooms up to 4 inches across. They appear on flower spikes that can grow to 10 feet high, spreading 2 to 3 feet wide. Plant breeders have produced some dwarf types that are grown mostly as annuals. Colors include white, yellow, pink, crimson and red. Flowers can be single, semidouble or fully double. Fully double forms resemble a powder puff. It is these varieties that are most available. Native to China.

Recommended Varieties — 'Summer Carnival', mixed colors, grows to 5 feet high. It won an All-America award for its earliness and superb color range. 'Majorette', mixed colors, also won an All-America award for its smaller size — 2-1/2 feet. 'Chater's Giants' grow to 10 feet high. All are fully double forms.

How to Grow — For blooms the first year, start seeds indoors 6 to 8 weeks before last frost date. Barely cover seeds with soil because they need light to germinate. Germination takes 5 to 18 days at 70F to 85F (21C to 30C) soil temperature. Soaking seeds overnight speeds germination. Set out seedlings after all danger of frost has passed.

Space plants 12 inches apart in full sun. Plants prefer a deep, fertile loam soil and plenty of moisture. They are heavy feeders and benefit from applications of liquid fertilizer at flowering time. Although newer dwarf varieties are perennial, they are generally weak and usually fail after the first season. Taller varieties will self-sow, but volunteers of double-flower types will revert back to single-flower form.

The worst problem with hollyhocks is rust disease, identified by brown pustules on undersides of leaves. Dusting plants with sulfur or spraying with zineb offers some control. It is best to destroy severely infected plants. Anthracnose is another destructive disease, identified by black blotches on stems and leaves. Control with sprays of Bordeaux mixture. Prune and destroy infected plant parts in fall.

Uses — Tall forms are an old-fashion favorite, useful as background highlight in borders or as temporary screen. Dwarf forms can be used in beds and borders for summer displays.

'Chater's Giants' hollyhock has attractive, double, pompon-type blooms.

'Futura Rose' impatiens.

IMPATIENS
Impatiens wallerana

Wild species of this popular, shade-loving annual are widely dispersed throughout the world. Most modern garden varieties were developed from plants native to India and Africa.

Plants create a mound of everblooming flowers. In addition to solid colors of white, pink, salmon, red and purple, there are bicolors with white stars at their centers. Although most are single flowers, a few double kinds are available. Heights vary according to variety. Dwarf types grow to 1 foot high. Some of the taller species can reach up to 3 feet high, spreading 3 feet wide.

Recommended Varieties—'Elfins' produce medium-size flowers on dwarf, compact plants that are perfectly uniform in growth habit. They branch out naturally from the base so no pinching is necessary to encourage spread. Available colors are red, pink, orange, purple and white.

The 'Futura' series is similar to 'Elfins' in growth habit but have larger flowers, which create more spectacular displays. Look for another major improvement—'Super Elfins'. These are earlier flowering and lower growing than the original 'Elfins'. They have a natural spreading habit, grow more compact and have larger flowers.

Largest flowers of any impatiens is 'Blitz', an All-America award winner. Individual, orange-scarlet flowers measure up to 2-1/4 inches across. Plants grow to 12 inches high. Dark-green leaves help enhance the bright, glowing flower color. Flowers appear within 60 days of sowing seeds and bloom for many months. Unfortunately, 'Blitz' does not come in any other separate colors and no mixture is currently available.

'Grande' is the largest-flowering impatiens mixture. Seven separate colors and a mixture are available. Flowers measure 2 inches across on plants that grow 12 to 14 inches high. 'Grande Orange' is one of the most spectacular of all impatiens. Another outstanding orange impatiens is 'Tangeglow', with large, tangerine flowers and long spurs.

Varieties such as 'Elfin' and 'Grande' are solid color with single flowers. Some interesting new flower forms have emerged in recent years, including double flowers and bicolor singles. Best of the bicolor singles are 'Twinkles' and 'Ripples'. 'Ripples' have slightly larger flowers. The bicolor effect is produced by a white star at the center of each flower. Remaining petal color can be red, pink, rose or fuchsia.

A special strain of impatiens developed from wild species collected in New Guinea have exotic, variegated leaves and extra-large flowers. 'New Guinea' impatiens are generally more difficult to grow than regular impatiens. Some varieties require full sun rather than shade.

How to Grow—Start seeds indoors 10 weeks before last frost date. Plant after all danger of frost has passed. Germination takes 8 days at 70F to 80F (21C to 27C) soil temperature. Light aids germination so press seeds into soil surface just enough to anchor them. Water with a light mist. To keep soil surface from drying out, cover seed tray with clear plastic bag.

Potting soil, trays and pots should be sterile because impatiens are extremely sensitive to soil-borne diseases such as damping-off. Even if you use sterile

Mixed colors of 'Elfin' impatiens brighten shady island bed.

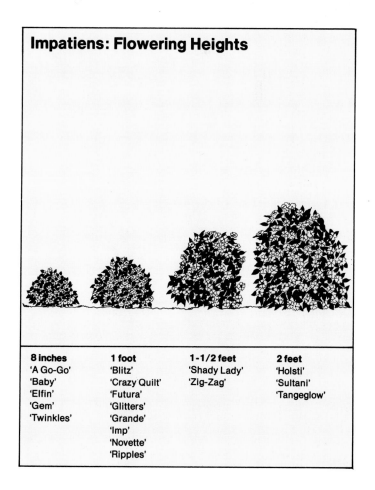

Impatiens: Flowering Heights

8 inches	1 foot	1-1/2 feet	2 feet
'A Go-Go'	'Blitz'	'Shady Lady'	'Holsti'
'Baby'	'Crazy Quilt'	'Zig-Zag'	'Sultani'
'Elfin'	'Futura'		'Tangeglow'
'Gem'	'Glitters'		
'Twinkles'	'Grande'		
	'Imp'		
	'Novette'		
	'Ripples'		

'Ripples Rose' impatiens has a white star in center of each flower, creating a bicolor effect.

materials, it is best to spray soil surface with captan or benomyl fungicide at time of seeding.

In the garden, the most important requirement for impatiens is *cool soil,* which is why they grow well in light shade. Soils that contain plenty of moisture-holding organic matter such as peat moss, garden compost or leaf mold are required. Space plants 12 inches apart and water regularly.

Inside your home, impatiens will grow in a variety of light conditions. Room temperature of 70F (21C) is ideal. Bright, filtered light helps produce the best displays.

Impatiens can be propagated readily from stem cuttings. Suspend a 4- to 5-inch-long section of stem in water. It will soon sprout roots, which can be potted to grow into a new flowering plant.

Maintain winter temperatures above 55F (13C). Because impatiens love humidity, mist leaf surfaces as often as possible. After several months of flowering, plants may become spindly. Prune to encourage new basal growth. Slugs are a common pest and can be controlled by slug baits.

Uses—No flowering annual performs better in shade than impatiens. They are colorful and long-lasting. After they pass the seedling stage, they branch out to create a beautiful, flowering ground cover. They are also popular for beds, borders, hanging baskets and tubs.

KALE, ORNAMENTAL
Brassica oleracea

Also called *flowering cabbage,* these hardy annuals are grown for the colorful rosette of leaves that forms at the center of each plant. Leaf color is usually creamy white or rose-pink, and lasts for several weeks during cool weather. Plants grow to 1 foot high and spread 1-1/2 feet wide.

Recommended Varieties—Usually sold as mixtures and not by variety name. Separate colors are sometimes available.

How to Grow—Start seeds indoors 6 to 8 weeks before time to plant outdoors. Seedlings tolerate mild frosts if *hardened-off*—exposed to cool temperatures gradually. Plants can be set outdoors several weeks before last frost date. Germination takes 3 to 10 days at 65F to 85F (19C to 30C) soil temperature. Pre-chilling seeds at 40F (5C) for 3 days ensures maximum germination.

Space plants 1-1/2 feet apart in full sun. Soil should be fertile loam, preferably rich in organic matter such as compost. Keep soil moist, especially during dry spells. Although plants are tolerant of hot weather, leaf color will not be as intense unless nights are cool. In hot-summer areas, time plantings so they mature in cool, fall weather.

Plants are prone to damage by chewing insects, especially caterpillars. Control with Sevin chemical spray or *Bacillus thuringiensis* organic control.

Uses—Effective as bedding plants for low beds and borders, also for edging. Plants do well in containers, especially large tubs and window boxes.

Ornamental kale is one of the more unusual annuals to grow for color in the garden.

KOCHIA
Kochia childsi

Kochia, pronounced *ko-kia,* is also called *burning bush* because of its reddish fall color. It is grown as a tender annual for its light-green, feathery foliage and bushy habit that resembles that of a dwarf evergreen cypress tree. Plants grow 2 to 3 feet high and spread 2 feet wide. They remain decorative through summer until fall frosts. Native to Mexico.

Recommended Varieties—'Acapulco Silver' differs from regular kochia because of the white leaf tips at top of plant, giving it a frosted appearance in summer. It is an All-America award winner.

How to Grow—Sow seeds outdoors after all danger of frost has passed. Or start seeds indoors 4 to 6 weeks before last frost date. Germination takes 6 days at 70F to 85F (19C to 30C) soil temperature. Exposure to light improves germination.

Space plants 1-1/2 feet apart in full sun. Kochia tolerate poor soil and dry conditions. Growth is slow during cool weather.

Control leaf hoppers to prevent spread of aster-yellows disease. Use Sevin chemical spray or pyrethrum organic spray.

Uses—Background to create temporary hedge. Also popular as accent used singly in beds of mixed annuals.

Kochia is grown mostly for its foliage, which resembles the needles of an evergreen.

LARKSPUR
Consolida ambigua

Larkspurs are hardy annuals closely related to delphiniums. Larkspurs resemble delphiniums but flowers are smaller. In the cool, coastal valleys of California and the Pacific Northwest, they are spectacular summer-flowering plants. Larkspurs are mostly sold as mixtures of white, pink, light blue, deep blue and purple. Plants grow to 2 feet high and spread 2 feet wide. Native to southern Europe.

Recommended Varieties—'Imperial Giant' is the most popular mixture.

How to Grow—Sow seeds outdoors as soon as soil can be worked in spring. Cover seeds with 1/4 inch of fine soil. For earlier blooms, start seeds indoors 6 to 8 weeks before time to plant outdoors. Germination takes 10 to 20 days at 60F to 70F (16C to 21C) soil temperature.

Space plants 12 inches apart in full sun. Soil should be slightly alkaline, loose, fertile and well drained. Keep soil moist but avoid getting water on foliage. Pick faded flowers to encourage continual bloom.

Foliage browns and mildews easily. Prevent by using a general-purpose garden fungicide. Several virus diseases can infect larkspur. These are best prevented by controlling insect carriers—notably aphids and leaf hoppers. Remove infected plants from garden. Use Sevin chemical spray or pyrethrum organic spray. Stem borers, leaf miners and cutworms are potential pests that can be controlled by the same sprays.

Uses—Beds and borders, particularly as background plant. Popular as cut flower. In addition to fresh use, flower stems are easy to dry for dried-flower arrangements.

'Imperial Giant' larkspur shows main assortment of colors available.

Flowers of 'Loveliness' lavatera have a satinlike sheen. Plants are heat resistant.

LAVATERA
Lavatera trimestris

Lavatera, also known as *tree mallow,* is a hardy annual native to the Mediterranean. It closely resembles the wild mallows widely distributed throughout North America. Flowers are large, prolific and eye-catching in shimmering white or pink, up to 4 inches across. They appear from midsummer to fall frost. Plants grow 3 to 4 feet high and spread 2 feet wide. Leaves are shaped like maple leaves.

Recommended Varieties—'Loveliness' is the most widely available. 'Tanagra' has larger flowers. It won a Fleuroselect award in 1973.

How to Grow—Lavatera dislikes transplanting. Sow seeds directly in the garden after all danger of frost has passed. Plant 1/4 inch deep. Germination takes 7 to 21 days at 70F (21C). Soak seeds in water overnight or file seed coat to aid penetration of moisture.

Space plants 1 to 2 feet apart in sandy soil. Water is necessary only after soil becomes dry. Like most members of the mallow family, plants are highly susceptible to rust disease. Brown pustules on undersides of leaves are signs of rust. In susceptible areas, dust with a sulfur-based fungicide. Remove and destroy rust-infected leaves as soon as they are noticed.

Uses—Accent plant in mixed beds and borders. Also effective as a background because of their height. Flowers are edible and are useful for cutting.

LINARIA
Linaria maroccana

These hardy annuals are also called *toadflax.* Dainty, snapdragonlike flowers closely resemble wild snapdragons known as *butter and eggs,* common to waysides in North America. Colors include white, yellow, pink, red, purple, blue and many bicolors. Flowers last several weeks during summer. Plants grow 8 to 12 inches high and spread 6 inches wide. Native to Morocco.

Recommended Varieties—'Fairy Bouquet' won an All-America award for its compact growth habit and multitude of bright colors.

How to Grow—Sow seeds outdoors as soon as soil can be worked in spring. Or start seeds indoors 6 weeks before time to plant outdoors. Germination takes 8 days at 60F (16C) soil temperature. Chilling seeds for 3 days at 40F (5C)—about the temperature in the vegetable bin of the refrigerator—encourages maximum germination.

Space plants 6 inches apart in full sun. Soil should be sandy and fertile. Water regularly. Plants flower best during cool, sunny weather. Generally free of pests and diseases.

Uses—Low, edging plant for beds and borders. Popular in rock gardens. Sometimes grown as container plant in greenhouse during winter.

'Fairy Bouquet' linaria won an All-America award for its extensive color range. Flowers resemble miniature snapdragons.

LIVINGSTONE DAISY

Dorotheanus bellidiformis

There is a vast family of succulent plants from South Africa commonly known as *ice plants*. They are tender annuals characterized by intensely colored, daisylike flowers, and a love of open, sunny locations. The most popular and easiest to grow are Livingstone daisies. They are often identified by an old botanical name, *Mesembryanthemum criniflorum*. They do best in cool, sunny areas of coastal California, where they flower profusely for several weeks during spring. Color range is extensive, including crimson, white, pink, purple, yellow and orange. Some are bicolor with a contrasting pale zone around dark centers. Fleshy leaves are covered with icelike crystals. Plants grow 8 inches high and spread 12 inches wide.

Recommended Varieties—Usually offered as a mixture and not by variety name. However, a few yellow varieties have started to make an appearance. 'Lunette' and 'Yellow Ice' are examples.

How to Grow—Start seeds indoors 10 weeks before your last frost date. Seeds germinate in 6 to 16 days at 60F (15C) soil temperature. Total darkness is needed for maximum germination.

Space plants 6 inches apart in full sun. Soil should be sandy. Plants tolerate drought and salt spray. Water sparingly after they are established. Where summers get hot and humid, plants have a tendency to burn. Time plantings so flowering occurs in the season when nights are still cool. Flowers close on cloudy days.

Mealy bugs can be a problem pest. Control with malathion chemical spray or use an organic insecticidal soap.

Uses—Mass planting in beds and borders. Popular as a ground cover in rock gardens, along slopes and cascading over dry walls.

Livingstone daisies create colorful border.

LOBELIA

Lobelia erinus

Lobelias prefer cool conditions to bloom well. They are generally classified as bedding types—*Lobelia erinus*—and hanging-basket types—*Lobelia erinus pendula*. They are challenging to grow from seeds, but easy from nursery-grown transplants. After planting, lobelias are free-flowering until fall frost. Most come in shades of blue, but white and red are also available. Plants grow 4 to 6 inches high and spread 6 inches wide. Tender annuals from South Africa.

Recommended Varieties—For edging, the best effect is achieved by planting separate colors such as 'Crystal Palace', deep violet-blue; 'Rosamond', wine-red with white eyes; and 'Heavenly', deep sky-blue.

How to Grow—Start seeds indoors 10 to 12 weeks before last frost date. Plant after all danger of frost has passed. Germination takes 10 days at 70F to 85F (21C to 30C) soil temperature. 'Heavenly' is an exception, preferring 50F to 60F (10C to 16C) soil temperature. Lobelia seeds need exposure to light for best germination. Press seeds into soil to anchor them.

Space plants 6 inches apart in full sun or partial shade. Soil should be fertile loam or sandy soil. Apply mulch around plants to keep soil cool. Water frequently in areas with hot summers.

Uses—Excellent for edging beds and borders. Effective in hanging baskets, window boxes and tubs.

'Rosamond' lobelia has red flowers with white centers.

Marigold garden features 'Orange Fireworks', front, 'Primrose Lady' and 'Sweet 'n Gold'.

MARIGOLD
Tagetes species

The late David Burpee, dean of American seedsmen, once said: "No garden flower is less trouble than the marigold to grow, has a longer season from the start of blooming until the frosts come, or has more decorative value both inside and outside the house." Mr. Burpee spoke about his favorite flower. His carefully chosen words met with enthusiastic agreement with those in attendance.

Marigolds are tender annuals native to the desert regions of Mexico. Four popular kinds are grown in home gardens: American, *Tagetes erecta;* French, *T. patula;* signet, *T. signata;* and triploid hybrids. Triploid hybrids are man-made crosses between tall American and dwarf French varieties. The result is an extremely early flowering, vigorous plant that produces more flowers over a longer period than others. Among these four classifications are many sizes and growth habits for every garden situation. Colors include white, yellow, orange and red.

Flowers can be double or single, varying from tiny, crested, 1-inch blooms of 'Petites' to 5-inch, globular blooms of 'Climax'. Plants vary in height from 6 inches to more than 3 feet, spreading up to 2 feet wide.

Leaves of most marigolds have a spicy, pungent odor—a form of natural repellent against foraging animals and insect pests. Odorless kinds are available, but many gardeners consider this valuable insect-repellent property a control for nematodes. At one time plant breeders thought that if they could breed out the oil responsible for the odor, they might increase marigold sales. But the odorless marigolds are not very popular except among flower arrangers. Few gardeners find the odor objectionable, and the odorless kinds are more prone to pest damage.

Recommended Varieties—In the past 50 years of plant breeding, more time and money has been spent on improving the marigold than any other flowering annual. In addition to Burpee, plant breeders such as Bodger, Harris, Denholm, Goldsmith, Hurst, Waller and Ferry Morse have made significant contributions in developing varieties.

Among odorless marigolds the most popular are 'Orange Hawaii' and 'Golden Hawaii'. These are American marigolds. Flowers are large, fully double, up to 4 inches across. Plants grow to 2-1/2 feet high. The following varieties have the typical marigold odor.

French marigolds: These are free-flowering, trouble-free plants excellent for bedding, edging, window boxes and for making dainty flower arrangements. An advantage they have over their taller, larger-flower American cousins is the addition of red to the color range. Some French marigolds are double and others have single flowers like a daisy. A popular feature of double-flower varieties is a crest—usually bright yellow—appearing on the center of flowers.

The most popular crested French marigold is the 'Petite' series. 'Petites' won an All-America award for their dwarf habit, 7 inches high, and early flowers. Recently, 'Petites' have been surpassed by the 'Boy' series. They have larger flowers and more prominent crests. They are just as free-flowering, not quite as early, and a little taller, 8 inches high. They generally make a better display.

Plant breeders John Mondry and Elwood Pickering inspect a field of marigolds near Santa Paula, California.

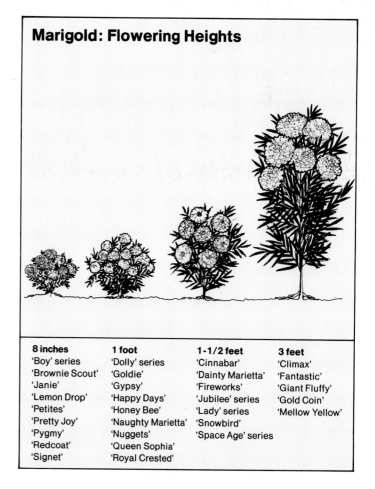

Marigold: Flowering Heights

8 inches	1 foot	1-1/2 feet	3 feet
'Boy' series	'Dolly' series	'Cinnabar'	'Climax'
'Brownie Scout'	'Goldie'	'Dainty Marietta'	'Fantastic'
'Janie'	'Gypsy'	'Fireworks'	'Giant Fluffy'
'Lemon Drop'	'Happy Days'	'Jubilee' series	'Gold Coin'
'Petites'	'Honey Bee'	'Lady' series	'Mellow Yellow'
'Pretty Joy'	'Naughty Marietta'	'Snowbird'	
'Pygmy'	'Nuggets'	'Space Age' series	
'Redcoat'	'Queen Sophia'		
'Signet'	'Royal Crested'		

'Snowbird' white marigold was produced from seeds that won $10,000 prize for Mrs. Alice Vonk, of Sully, Iowa. Burpee Seeds sponsored the contest, which went on for 50 years.

'Inca Orange' marigold with silver-gray dusty miller.

A number of French marigolds have flatter petals than 'Boys' or 'Petites' and exhibit two color zones. Outstanding among these is 'Queen Sophia', 10 inches high, which won an All-America award. It has more open flower form and russeted petal centers with bright-orange edges, creating a bicolor effect.

Bicolor French marigolds are popular for bedding. An outstanding variety with the more traditional rounded flower form is 'Glowing Embers'—10 inches high. It flowers 10 to 14 days earlier than 'Honeycomb', which has maroon petals with a gold-yellow border.

Among single-flower French marigolds, 'Naughty Marietta', 12 inches high, is a popular variety, displaying yellow petals splashed with red.

Signet marigolds: These have tiny, single flowers, and lots of them. Foliage is fine and feathery but plants often produce so many flowers they completely hide foliage. Signet marigolds make dense, mounded plants good for edging, rock gardens and window boxes. Space plants close together and they make a beautiful, temporary ground cover. Best varieties are 'Lemon Gem' and 'Orange Gem', both 8 inches high.

Triploid hybrid marigolds: Walk into a seedsman's trial garden at the height of summer. The brightest displays generally prove to be triploid hybrid marigolds. They seem to grab all the sunlight and hand it back to you, outshining and outlasting other flowering annuals.

Triploid hybrid marigolds are called *mule marigolds* in the United States, and *Afro-French* marigolds in England. The English still insist on calling American marigolds African, even though they are native to America. These incredibly free-flowering hybrids are the result of a difficult, man-made cross between the dwarf French marigold and the tall American marigold. They combine the best qualities of both parents: compact habit from the French and large flower size from the American. Plants are *sterile*—unable to produce viable seeds. All plant vigor is directed toward producing profuse numbers of flowers early and over a long period. Seeds are expensive, but the results are worth the cost. It is best to start seeds indoors and transplant seedlings to the garden.

The first triploid hybrids were 'Nuggets', 10 inches high, available in yellow, orange and red plus a mixture. These are still popular even though the 2-inch flowers are relatively small by comparison to other triploids. 'Red Seven Star', 14 inches high, has a more impressive flower size—2-3/4 inches. I would rate 'Red Seven Star' and 'Copper Canyon', which is not as available, the best of the triploid hybrids.

For good, clear-yellow flowers larger than those of 'Nuggets', try 'Honey Bee', 12 inches high, with flowers up to 2-1/2 inches across.

American marigolds: Most American marigolds are tall-growing plants that are best used as backgrounds and in borders. They take longer to bloom than French marigolds, and do not have red in their color range. Flowers are much larger—up to 4 inches across—and are "super-double," creating a globe shape.

In 1976, white was added to the color range. Seedsman David Burpee searched for more than 50 years for a large-flower marigold as pure white as 'Snowstorm' petunia. His award of $10,000 went to an Iowa home gardener, Mrs. Alice Vonk, who submitted seeds that produced the first white.

Tallest of the American marigolds and producing the largest flowers is the 'Climax' series, 3 feet high. 'Gold Coin' series have flowers that are almost as large and less prone to becoming lanky.

American marigolds such as the 'Dolly' types, 10 inches high, are also available. They have never been popular, probably because the large flowers and small plants seem out of proportion. They can look appealing in containers mixed with other dwarf annuals.

Far more popular are the semitall American marigolds, or *hedge* marigolds. 'Lady' hybrids, 15 inches high, are capable of producing more than 100 fully open flowers per plant. Flowers are rounded. Colors include yellow, gold, orange, primrose and a mixture.

'Jubilee' hybrids are slightly taller—to 18 inches. They are widely acclaimed for their sturdy growth habit and resistance to wind and rain. They produce abundant amounts of super-double blooms.

How to Grow—Except for triploid hybrid marigolds, sow seeds in the garden after all danger of frost has passed. Barely cover seeds with soil because light improves germination. Germination of triploid hybrids is sometimes substandard, so it is best to start seeds indoors. Sow seeds 6 to 8 weeks before last frost date. Germination takes 7 days at 70F to 85F (21C to 30C) soil temperature.

Marigolds require a sunny location. Soil should not be overly fertile. Be careful not to overwater. Excessive feeding and moisture encourages foliage growth at the expense of flowers—particularly taller forms.

Dwarf French varieties and signet marigolds tolerate crowding, but proper spacing is necessary for the triploids and Americans. Space triploids at least 12 inches apart. Space Americans 18 inches apart. Soil should be warm and well drained. Avoid planting in clay soils. As flowers fade, pick dead blooms often, and plants will continue flowering until fall frosts.

Many varieties of marigolds are subject to a problem called *heat check*. High heat causes plants to stop blooming. Avoid by choosing varieties resistant to heat check such as 'Janie' and the triploid hybrids.

Marigolds are seldom bothered by insects and diseases, less so than most annuals. A few problems occasionally occur. Slugs are fond of marigold foliage. They strip leaves from new transplants and seedlings unless controlled by slug bait. Japanese beetles eat the flowers. Control them with traps or biological controls. Aster yellows, a virus disease sometimes transmitted by leaf hoppers, can be a problem, particularly with odorless varieties.

Uses—Dwarf French and dwarf signet marigolds are excellent for edging beds and borders. These types are also suitable for planting in containers such as tubs and window boxes. Dwarf French, triploid hybrids and semidwarf American marigolds are favorites for summer bedding, used as mass plantings in beds and borders. Tall American marigolds are good for cutting and as backgrounds in beds and borders. Petals of marigold flowers are edible and make an excellent substitute for saffron in cooking.

'First Lady' marigold shows its extraordinary flowering capacity.

Flowers of 'Cinnabar' marigold have a daisylike form.

Hunnemannia, or tulip poppy, produces yellow, satinlike flowers that accept heat.

MEXICAN TULIP POPPY
Hunnemannia fumariifolia

This tender annual from Mexico produces yellow, tulip-shape flowers that appear in summer. In mild-winter areas such as southern California, the Gulf Coast and Florida, it grows as a perennial. Plants grow to 2 feet high and spread 1 foot wide.

Recommended Varieties—Not normally sold by variety name.

How to Grow—Surface-sow seeds outdoors after all danger of frost has passed. For earlier flowers, start seeds 4 to 6 weeks before last frost date. Germination takes 7 to 18 days at 70F to 85F (21C to 30C) soil temperature. Seeds require regular moisture for optimum germination. Handle seedlings carefully because roots are sensitive to rough transplanting.

Space plants 12 inches apart in full sun. Sandy, slightly alkaline soil is best, but plants tolerate poor soil. Water only during dry spells. Plants are generally free of pests and diseases.

Uses—Mostly used as an accent in mixed beds and borders. Often included in Southern and Western wildflower mixtures. Naturalizes in open spaces.

MIGNONETTE
Reseda odorata

This hardy annual is not a glamorous-looking plant, but it does have a romantic history. It also has a quality that is increasingly difficult to find among modern annuals—*fragrance*. Native to North Africa and Egypt, the Emperor Napoleon found it growing along the banks of the Nile River. He collected seeds and sent them to his Empress Josephine who was fond of flowers. Mignonette became popular throughout France in floral arrangements. It is widely available today.

Mignonette grows a clump of mostly green flower spikes, closely set with insignificant yellow or orange flowers. Plants grow 12 to 18 inches high and spread 12 inches wide.

Recommended Varieties—Not much choice among varieties, but 'Red Monarch' has the distinction of reddish-orange flowers.

How to Grow—Sow seeds outdoors in early spring, or start indoors 6 weeks before time to plant outdoors. Germination takes 4 to 10 days at 70F to 85F (21C to 30C) soil temperature. Exposure to light improves germination.

Space plants 6 to 12 inches apart in full sun. Prefers moist soil. Generally free of pests and diseases, although caterpillars sometimes eat leaves. Control with Sevin chemical spray or Dipel organic spray.

Uses—Mostly grown for cutting to add fragrance to indoor flower arrangements.

Mignonette is usually grown for cutting. Cut flowers will fill a room with their pleasant fragrance.

MIMULUS
Mimulus hybridus

Mimulus is also known as *monkey flower* because the velvety, freckled flower design resembles a monkey's face. It is a tender annual. Recently developed cultivated hybrid varieties are mostly dwarf, mound-shape plants. They are available in a rich range of colors, including red, yellow, orange and white. Many of the funnel-shape flowers have exotic, spotted patterns with contrasting colors. Plants grow 12 inches high and spread 12 inches wide. Flowers appear continually during cool weather. Native to Chile.

Recommended Varieties—'Velvet' hybrid is an American strain. Flowers are predominately red and yellow shades.

How to Grow—Start seeds indoors 10 weeks before last frost date. Germination takes 14 days at 60F (15C) soil temperature. Exposure to light aids germination.

Space plants 6 inches apart in full sun or light shade. Soil should be cool and moist, preferably enriched with plenty of organic matter. Plants cease to flower in hot weather. Pick faded flowers to promote continual bloom.

Uses—Bedding plant in moist, shaded locations and around the perimeter of ponds or garden pools. Suitable for container plantings in tubs and window boxes.

MOONFLOWER
Ipomoea alba

These tender annuals are fast-growing vines that need a strong trellis or fencing for support. Moonflowers resemble large, white, morning glories but bloom at night all summer. Flowers begin to open in the late afternoon and remain open until midmorning of the following day. The 6-inch flowers are pollinated by night-flying moths. Plants grow to 15 feet high and have large, decorative, heart-shape leaves. Native to the tropics of South America.

Recommended Varieties—Not normally sold by variety name.

How to Grow—Seeds have an extremely hard coat. To speed germination, soak seeds overnight in lukewarm water or notch seed coat with file to allow moisture penetration. Seeds may be sown outdoors after all danger of frost has passed. Or start seeds indoors 4 weeks before last frost date. Cover with 1 inch of soil. Germination takes 10 days at 70F to 85F (21C to 30C) soil temperature.

Space plants 12 inches apart in full sun. Loose, fertile, sandy soil suits them best. Overwatering can encourage too much leaf growth at expense of flowers, especially if soil is high in nitrogen. Sturdy support for heavy vines is essential.

New transplants should be protected from slugs and snails. Use slug bait or remove pests by hand. Japanese beetles can cause damage. Control with Sevin chemical spray or traps.

Uses—Climbs around porch or other structure close to the house. Locate so flowers can be highlighted by moonlight. Makes a thick, luxurious screen.

Mimulus, or monkey flower, has been hybridized to make them more heat tolerant and suitable to grow as early summer bedding plants.

Moonflower is a spectacular vining annual. Flowers open in late afternoon and last until the following morning.

'Heavenly Blue' morning glory is a fast-growing, flowering vine.

'Japanese Imperial Giant' has largest blooms of morning glories.

MORNING GLORY
Ipomoea imperialis

Morning glories are tender annuals with the distinction of being America's most popular flowering vine. Plants grow up to 10 feet long. Flowers are shaped like trumpets growing up to 5 inches across. They come in red, white, blue and bicolors. Flowers last only one day and generally close up in the afternoon, but are produced continually all summer. Widely dispersed throughout tropical and temperate areas of the world.

Recommended Varieties—The most popular morning glory is 'Heavenly Blue'. It produces lovely, sky-blue flowers 4 inches across in great profusion on vigorous vines. 'Pearly Gates' has 4-1/2-inch white flowers. 'Scarlet O'Hara' is crimson with large flowers. Both won All-America awards. 'Japanese Imperial Giant' has the largest flowers, up to 5 inches across. Most have white margins.

A class of dwarf morning glory, 'Dwarf Variegated', comes from Japan. They have variegated leaves and a neat, spreading habit. Plants are excellent in containers and window boxes where they can create a cascade effect. Plants grow about 6 inches high and spread about 12 inches wide.

How To Grow—Pea-size seeds have extremely hard coats. Before planting, soak overnight in lukewarm water. Or file seed coat to allow penetration of moisture. Sow seeds directly in the garden after all danger of frost has passed. Or start indoors 4 weeks before last frost date. Cover seeds with 1 inch of soil. Germination takes 7 days at 70F to 85F (21C to 30C) soil temperature.

Space plants 12 inches apart in full sun. Plants tolerate a wide range of soil conditions and are drought-resistant. Avoid overwatering and do not give plants fertilizer high in nitrogen. This tends to promote too much foliage growth at the expense of flowers. Heavy vines require strong trellis or fencing for support. For winter blooms in greenhouse or sun room, start seeds in September in 6-inch pots. Provide bamboo poles for supports.

Slugs and snails like to eat young transplants. Control with slug bait or remove by hand. Infestations of Japanese beetles can be a problem. Control with Sevin chemical spray or beetle traps.

Uses—Screen to cover bare fences and to decorate posts and arbors. Dwarf varieties can be used as temporary ground covers and container plants.

NASTURTIUM
Tropaeolum majus

Nasturtiums are hardy annuals available in many distinct types. Some are dwarf and bushy, growing to 1 foot high and spreading 2 feet wide. Others are climbing, reaching up to 6 feet high. Flowers can be single or double, measuring to 2-1/2 inches across. Colors include white, yellow, orange, red, pink and mahogany. Under cool conditions plants bloom continually, matching petunias for dramatic floral effect. Native to the Andes Mountains.

Recommended Varieties—For years, 'Double Dwarf Jewel' has been the leading variety. These grow 12 inches high and produce flowers that face sideways. A long spur protrudes below petals. Spur is filled with sweet nectar and attracts hummingbirds. 'Whirlybird' is a spurless nasturtium developed by a California plant breeder. Absence of spurs cause flowers to face upward, presenting a more dramatic and colorful effect. Plants are dwarf, bushy and uniform, growing to 12 inches high.

How to Grow—Sow seeds directly in the garden as soon as soil warms in early spring. Cover seeds with 1 inch of soil. For earlier blooms start seeds indoors 6 weeks before time to plant outdoors. Germination takes 10 to 14 days at 65F (19C) soil temperature.

Space plants 12 inches apart in full sun. Nasturtiums tolerate poor soils, even sandy or stony soils. Soils that are overly fertile may produce too much leaf growth at the expense of flowers. Keep soil moist in warm-summer areas. In areas with cool summers, nasturtiums are remarkably free-flowering. They will stop flowering when subjected to prolonged heat. The Pacific Coast, cool parts of Canada and coastal Maine are good growing regions for nasturtiums.

Nasturtiums are loved by aphids. Plants are often located near vegetable gardens as a trap plant to lure aphids away from vegetables. Sevin or malathion are effective chemical sprays to use against aphids. Nicotine sulfate is an organic spray.

Uses—Dwarf varieties are good for beds, borders and container plantings, including hanging baskets. Tall, climbing types can be trained up a trellis, fence or arbor as a flowering vine. Flowers have long stems that are excellent for cutting. All parts of nasturtium—leaves, stems, flowers and seeds—are edible. Flowers are particularly popular in salads.

'Whirlybird' nasturtium being used as ground and slope cover.

NEMESIA
Nemesia strumosa

Nemesias are free-flowering plants popular for summer bedding in areas with cool summers. They produce masses of flowers that resemble small pansies but with a large lower lip. Colors include red, yellow, orange, rose-pink, white and light blue. Some have contrasting centers that create a beautiful, bicolor effect. Flowers measure up to 2 inches across and have a sweet scent. Plants grow 12 to 18 inches high and spread 6 to 8 inches wide. Tender annuals native to South Africa.

Recommended Varieties—'Carnival Mixed Colors', 9 to 12 inches high, are neat and compact. Plants are smothered in blooms. Among separate colors, the most interesting is 'Blue Gem', producing dome-shape plants covered in sky-blue flowers.

How to Grow—Sow seeds directly in the garden in early spring after danger of frost has passed. Cover seeds with 1/8 inch of fine soil. For earlier blooms, start seeds indoors 6 to 8 weeks before last frost date. Germination takes 5 to 10 days at 60F (16C) soil temperature. Seeds are sensitive to temperatures above 70F (21C).

Space plants 12 inches apart in full sun or partial shade. They do best in moist, fertile soil, and cease to flower during periods of prolonged heat. Some chewing insects can be a nuisance. Spraying with Sevin chemical spray or pyrethrum organic spray is generally effective.

Uses—Mass plantings in beds and borders, rock gardens, dry walls and shade gardens. Gardeners with sun rooms or greenhouses can grow them in containers for winter flowers.

Nemesia 'Mixed Colors' shows assortment of colors available.

Nemophila, or baby blue eyes, is a California wildflower commonly used to edge beds and borders.

'Niki Red' nicotiana, rear, creates a stunning background for French marigold 'Queen Sophia' and verbena 'Sangria'. This planting is part of an All-America display garden.

NEMOPHILA
Nemophila menziesii

This hardy annual is a California wildflower also known as *baby blue eyes*. It is valued for its ability to produce masses of delicate, cup-shape, sky-blue flowers under cool, sunny conditions. Neat, compact, mounded plants grow 9 inches high and spread 9 inches wide.

Recommended Varieties—Not normally sold by variety name.

How to Grow—Sow seeds outdoors as soon as soil warms in early spring. Or start seeds indoors 6 weeks before time to plant outdoors. Germination takes 5 to 10 days at 60F (16C) soil temperature. Seeds are sensitive to temperatures above 70F (21C).

Space plants 6 inches apart in full sun. Nemophila tolerates a wide range of soil conditions, even poor soil. Keep soil moist during dry spells. Plants readily self-seed and are rarely troubled by pests or diseases.

Uses—Excellent for edging beds and borders and for naturalizing along waysides and in wildflower meadows.

NICOTIANA
Nicotiana alata

Nicotiana is also known as *flowering tobacco*. These tender annuals have been grown for many years, but old, traditional varieties had many shortcomings. Flowers would close in the afternoon, and plants would grow tall and weedy to 3 feet high. Recently, plant breeders have introduced improved hybrids that are semidwarf, growing 1-1/2 feet high. Flowers grow to 2 inches across and remain open all day. Flowering continues through summer, matching petunias for sheer brilliance. Colors include white, lime-green, yellow, pink, red and purple. Petals have a shimmer to them that intensifies the color impact. Native to South America.

Recommended Varieties—'Niki' series of semidwarf hybrids is outstanding, particularly 'Niki Red', winner of an All-America award. Other separate colors are available, including an eye-catching white.

Among non-hybrid types, 'Lime Green', an unusual pale green, is popular with flower arrangers. This old-fashion favorite has been surpassed by 'Really Green', a selection from 'Lime Green'. It grows to 30 inches high and has the deepest green available.

How to Grow—Start seeds indoors 6 to 8 weeks before last frost date. Plant after all danger of frost has passed. Light aids germination so press seeds into soil surface just enough to anchor them. Keep seeds moist with a fine spray. Germination takes 5 to 12 days at 70F to 85F (21C to 30C) soil temperature.

Space plants 12 inches apart in full sun. Soil should be fertile, well-drained loam. Plants tolerate dry spells but prefer regular water.

A few virus and fungus diseases cause leaf blemishes, but they are rarely serious enough to affect flowering display. Several kinds of beetles are attracted to nicotiana, including Colorado potato beetle, flea beetle and cucumber beetle. These can be controlled with Sevin chemical spray or pyrethrum organic spray.

Uses—Excellent as summer bedding plants in beds and borders.

NIEREMBERGIA
Nierembergia hippomanica

This low-growing, tender annual is actually a tender perennial in frost-free areas. A drawback is that it tends to get weedy after the first year. Grown as an annual to flower the first year, it creates a beautiful mound of small, cup-shape flowers. Although individual flowers measure only 1/4 inch across, there are lots of them, produced continually through summer. Plants are sometimes smothered in flowers. Usual color is purple, but white is available. Foliage is delicate and fine. Plants grow to 12 inches high and spread 12 inches wide. Native to Argentina.

Recommended Varieties— 'Purple Robe' won an All-America award for its neat, compact habit and long flowering period.

How to Grow—Start seeds indoors 10 weeks before last frost date. Cover seeds lightly with soil. Germination takes 6 to 14 days at 70F to 85F (21C to 30C) soil temperature.

Space plants 6 inches apart in full sun or partial shade in sheltered location. Keep soil moist. For indoor flowers in a greenhouse or sun room, start seeds indoors 4 months before flowering. Plants are generally free of pests and diseases.

Uses—Popular for edging beds and borders.

NIGELLA
Nigella damascena

Flowers of nigella resemble cornflowers. Most are blue but mixtures include white and pink. Flowers appear through summer. After flowers fade, large, balloonlike seed pods form. They can be used in dried arrangements. Plants grow 12 to 24 inches high and spread 8 to 12 inches wide. Foliage is delicate and feathery. Hardy annuals native to the Mediterranean.

Recommended Varieties— 'Persian Jewels' is a good mixture.

How to Grow—Plants dislike transplanting. Sow seeds directly in the garden in early spring after soil warms. Germination takes 8 to 16 days at 60F (16C) soil temperature. Nigella reseeds readily.

Space plants 12 inches apart in full sun. Keep soil moist. Plants prefer cool conditions for continual flowering and largest blooms.

Uses—Fresh flowers for cutting. Plant in mixed beds and borders where touch of blue is desired. Seed pods are valued for use in dried arrangements.

'Purple Robe' nierembergia in companion planting with 'White Cascade' petunias.

Nigella, or love in the mist, is an old-fashion annual popular for cutting.

Pansies growing as bedding plants for a spring display.

PANSY
Viola tricolor

Pansies are strictly classified as hardy biennials. However, recently developed hybrid varieties bloom so early they can be treated as hardy annuals. If seeds are sown in winter, flowers will appear in early spring. Some will bloom all four seasons of the year. Older varieties cannot tolerate hot weather and stop flowering in summer. Colors include red, white, blue, purple, yellow and orange. The most popular varieties are handsomely blotched with black markings on petals. Flowers measure up to 4-1/2 inches across. Plants grow to 6 inches high and spread 6 inches wide.

Recommended Varieties—Hybrids produce best displays and largest flowers. Some are available in plain colors; others have black blotches. The most popular hybrid is the 'Majestic Giants', developed in Japan and winner of an All-America award. Individual flowers measure up to 4 inches across in bright colors with bold, black blotches.

The 'Imperials', also from Japan, have larger flowers. Seed supply has been unreliable except for 'Imperial Blue'. It won an All-America award for its large flower size and long bloom period. Many less-expensive standard varieties are available, and every seed catalog offers a favorite strain. 'Roggli Elite Swiss Giants', developed in Switzerland, is widely available.

Climbing pansies: One of the most interesting pansies for indoor culture in greenhouse conditions is a climbing variety. It is offered by Geo. W. Park Seed Co. A fine display of climbing pansies can be seen during winter and early spring at Longwood Gardens, Pennsylvania. This special strain, developed in the Pacific Northwest, can climb several feet high when grown in pots and trained to a trellis.

How to Grow—Seeds germinate in 8 to 12 days at 70F (21C) soil temperature. There are two ways to start seeds, depending on if you are growing standard varieties or hybrids. The traditional method is to plant seeds in summer in a specially prepared seedbed inside a *cold frame.* This is a boxlike structure, usually with a glass top. See page 42. Locate in lightly shaded area to prevent sun scorch and rapid drying of soil. The seedbed should be weed-free with a level surface, rich in organic matter and well drained. As a precaution against damping-off disease, spray soil surface with benomyl. Sow seeds in rows 4 inches apart. Cover with 1/8 inch of fine soil. Firm surface so seeds are in contact with soil. Keep moist with fine spray. If germinating seeds dry out they usually die.

When plants begin to set buds, transplant to permanent locations. Space 6 inches apart and water well. Pansies are hardy and can survive mild frosts. In mild-winter areas where the ground does not freeze, little or no protection is required. In Northern states where alternate thawing and freezing may injure plants, lightly cover them with loose straw or shredded leaves *after* ground freezes. If plants are grown in a cold frame, the success rate is much higher.

With hybrids, sow seeds indoors in seed trays in December or January. Transfer to individual 2-inch pots when seedlings are large enough to handle. Keep seedlings in a cool place—50F (10C)—and feed with diluted liquid fertilizer. Harden-off plants for a week in a cold frame and transplant to outdoor garden 3 weeks before last frost date.

'Imperial Blue' pansy won an All-America award for its large flowers and ability to bloom through all four seasons.

Climbing pansies are a special strain that can be trained to grow up a trellis or other support. They are best grown through winter in a cool greenhouse.

'Majestic Giants' pansy, showing the main assortment of colors available.

Space plants 6 inches apart in full sun or partial shade. Plants prefer cool, moist soil, preferably improved with plenty of organic matter. Remove flowers when they fade to prevent seed pods from forming. This allows plants to bloom continually.

Common diseases that affect pansies are leaf spots and root rots. During cold, wet, windy weather, apply sprays after rains to control. Root rot is also caused by a fungus. It dwarfs plants and turns leaves yellow, followed by black rotting of roots. Remove and destroy diseased plants and plant new crops in sterilized soil. Slugs can be serious pests, eating pansy leaves. These can be controlled by slug bait.

Uses—Colorful in beds and containers such as tubs and window boxes. Pansies are one of the most welcome sights of early spring. No other flowering annual can outshine them for colorful mass displays early in the year. Favorites in hanging baskets. They are exceptional for edging beds or borders of spring-flowering bulbs such as tulips and daffodils.

PENSTEMON
Penstemon gloxinioides

Although penstemons are actually tender perennials, some varieties of the gloxinia-flower kinds can be treated as tender annuals. If seeds are sown early in the season, they will flower the first year. Penstemons are also called *bearded tongue* for a conspicuous bearded stamen within each blossom. Summer-blooming flowers are tubular like foxgloves, borne on long spikes. Colors include white, red, rose-pink and lavender. Plants grow 2 feet high and spread 1 foot wide. Developed from species native to Mexico and California.

Recommended Varieties—'Giant Floradale', 2 feet high, has a good mixture of colors. It has long flower spikes studded with large florets with contrasting white throats.

How to Grow—Where the ground does not freeze, sow seeds outdoors in fall for flowers the following spring. In other regions start seeds indoors 10 weeks before last frost date. Germination takes 8 to 18 days at 60F (15C) soil temperature. Exposure to light improves germination of seeds.

Space plants 12 inches apart in full sun. Soil should be loose and fertile. Water regularly during dry spells. Plants flower best during cool, sunny conditions such as those found in coastal California and the Pacific Northwest. Aphids and other chewing insects may attack penstemon. Spray with Sevin or malathion chemical spray or a pyrethrum organic spray.

Uses—Beds and borders and for cutting.

'Giant Floradale' penstemon does best in cool-summer areas.

PEPPER, ORNAMENTAL
Capsicum annuum

Ornamental peppers are tender annuals. Although flowers are usually small and insignificant, they are quickly followed by beautiful yellow, orange and red fruit. Most fruit are cone shape, round or sharply tapered. Plants grow 9 to 12 inches high and spread 9 to 12 inches wide. Native to South America.

Recommended Varieties—'Holiday Cheer', 8 inches high, won an All-America award for its unique, round fruit. 'Fiesta', 9 inches high, produces an abundance of colorful, slender, tapered fruit.

How to Grow—Start seeds indoors 8 to 10 weeks before last frost date. Cover seeds with 1/4 inch of fine soil. Germination occurs in 6 to 14 days at 70F to 85F (21C to 30C) soil temperature. Plant seedlings after all danger of frost has passed. Plants started from seeds in July will have colorful fruit by Christmas for indoor decoration.

Space plants 9 inches apart in full sun. Soil should be fertile loam. Keep soil moist. Feed plants every 2 weeks with a liquid fertilizer after plants begin to flower. Because fruit are exceedingly hot, plants are generally free of pests and diseases.

Uses—Edging beds and borders. Christmas peppers are often grown in pots for sale at Christmas.

PERILLA
Perilla frutescens

Perilla is a tender annual commonly grown for its colorful, purple leaves that resemble coleus. Plants grow to 3 feet high and spread 2 feet wide. Native to India.

Recommended Varieties—Not normally sold by variety name. Sometimes sold as beefsteak plant.

How to Grow—Sow seeds outdoors after all danger of frost has passed. Or sow seeds indoors 5 to 6 weeks before last frost date. Germination takes 15 to 20 days at 70F to 85F (21C to 30C) soil temperature. Do not cover seeds because they need light to germinate. Take care not to disturb roots when transplanting.

Space plants 15 inches apart in full sun. Plants tolerate wide range of soil conditions. Provide with regular water. Plants may need staking in rich, fertile soils. Control height by pinching out growing tip. Plants are generally free of pests and diseases.

Uses—Background to create contrast for more brightly colored annuals such as marigolds, petunias and zinnias.

'Holiday Cheer' ornamental pepper won an All-America award for its value as a colorful bedding plant.

Close-up of perilla shows its shiny, textured, bronze-color leaves.

'Red Cascade' grandiflora petunia.

PETUNIA
Petunia hybrida and other species

The best-selling hybrid petunias are classified as *grandifloras*—meaning large flowers—and *multifloras*—meaning many flowers. Petunias have come a long way since the French botanist, Petun, for whom the genus is named, collected seeds in Argentina. He introduced them to Europe in the mid-1850s.

Breeding petunias to create improved varieties began in Ventura, California, as early as 1880 with work on the *superbissima* types. Mrs. Theodosia Burr Shepherd started the first flower-seed business in California, producing petunias with extremely large flowers—up to 7 inches across. These became known as '*Giants of California*'. They were the leading petunias until the 1930s, when Ernst Benary of Germany and T. Sakata of Japan began introducing large-flower, fringed hybrid types that became known as *grandiflora* petunias. Today, 'Giants of California' are seldom seen in home gardens, although a few specialist seed sources offer them. Their flowers are still the largest petunias available.

Closely related to tobacco, popular petunia hybrids are derived mostly from three species found in South America. Color range is extensive, including white and shades of red, purple, blue and yellow, plus many bizarre bicolors.

The two biggest selling classes are hybrid grandifloras and hybrid multifloras. Each of these are divided into two more groups—singles and doubles. Grandifloras have the largest flowers and are the most popular. But the smaller-flower multifloras produce a better display. What they lack in size they make up for in vigor and profuse bloom. Although plant breeders consider the development of double-flower varieties a significant breakthrough for petunias, they have not matched the appeal of the best-selling singles. Plants grow 12 to 15 inches high and spread 2 feet wide. They flower continually through summer until fall frost.

Grandifloras: Best-selling grandifloras are 'White Cascade', 15 inches high, and 'Red Cascade', 14 inches high. 'White Cascade' produces flowers up to 4-3/4 inches across. Outdoors, 'White Cascade' tends to suffer from smog and rainy weather. But it excels when grown in a protected or indoor environment such as a greenhouse, especially in a hanging basket. For outdoor displays, 'Glacier', 12 inches high, is more dependable and earlier than 'White Cascade', although flowers are slightly smaller.

The super grandiflora 'Cascade' types with frilled petals originated as a mutation from 'White Cloud', an old, plain-edge variety. This mutant was used to develop 'Sea Foam'. From 'Sea Foam' came the first of the 'Cascades'. Following the success of 'Cascades', other plant breeders set their sights on even larger flowers. Latest to come along are 'Titans' from Japan, which have individual blooms up to 4-1/2 inches across.

Two other dependable grandiflora strains are the 'Magic' and the 'Ultra' series, developed for better branching habit and more reliable garden performance than 'Cascades' or 'Titans'.

Plant breeders have attempted to bring a rich yellow petunia into the color range. Earlier attempts were not satisfactory because flowers were small and the plants were weak. However, 'California Girl' and 'Sunburst' are two strong-growing yellow grandifloras.

'Star Joy' multiflora petunia is a beautiful bicolor, exhibiting a star pattern.

'Appleblossom' grandiflora petunia.

'California Girl' grandiflora petunia was the first commercially successful yellow petunia.

A number of bicolor grandiflora petunias have been developed. They include flowers in red and blue with a white star at center, formed by white stripes running down the petal center to the middle. 'Allstar', red; and 'Telstar', blue; are two that have a uniform star pattern.

More recently, the bicolor pattern has been developed to occur as a ring around the outer petal edge, which creates a frosted effect. 'Blue Picotee' and 'Red Picotee' are two of the best with this frosted pattern. They are especially appealing when used in delicate flower arrangements.

Among double grandiflora petunias, the 'Bouquet' series is popular. 'Circus', a salmon-red and white bicolor, won an All-America award for its exotic flower display and compact, basal branching habit.

Multifloras: Improvements in breeding in terms of color and pattern designs have also been done for multifloras, which are unequalled for mass plantings. They are generally more vigorous and colorful than grandifloras when seen from a distance.

'Joy' series is tops among multifloras. These come in clear colors and bicolors, such as 'White Joy', 'Red Joy', 'Sky Joy', light blue; 'Blue Joy', deep blue; 'Starlight Joy', deep blue with white star; and 'Star Joy', rosy-red with white star. The Joys have a "sister" series—the 'Plums'. Blooms are deeply veined. Plants have added benefit of being the most weather tolerant and have the most resistance to botrytis blight.

Two outstanding double multiflora petunias are the 'Tarts' and the 'Delights'.

How to Grow—Start seeds indoors 8 to 10 weeks before last frost date. Plant after all danger of frost has passed. Germination takes 7 to 10 days at 70F to 85F (21C to 30C) soil temperature. Seeds are tiny and need light to germinate. Press seeds into the soil surface, just enough to anchor them. Use seed trays to get them started. When seedlings are large enough to handle, transfer them to individual 2-inch pots prior to transplanting. To ensure successful germination, keep soil surface moist by misting. Seeds should not be disturbed or allowed to dry out. If there is any danger of the soil drying out, place seed tray in clear plastic bag to retain moisture.

Space plants 12 inches apart in full sun in fertile, sandy soil that has good drainage. When choosing varieties, read catalog descriptions carefully to avoid problems relevant to your local conditions. For example, some petunias are more susceptible to pollution than others. Other varieties recover rapidly from excessive rainfall. Flowers of grandiflora petunias droop sadly after rain, and can take some time to produce another attractive floral display.

Petunias are troubled by few pests and diseases, but mosaic virus can be a problem. Leaves of diseased plants crinkle, curl and become mottled with yellowish-green and dark-green patches. Diseased plants remain stunted and flowers are deformed. Control this virus by keeping aphids off plants because they transmit the disease. Handling plants after smoking or chewing tobacco infected with tobacco mosaic can pass on the disease. Aphids are easily destroyed by many insect sprays including diazinon, malathion and insecticidal soap. Or control by washing them off with water from a garden hose. Slugs and snails can chew

'Plum Blue' multiflora petunia is vigorous and compact grower.

transplants down to bare stems. Control with slug bait or hand-pick in early morning after rain.

Uses—Mass displays in beds and borders. Also popular in containers, especially window boxes, tubs and hanging baskets. In addition to outdoor displays, petunias can be grown indoors during winter as a flowering container plant in a greenhouse or sun room.

'FIRE CHIEF' PETUNIA

Scotty Sinclair, a plant breeder for many years with Bodger Seeds of California, developed the world's first red petunia. 'Fire Chief' won a gold medal in the All-America Selections. "Color and fragrance are the biggest challenges in plant breeding," said Sinclair. "All species of flowers have one primary color missing. Usually a mutation or an accident of nature produces the missing colors. There are still no yellow sweet peas or blue zinnias, and until 1950 there was no red petunia."

'Fire Chief' was not a mutation or sport. It was produced scientifically by hybridization. Sinclair bred two salmon-pink petunias and got a red. "Color is controlled by genes" said Sinclair. "When you cross two same-color genes you get a more intense color—if you have the right genes together. Even then, it requires luck to get such a vibrant red."

PHACELIA
Phacelia campanularia

This native California wayside plant is a hardy annual. It produces beautiful, blue, cup-shape flowers. Plants grow 9 inches tall and spread 9 inches wide.

Recommended Varieties—Not normally sold by variety name.

How to Grow—Sow seeds outdoors directly in the garden as soon as soil warms in spring. Germination takes 5 to 12 days at 60F (15C) soil temperature. Exposure to light aids germination. Seeds are sensitive to temperatures above 65F (19C). Sow seeds indoors in September and plants will flower in pots during winter in a greenhouse or sun room.

Space plants 6 inches apart in full sun. Soil should be loose and fertile. Water plants regularly during dry spells. Plants tolerate heat. Seedlings may need protection from slugs and snails. Use slug bait or hand-pick during early morning and early evening following rain.

Uses—Edging beds and borders and container plantings such as window boxes.

'Rose Joy', 'Salmon Joy' and 'White Joy' multiflora petunias create a stunning island bed.

Phacelia is a California wildflower widely used for edging beds and borders.

Mass planting of annual phlox covers an enormous flower bed near Orlando, Florida.

Selection of pimpernel blossoms shows main assortment of colors.

PHLOX
Phlox drummondi

Annual phlox is a hardy, heat-resistant, summer-flowering annual. Flowers are single, borne in clusters on compact, mound-shape plants. Colors include white, blue, red, pink and lavender. Some are bicolor with white stars in the center. Petal tips can be smooth or fringed. Plants grow 8 to 15 inches high and spread 8 inches wide. Native to Texas.

Recommended Varieties—'Twinkle', mixed colors, 8 inches high, won an All-America award for its exotic, pointed petals and beautiful, star patterns. 'Dwarf Beauty' is a compact, free-flowering mixture, with plain-edge petals, growing to 8 inches high.

How to Grow—Sow seeds outdoors in spring as soon as soil can be worked. Cover seeds with 1/8 inch of fine soil. Seedlings are hardy and will tolerate mild frosts. For earlier flowers, start seeds indoors 6 to 8 weeks before time to plant outdoors. Keep seed tray in total darkness until seedlings emerge. Germination takes 6 to 15 days at 55F to 65F (13C to 19C) soil temperature. When thinning seedlings don't discard smallest or weakest plants. These generally produce the best colors.

Space plants 12 inches apart in full sun in fertile, loose soil. Water regularly during dry spells. Feed plants with a diluted liquid plant food when flower buds appear. Pick faded flowers to encourage continual bloom.

Potential insect pests include beetles, phlox plant bug, mites and nematodes. The beetles and phlox plant bug can be controlled by Sevin or malathion chemical spray or rotenone-pyrethrum organic spray. Control mites with dicofol or wash plants with insecticidal soap. To control nematodes, sterilize soil by fumigation. This is best done by a professional exterminating company.

Several fungus diseases such as powdery mildew can infect plants. Benomyl can reduce infestations.

Uses—Massed plantings in beds and borders. Popular as edging and in rock gardens. Valued as cut flower by flower arrangers.

PIMPERNEL
Anagallis linifolia

These are tender perennials usually grown as tender annuals. Pimpernel are large-flower cousins of the scarlet pimpernel, a weed common throughout North America. Colors include blue, purple and red. Plants grow 12 inches high and spread 6 inches wide. Flowers are produced during summer under cool, sunny conditions. Native to the Mediterranean.

Recommended Varieties—Not normally sold by variety name. Sometimes the mixture is sold as grandiflora.

How to Grow—Sow seeds directly in the garden after all danger of frost has passed. Lightly cover seeds with fine soil because light aids germination. Or start seeds indoors 6 to 8 weeks before last frost date. Germination takes 10 to 21 days at 60F (16C) soil temperature. Seeds are sensitive to temperatures above 60F (16C).

Space plants 6 inches apart in full sun. Plants prefer cool, loam soil. Water regularly during dry spells. Generally free of pests and diseases.

Uses—Edging beds and borders. Planted as clumps in rock gardens. Does best in cool regions.

POLYGONUM
Polygonum capitatum

This tender perennial from India is often grown as a tender annual. Also known as *knotweed,* polygonum is a ground-hugging, spreading plant. Decorative leaves are bronze and shaped like hearts. Numerous flowers are small, round and pink, produced continually through summer until fall frost. They are perennials in mild climates where freezing does not occur. Plants grow 3 to 4 inches high and spread 2 feet wide.

Recommended Varieties—Not normally sold by variety name, although polygonum is sometimes listed as 'Magic Carpet'.

How to Grow—Sow seeds directly in the garden after all danger of frost has passed. Barely cover seeds with soil. For earlier flowers, start seeds indoors 6 to 8 weeks before last frost date. Germination takes 20 days at 70F to 85F (21C to 30C) soil temperature.

Space plants 12 inches apart in full sun or light shade. Plants tolerate high heat and a wide range of soils, even poor soil. Water regularly during dry spells.

Japanese beetles sometimes attack plantings. Control with Sevin chemical spray or pyrethrum organic spray.

Uses—Ground cover for problem slopes. Effective as edging for beds and borders. Decorative in rock gardens where it will grow up and over rocks. Widely used in hanging baskets outdoors and indoors.

POPPY, ICELAND
Papaver nudicaule

Iceland poppies are perennials but bloom the first year if seeds are sown early. Flowers are silky and shimmering, measuring up to 4 inches across. They bloom best during cool, sunny weather. Colors include red, pink, white, orange and yellow. Flowers can be single or double. Plants grow 15 to 18 inches high and spread 12 inches wide. Native to Canada and the Pacific Northwest.

Recommended Varieties—'Champagne Bubbles' hybrid, 18 inches high, has the largest flowers. It blooms early and has strong stems.

How to Grow—Sow seeds outdoors in early spring as soon as ground can be worked. Barely cover the tiny seeds with soil. Because darkness aids germination, keep seed tray in a dark place until seedlings are up. Germination takes 6 to 14 days at 60F to 70F (16C to 21C) soil temperature. Seeds may be sown in fall of the previous year in mild-winter areas for early spring flowers. In areas subject to severe winters, plants are often grown in cold frames and in cool greenhouses. Where summers are hot, start seeds indoors in flats. Transplant seedlings in individual peat pots. Harden-off seedlings before transplanting and they can be set out several weeks before the last frost date. Avoid disturbing roots or plants will not transplant well.

Space plants 12 inches apart in full sun. They do best in fertile loam or sandy soil. Keep soil moist. Plants need cool conditions to flower well.

Aphids can infest tender new growth. Spray with malathion or Sevin chemical insecticides. Or wash plants with insecticidal soap as an organic control. Root-knot nematodes are troublesome in some regions.

Polygonum makes a colorful ground cover, popular for decorating dry slopes.

Long stems of Iceland poppies make blossoms excellent for cutting.

Red Shirley poppies and white Queen-Anne's lace are perfect companions in a wildflower planting.

'Sunglo' mixed colors portulaca create a beautiful border.

POPPY, SHIRLEY
Papaver rhoeas

Shirley poppies are hardy annuals similar in appearance to Iceland poppies. There are a few differences. Shirley poppies are native to Europe rather than North America, and the color range is richer in reds and absent in orange and yellow. Sometimes called *corn poppies,* they are the poppies often depicted by French impressionist painters, growing prolifically in meadows and fields. Flowers measure up to 3 inches across, usually single or semidouble. Colors include white, pink, purple and red. They have powdery yellow centers and some are bicolors, with white or black markings at the base of each petal. Plants grow 2 to 3 feet high and spread 1 foot wide.

Recommended Varieties—Generally sold simply as 'Double-Flowered' and 'Single-Flowered' in a mixture of colors.

How to Grow—Poppies do not transplant well. Surface-sow seeds directly in the garden several weeks before last frost date. Seedlings will tolerate mild frosts. Germination occurs in 8 days at 60F to 70F (16C to 21C) soil temperature.

Space plants 12 inches apart in full sun. Plant in fertile loam or sandy soil. Keep soil moist. Plants bloom best when nights are cool. It is characteristic of Shirley poppies for flower stems to bend over as though wilted. This is natural and stems usually straighten as buds open. Generally free of pests and diseases. Aphids and nematodes can be problems. See Iceland Poppy, page 131, for controls.

Uses—Plant in clumps in beds and borders. Popular for naturalizing in wildflower meadows. Combine with Queen-Ann's lace for an eye-catching red and white contrast. Long flower stems are excellent for cutting. Pick flowers when in bud and seal stem ends with a flame to prevent rapid wilting and petal drop.

PORTULACA
Portulaca grandiflora

This low-growing succulent is the most reliable, tender annual for dry areas exposed to high heat. Narrow, fleshy leaves spread a thick carpet up to 24 inches wide and 6 inches high. They are covered with 2-1/2-inch, ruffled, roselike flowers in white, yellow, orange, red, magenta and cream. Some varieties are cup shaped; others have double flowers. Flowers open in sunny weather and close at night, in shade and during cloudy weather. Older varieties close in the afternoon, but recent hybrids stay open all day during sunlight. Native to South America.

Recommended Varieties—Hybrids are more expensive than standard varieties but worth the additional cost. They not only have larger flowers, they have a wider spread, and many are available in separate colors. 'Sunglo' hybrids, 6 inches high, a popular mixture, is also available in an extensive range of separate colors. The best are 'Flame', orange-red; 'Orchid', light pink; and 'Rose', magenta. Another exceptional fully double hybrid strain is 'Sunnyside', 6 inches high, available in 10 separate colors and a mixture.

How to Grow—Seeds may be surface-sown directly in the garden after all danger of frost has passed. But seeds are tiny and better results are obtained by starting them indoors 6 weeks before last frost date. Prechilling seeds for 14 days at 40F (5C) improves germination. Do not cover seeds with soil because they need light to germinate. Germination takes 7 days at 70F to 85F (21C to 30C) soil temperature.

Space plants 12 inches apart in full sun. Plants tolerate a wide range of soil conditions, even poor soil. Loose loam or sandy soil is best. Portulaca is heat and drought resistant. Water only after soil has dried out. Pests and diseases rarely trouble this popular plant. It is the closest you can get to a foolproof, flowering annual.

Uses—Edging beds and borders. Use to cover dry slopes as flowering ground cover. Grow in containers, especially window boxes.

'Sunglo Orange' portulaca is one of the most eye-catching flowers in this popular hybrid series.

PRIMULA
Primula species

Primulas are generally regarded as hardy perennials. However, many kinds can be treated as hardy annuals to flower the first year from seeds started indoors. Grown in a cool greenhouse, some species make magnificent flowering container plants, providing color indoors during early spring. *Primula polyanthus, P. malacoides,* fairy primrose, and *P. obconica,* top primrose, are the three most popular. With the exception of *P. polyanthus,* a cross between European species, these primulas are native to China.

Primula malacoides and *P. obconica* are grown almost exclusively as container plants for indoor color. *P. malacoides* can be grown as an outdoor bedding plant in shade in areas of coastal California having mild winters and cool summers. *P. polyanthus* can be grown for outdoor bedding and as flowering container plants indoors. It is the more colorful of the three, providing clusters of 2-inch flowers in white, yellow, red, blue, rose-pink and apricot. Many have contrasting yellow eyes. Flowering lasts several weeks in spring.

Plants grow to 6 inches high and spread 6 inches wide. Plants need at least 7 months to produce flowers when grown from seeds, which is why most people prefer to buy them as nursery-grown transplants.

Recommended Varieties—The most popular variety of *P. polyanthus* is the hybrid 'Pacific Giants', available as a mixture and as several separate colors. They are outstanding planted in massed beds and as an edging.

How to Grow—Place seeds in refrigerator for 3 to 4 weeks to help break dormancy. Thinly sow into seed flats, pressing seeds into soil surface. Do not cover seeds because they need light to germinate. Keep soil surface moist at all times by misting lightly. If seeds dry out for even an hour or two, they will probably die. Germination can be erratic, but usually takes 12 to 21 days at 60F to 70F (16C to 21C) soil temperature.

Sow seeds in September for spring flowers. When large enough to handle, transplant seedlings to 2-1/2-inch peat pots. As they grow, transplant again into 4-inch pots. Grow transplants in a cool, 50F (10C) greenhouse until danger of heavy frost has passed. They can then be transplanted outdoors. If you do not have a greenhouse, plants can be grown through winter in cold frames. Sink pots into soil or peat until time to transplant.

Hybrid varieties can be grown in sun or partial shade

'Pacific Giants' primula polyanthus is a favorite pot plant to grow indoors.

'Splash' salpiglossis is one of the most colorful annuals. It does best where summers are cool.

Unusual brown flower is one of the colors in the 'Splash' series.

if conditions are cool. Space plants 6 inches apart. Soil should be acid, loose, well drained and high in organic matter. Leaf mold, peat moss or compost are recommended. Water plants regularly and never allow soil to dry out.

Several species of aphids can infest leaves. Control by spraying with malathion or Sevin chemical insecticide. Or wash plants with insecticidal soap. Leaf spot, anthracnose and rust diseases are generally controlled with zineb.

Uses—Primulas are most often used for mass plantings in beds and borders, especially in partial shade. Popular as flowering container plants grown over winter in greenhouses and sun rooms for flowering around Mother's Day.

SALPIGLOSSIS
Salpiglossis sinuata

Salpiglossis is also known as *velvet flower* because of the velvety texture of its petals. Under cool, sunny conditions, salpiglossis are beautiful plants. They resemble petunias, but are taller and more dramatic in their color range. They do well in the Pacific Northwest and coastal California, but in many regions plants burn before they bloom. They are usually grown during winter as a cool greenhouse plant. Trumpet-shape flowers are among the most colorful in all the flower kingdom. They measure up to 2-1/2 inches wide. Colors include red, white, yellow, blue, purple and brown, usually with exotic veins in contrasting colors. Plants grow 2 to 3 feet high and spread 1 foot wide. Tender annual native to South America.

Recommended Varieties—'Splash', mixed colors, 2-1/2 feet high, matures earlier than other varieties and produces more flowers per plant. Flowers are generally larger and available in a wide color range.

How to Grow—Sow seeds outdoors after all danger of frost has passed. For best results, start seeds indoors 8 weeks before last frost date. Cover the tiny seeds with no more than 1/8 inch of soil. Germination is improved if seeds are kept in total darkness until they sprout. Germination takes 4 to 12 days at 70F to 85F (21C to 30C) soil temperature. Sow in early fall for winter flowers indoors.

Space plants 12 inches apart in full sun in a loose, well-drained soil rich in organic matter. Keep soil moist. Do not apply too much fertilizer because plants are sensitive to nitrogen burn. Tall varieties generally need a sheltered location and some kind of support.

Southern root-knot nematodes are the most destructive pests. Control by fumigating the soil. Consult with a professional pest-control service to do this. Planting a cover crop of marigolds the previous season may help control nematodes. Wilt disease and aster yellows are common. Destroy infected plants and reduce populations of insect pests such as leaf hoppers, which carry the disease. Sevin chemical spray or rotenone-pyrethrum organic spray are effective controls.

Uses—Beds and borders, and for cutting. Plants grown in a cool greenhouse during winter make attractive container plants.

SALVIA
Salvia species

Two kinds of annual salvias are popular among home gardeners. *Salvia splendens* produces mostly thick, red, flower spikes on dark-green plants. *S. farinacea* produces mostly slender, blue flower spikes on gray-green plants. *S. patens* and *S. horminum* are less familiar annual species. All prefer warm weather and are grown as tender annuals.

Salvia splendens, scarlet sage, grows 10 to 30 inches high and spreads 10 to 24 inches wide, depending on the variety. Tubular flowers are arranged in spikes. Vibrant red coloring contrasts with the dark-green leaves, making this species popular as summer bedding plants. Other colors include pink, dark purple and white. Native to Brazil.

Salvia farinacea grows 2 feet high and spreads 2 feet wide. It is most often used for backgrounds in beds and borders of mixed annuals. In addition to popular blue varieties, a variety with white flowers is available. Both are attractive as cut flowers. *S. farinacea* is actually perennial, but is best treated as an annual. It will flower the first year if seeds are started early indoors. Native to New Mexico and Texas.

Recommended Varieties—If growing conditions are poor, differences between varieties of red salvias are difficult to detect, except for plant height. Under favorable conditions of partial sunlight, ample moisture and cool nights, some varieties stand out. 'Carabiniere', 10 to 12 inches high, is the only salvia to win a First-Class Certificate from the Royal Horticultural Society. This is mostly because of its unusually long, stocky, flower spikes. The best *Salvia farinacea* is 'Victoria', a deep-blue selection developed from 'Catima'. 'Victoria' is an award winner in the Fleuroselect trials. It has been outstanding wherever I have seen it growing in North America.

How to Grow—Start seeds of *Salvia splendens* indoors 8 weeks before last frost date. Plant transplants after all danger of frost has passed. Do not cover seeds with soil. Germination takes 4 to 12 days at 70F to 85F (21C to 30C) soil temperature. Start *S. farinacea* 10 weeks before the outdoor planting date.

Salvia splendens does best in a sunny or partially shaded location. Plant in fertile, loam soil that drains well. Regular watering is essential to keep plants blooming during hot weather. Space plants 12 inches apart. Although these salvias accept heat, high humidity deters bloom production. *S. farinacea* is much more tolerant of high heat and humidity. Space plants 1-1/2 feet apart.

Seedlings are highly susceptible to damping-off disease. Use sterilized seed-starting materials and spray soil surface with benomyl. Otherwise, salvias are generally free of insects and diseases.

Uses—*Salvia splendens* is often used for massed display in beds and borders. *S. farinacea* is often used as background plant and for cutting.

'Bonfire' salvia creates a stunning contrast to yellow gloriosa daisies.

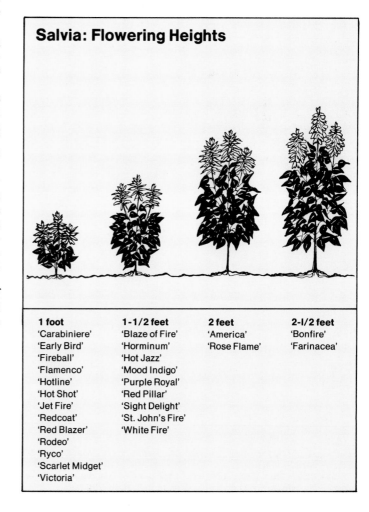

Salvia: Flowering Heights

1 foot	1-1/2 feet	2 feet	2-1/2 feet
'Carabiniere'	'Blaze of Fire'	'America'	'Bonfire'
'Early Bird'	'Horminum'	'Rose Flame'	'Farinacea'
'Fireball'	'Hot Jazz'		
'Flamenco'	'Mood Indigo'		
'Hotline'	'Purple Royal'		
'Hot Shot'	'Red Pillar'		
'Jet Fire'	'Sight Delight'		
'Redcoat'	'St. John's Fire'		
'Red Blazer'	'White Fire'		
'Rodeo'			
'Ryco'			
'Scarlet Midget'			
'Victoria'			

Flowers of 'Gold Braid' sanvitalia resemble miniature sunflowers but plants are related to zinnias.

Schizanthus does well where summers are cool. In warm-summer areas it is usually grown in a cool greenhouse during winter.

SANVITALIA
Sanvitalia procumbens

This tender annual flowers continually from summer to fall frost. It creates a low, spreading carpet of fine leaves covered with masses of miniature, zinnia-type flowers 3/4 inch across. Flowers have pointed, gold-yellow petals radiating from purple centers. Plants grow 6 inches high and spread 6 to 8 inches wide. Native to Mexico.

Recommended Varieties—Not normally sold by variety name, but sometimes listed in seed catalogs as creeping zinnia.

How to Grow—Sow seeds outdoors after all danger of frost has passed. Barely cover seeds with fine soil because light aids germination. Seeds germinate in 3 to 7 days at 70F to 85F (21C to 30C) soil temperature.

Plant in full sun. Plants tolerate crowding but it is best to thin them to 6 inches apart. Accepts heat, drought and poor soils. Generally free of pests and diseases.

Uses—Makes a beautiful flowering ground cover. Useful for edging beds and borders, rock gardens and hanging baskets. Plants will cascade over walls and balconies.

SHIZANTHUS
Shizanthus

In areas with cool summers, schizanthus, also known as *butterfly flower,* can rival the most colorful flowering annuals. Orchidlike flowers are thickly clustered on strong stems. Flowers bloom during summer but burn where summers are hot. Colors include white, yellow, orange, pink and purple. They have contrasting yellow throats and are heavily spotted or freckled. Plants grow 12 to 24 inches high and spread 12 inches wide.

Recommended Varieties—'Bouquet' and 'Hit Parade' are dwarf types growing to 12 inches high. Flowers are large, available in complete range of colors.

How to Grow—Plants grow slowly. Start seeds 12 weeks before last frost date. Plant after all danger of frost has passed. Germination takes 8 days at 60F to 70F (16C to 21C) soil temperature. Seeds are fine and should be covered lightly with soil. Darkness aids germination. Store seed flats or containers in total darkness until seedlings emerge. Seeds are sensitive to temperatures above 70F (21C).

Space plants 12 inches apart in full sun. Soil should be loose, fertile loam enriched with plenty of organic matter. Keep soil moist.

Aster yellows disease sometimes infects plants. Destroy infected plants, and control leaf hoppers, which transmit the disease. Sevin chemical spray or rotenone organic spray help control leaf hoppers. Seedlings are susceptible to damping-off disease. Control by using sterilized pots and implements and spray soil with benomyl. Where anthracnose is prevalent, avoid wetting foliage with overhead watering. Spray with Bordeaux mixture or other copper-base fungicide.

Uses—Excellent for mass displays in beds and borders in regions where summers remain sunny and cool. For this reason, schizanthus is often used for bedding in the Pacific Northwest and other areas as winter-flowering greenhouse plants.

SHASTA DAISY
Chrysanthemum maximum

Shasta daisies are hardy perennials, flowering the second season when grown from seeds. Special, early flowering dwarf kinds are becoming available. They can be grown as hardy annuals, flowering the first year from seeds sown indoors early in the season. Flowers of annual types are smaller than perennial varieties, and there are not yet any double flowers. Flowers are pure-white with yellow centers, measuring up to 2-1/2 inches across. Plants grow 12 inches high and spread 12 inches wide. Flowers bloom continually all summer. Native to Europe.

Recommended Varieties—'Silver Princess', also listed as 'Miss Muffet', grows as a beautiful mound of leaves just 12 inches high, with many flowers held on strong, wiry stems.

How to Grow—Seedlings tolerate mild frosts if they are hardened-off. Start seeds indoors 8 weeks before time to plant outdoors. Transplanting can occur several weeks before the last frost date. Do not cover seeds with soil because they need light for germination. Germination takes 10 to 14 days at 70F to 75F (21C to 24C) soil temperature.

Space plants 12 inches apart in full sun in fertile loam soil. Keep soil moist and feed with liquid fertilizer at time of flowering to obtain largest flowers and longest bloom. Generally free of pests and diseases.

Uses—Mixed beds and borders, particularly for edging. Valued by flower arrangers for cutting.

'Silver Princess' Shasta daisy is a special dwarf variety that creates a cushion of flowers.

SHOO-FLY PLANT
Nicandra physaloides

This tender annual received its name because its blue flowers are repellent to insects. Flowers resemble miniature morning glories and are followed by yellow, lanternlike seed cases. These cases can be dried and used in flower arrangements. Plants grow 2 to 3 feet high and spread 2 feet wide. Native to Peru.

Recommended Varieties—Not sold by variety name.

How to Grow—Start seeds indoors 8 to 10 weeks before last frost date. Plant after all danger of frost has passed. Germination occurs in 15 to 20 days at 70F to 85F (21C to 30C) soil temperature.

Space plants 12 inches apart in full sun. Plant in fertile, well-drained garden soil. Water regularly during dry spells. Flowering is enhanced by feeding plants monthly with a diluted liquid fertilizer. Generally free of pests and diseases.

Uses—Mostly used as a curiosity in mixed beds and borders. Also grown as winter-flowering container plant in greenhouses. Decorative seed cases are used in dried arrangements.

Shoo-fly plant is grown mostly as a curiosity because of its trait of repelling insects.

Planting of snapdragons is a blend of separate colors, including red, pink and white.

SNAPDRAGON
Antirrhinum majus

Snapdragons are tender perennials that are best grown as tender annuals. Because they tolerate mild frosts, they are sometimes classified as hardy annuals, although this distinction is debatable. Native to the Mediterranean, they flower continually during sunny, cool weather, ceasing when days turn hot and humid.

By skillful hybridizing, a number of American and Japanese plant breeders have made some significant changes in snapdragons. Improved flower forms and a variety of growth habits make them more versatile for garden displays. Tall types are more colorful with different flower shapes, including "butterfly" flowers and "azalea" flowers. Dwarf kinds, barely recognizable as snapdragons, are available for low beds and borders. Plants are true miniatures, creating a magnificent, flowering carpet when massed together.

Old-fashion snapdragons grew long flower spikes studded with tubular flowers, ending in a dragon's mouth. Newer forms include *double florets,* greatly increasing the color effect; and *open florets,* where the "mouth" is open instead of closed. This presents a larger petal area and intensifies their display qualities compared to traditional varieties.

Colors include white, yellow, orange, rose-pink, salmon, crimson and some bicolors. Flowering height ranges from 6 inches for miniatures, to 3 feet for the tall types, which spread 12 inches wide.

Recommended Varieties—Generally, snapdragons can be classified as dwarf and tall. Among the best tall varieties are the 'Rockets', 3 feet high. Both mixtures and separate colors are winners of All-America awards. They have the traditional, snapdragon flower that has a closed mouth. 'Madame Butterfly', 2-1/2 feet high, is an azalea-flower type. Open florets are double and much larger than standard or single-flower, open-flower kinds. The mixture won an All-America award for its vigor and enchanting floral display.

Among dwarf varieties, 'Floral Carpet' is winner of the most awards, in both the All-America Selections and Royal Horticultural Society trials. Plants grow just 6 inches high and are available in separate colors, plus the award-winning mixture. The most eye-catching single color is 'Rose', an All-America award winner and recipient of a Royal Horticultural Society award of merit. 'Pixies' are similar to 'Floral Carpets' but have open florets. These have single flowers—classified as *butterfly flowers*—to distinguish them from the double *azalea flowers.* Available as a mixture and separate colors, 'Orange Pixie' is a winner of a Fleuroselect award, and especially noteworthy.

How to Grow—In cool climates, seeds can be surface-sown directly in the garden several weeks before the last frost date. For earlier flowers, start seeds indoors 8 weeks before time to plant outdoors. Germination takes 5 to 12 days at 70F to 85F (21C to 30C) soil temperature. Exposure to light aids germination.

Space plants 12 inches apart in full sun. Plants prefer loose, fertile loam or sandy soil. Pinch tops of young plants to encourage side branching. Keep soil moist and feed monthly with a diluted liquid plant food. Tall varieties may require staking to keep them erect. If plants stop blooming during hot weather, shear tops to within 6 inches of the soil level for repeat flowering during fall.

Flower spike of 'Bright Butterflies' snapdragon shows how individual florets open to display more color than closed flower form.

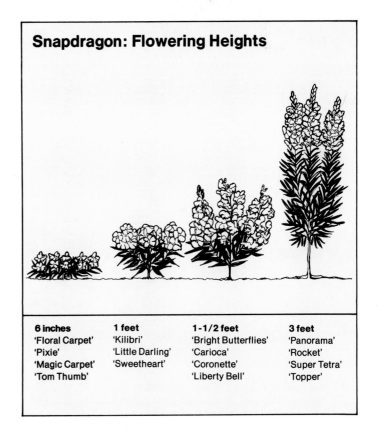

Snapdragon: Flowering Heights

6 inches	1 feet	1-1/2 feet	3 feet
'Floral Carpet'	'Kilibri'	'Bright Butterflies'	'Panorama'
'Pixie'	'Little Darling'	'Carioca'	'Rocket'
'Magic Carpet'	'Sweetheart'	'Coronette'	'Super Tetra'
'Tom Thumb'		'Liberty Bell'	'Topper'

Flower spike of 'Madame Butterfly' snapdragon shows how each floret is doubled, resembling an azalea flower.

Snow on the mountain, or euphorbia, is an eye-catching border plant in summer.

Aphids and mites are sometimes troublesome. Spray plants with malathion for aphid control. Spray dicofol for mite control. As an organic alternative, wash plants with an insecticidal soap.

By far the most troublesome disease is rust, a fungus disease. You can identify it by the tiny, brown pustules that form on leaves. Many rust-resistant strains are available. Sprays of sulfur-base fungicides help control.

Uses—Miniatures can be used as edging in beds and borders or massed as a flowering ground cover. They look good in containers, especially tubs. Taller varieties make excellent background plants in beds and borders and last long as cut flowers. Special varieties are available for growing in containers in cool greenhouses during winter.

SNOW ON THE MOUNTAIN
Euphorbia marginata

This tender annual has tiny, insignificant flowers, but leaves are highly ornamental—gray-green with brilliant white margins. It is closely related to the poinsettia. It oozes a milky sap when cut. If you accidentally get sap on your skin, wash it off immediately because it can cause irritation. Plants grow 2 feet high and spread 1-1/2 feet wide. Native to the United States, growing wild from Texas to Minnesota.

Recommended Varieties—Not normally sold by variety name.

How to Grow—Sow seeds outdoors after all danger of frost has passed. Or start seeds indoors 6 to 8 weeks before last frost date. Germination takes 14 days at 70F (21C) soil temperature. Pre-chilling seeds in the refrigerator for 2 months at 40F (5C) improves germination.

Space plants 12 to 18 inches apart in full sun. Plants tolerate poor soils, heat and drought. Generally free of pests and diseases.

Uses—Accent plant mixed with other annuals and as background. Contrasts well with dark-color annuals, especially blue and red.

SOLANUM, ORNAMENTAL
Solanum species

Several kinds of ornamental solanums or eggplants are popular as bedding plants for their colorful, long-lasting fruit. Some have fruit like cherries, turning from green to yellow and deep orange. Others are shaped like hen's eggs, turning from white to yellow. There are also red-fruit and purple-fruit kinds. Some bear poisonous fruit and should not be planted if children are around. Plants grow 9 inches to 2 feet high, depending on variety, spreading 9 to 24 inches wide. Tender annuals native to South America.

Recommended Varieties—'Golden Egg', 2 feet high, grows like a normal eggplant, but becomes loaded with decorative fruit the size and shape of a hen's egg. Fruit turn from white to yellow when ripe. They are edible although skins are tough and should be peeled before eating. 'Christmas Cherry', also 'Jerusalem Cherry', 9 inches high, was popular for bedding and as a container plant for Christmas gifts. But fruit is poisonous. The round-fruit, ornamental pepper 'Holiday Cheer' is a better choice. Fruit is not poisonous and matures much earlier. See Pepper, Ornamental—page 125.

How to Grow—Start seeds indoors 8 weeks before last frost date. Plant after all danger of frost has passed. Barely cover seeds with fine soil because exposure to light aids germination. Seeds germinate in 7 to 14 days at 70F to 85F (21C to 30C) soil temperature.

Space dwarf varieties 9 inches apart in full sun. Space taller varieties 1-1/2 to 2 feet apart. Soil should be fertile loam or sandy soil. Water regularly and feed with liquid plant food when plants begin to flower and when they set fruit.

Plants grown outdoors are highly susceptible to damage by Colorado potato beetles and flea beetles. To control, spray plants weekly with Sevin chemical spray or pyrethrum organic spray.

Uses—Dwarf varieties are popular for massed display in beds and borders and for edging. They are also effective as container plants, especially for use indoors during winter, such as in a greenhouse or sun room. Tall varieties are frequently grown in pots and are often used as a highlight in mixed beds and borders.

STATICE
Limonium sinuatum

These tender annuals are native to the Mediterranean. Masses of dainty, papery flowers are clustered together on stiff stems. Colors include white, yellow, rose-pink, lavender and blue. Most flowers have white centers. Plants grow 2-1/2 feet high and spread 2 feet wide. Flowers bloom all summer during warm weather. Also known as *German statice*.

Recommended Varieties—'Art Shades', mixed colors, and 'Grandstand' mixture, both 2-1/2 feet high, come in a bright color range. 'Petite Bouquet', 12 inches high, has a dense, compact habit. Separate colors are also offered by seedsmen.

How to Grow—Sow seeds outdoors after all danger of frost has passed. For best results, start seeds indoors 8 to 10 weeks before last frost date. Germination takes 6 to 18 days at 60F to 70F (16C to 21C) soil temperature. Flower heads are difficult to separate into individual seeds but can be germinated as a unit.

Space plants 12 inches apart in full sun. Soil should be fertile loam or sandy. Water only when soil becomes dry because roots are prone to root rot. Apart from root rot, which can be avoided by not overwatering, statice is rarely troubled by pests or diseases. Plants are tolerant of heat and drought.

Uses—Grown in cutting gardens for fresh arrangements. Also dries easily to make everlasting flowers in dried arrangements.

Ornamental solanum 'Golden Egg' is appealing as highlight in beds of mixed annuals. Fruit turn from white to yellow when ripe.

Annual statice is usually grown for cutting to create dried-flower arrangements.

Selection of stocks show main assortment of colors available.

STOCKS
Matthiola incana

Stocks are hardy annuals that bloom mostly in spring and summer. Two kinds of stocks are generally available. Tall, *column* stocks are usually grown for cutting in a cool greenhouse during winter or outdoors in cool-summer areas. They require up to 5 months of cool temperatures to bloom. Dwarf *bedding* stocks bloom in 7 weeks, allowing them to flower over most areas of North America before hot weather sets in.

Stocks cannot tolerate temperatures over 65F (19C), otherwise they do not set flower buds. Column-type stocks grow to 3 feet high. Dwarf bedding types reach only 15 inches high. Both kinds spread about 12 inches. Flowers are fragrant, mostly double, clustered around the stem. Colors include white, yellow, pink, rose, crimson, blue and purple. Native to southern Europe.

Recommended Varieties—For outdoor bedding, 'Trysomic 7-Weeks', mixed colors, 15 inches high, can do well where stocks have previously been difficult to grow. They are the earliest to flower from seeds. 'Great Imperial', mixed colors, 2-1/2 feet high, have large flowers on long stems that branch freely from the base. They are suitable for bedding and cutting.

Night-scented stocks *Matthiola bicornis:* These bloom at night, filling the air with a pleasant fragrance. For this reason they are often planted close to patios, decks and doorways where the scent can be appreciated. Flowers are single, much smaller than regular stocks. They are borne on branching plants that grow 2 feet high and spread 1-1/2 feet wide. Culture is same as regular stocks.

Virginia stocks *Malcomia maritima:* Masses of small, single flowers are borne on dwarf plants growing 6 to 12 inches high, popular for edging and low borders in areas where summers are cool. Not native to Virginia but from the Mediterranean.

How to Grow—Start seeds indoors 4 to 6 weeks before last frost date. Plant after danger of heavy frost has passed. Plants that are hardened-off will tolerate mild frosts. Barely cover seeds with soil because light improves germination. Germination occurs in 8 days at 65F to 75F (19C to 24C) soil temperature. Seeds are sensitive to drying out. Do not overwater because they are highly susceptible to root rot.

Space plants 12 inches apart in full sun. Soil should be fertile loam or sandy. Keep soil moist but do not overwater. Stocks are heavy feeders and should receive a diluted liquid fertilizer each week after being transplanted. When temperatures go above 65F (19C), plants are stressed and cease to flower.

Stocks are susceptible to a number of diseases. The two most common are bacterial blight and root rot. Bacterial blight affects indoor and outdoor plants, evidenced by a sudden wilting or collapse of young plants. No cure is known. Because the bacteria lives in soil, sterilizing planting beds before setting out plants will control this disease. The most common root rot is caused by a fungus that affects roots and lower stems. Plants wilt rapidly and die. Infected parts become black and soft, especially those close to soil. Control by growing plants in well-drained soil and do not overwater.

Uses—Beds and borders, and for cutting. Popular for growing in containers in cool greenhouse.

Night-scented stocks are prime choices if you want a fragrant garden. Stocks do best where summers are cool.

STRAWFLOWER
Helichrysum bracteatum

Strawflowers are native to western Australia, where they blanket the hillsides in summer like dandelions. They are tender annuals that flower continually from early summer to fall frost. Plants are not bothered by high heat and dry conditions. Flowers are shaped like daisies, up to 3 inches across, and shimmer in the sunlight. Colors include red, yellow, white, pink, orange, salmon and purple. Strawflowers grow to 3 feet high and spread 12 to 15 inches wide. Dwarf varieties are also available.

Recommended Varieties—Tall varieties are commonly sold only as 'Tall Double', but two dwarf varieties are superior. They are 'Hot Bikini', 2 feet high, an award winner in the Fleuroselect trials; and 'Dwarf Spangle', 2 feet high. Both are mixtures that bloom profusely in a brilliant color range. In spite of their dwarf habit, flowers produce strong stems long enough for cutting.

How to Grow—Sow seeds over soil surface directly in the garden. Seeds require light to germinate. For earliest blooms, start seeds indoors 6 weeks before last frost date. Germination takes 7 to 10 days at 60F to 70F (16C to 21C) soil temperature.

Space plants 12 inches apart in full sun. Soil should be loam or sandy, preferably alkaline. Plants tolerate poor soil, heat and drought. Remove faded flowers regularly, and water during dry spells to prolong the flowering display. They are reliable, trouble-free plants rarely bothered by pests or diseases.

Uses—Mixed beds and borders, also for cutting. Because petals have a papery texture and dry easily, they are among the most popular everlasting flowers for colorful dried arrangements. To dry, hang by their stems in a warm place. Cut flower head from stem and place on stiff wires. Dried flowers remain colorful for many months.

Strawflowers show the main assortment of flower colors available.

SUNFLOWER
Helianthus species

Sunflowers are tender annuals that tolerate hot summers. Although they are often listed in the vegetable section of seed catalogs because of their edible seeds, many varieties are grown as ornamentals. Flowers are mostly yellow with dark centers, up to 12 inches across. Single and double forms are available. Height varies according to variety—3 feet for dwarf kinds and up to 10 feet for tall kinds. Native to North America.

Recommended Varieties—'Teddy Bear', 3 feet high, grows huge, fully double, pompon-type flowers up to 8 inches across. Planted close together, they create a beautiful, temporary flowering hedge. 'Color Fashion', mixed colors, grows to 6 feet high. Plants are covered with single, 6-inch-wide flowers that resemble enormous black-eyed Susans. Colors include yellow, gold, brown and mahogany-red. Some have contrasting color zones that create a pinwheel effect.

How to Grow—Sow seeds directly in the garden after all danger of frost has passed. Cover seeds with 1 inch of fine soil. Germination occurs in 3 to 7 days at 70F to 85F (21C to 30C) soil temperature.

Space plants 2 feet apart in full sun. Sunflowers toler-

'Teddy Bear' sunflower is popular as background and for use in flower arrangements.

Sweet peas show main assortment of flower colors available.

ate a wide range of soil conditions, even poor soil, but produce the largest flowers in fertile loam. Water regularly and feed with liquid fertilizer when plants begin blooming.

Generally not troubled by pests or diseases. When seeds form they attract flocks of seed-eating birds, especially finches. When planted for ornamental value the birds are considered beneficial rather than pests.

Uses—Background plants in beds and borders. Double-flower kinds are valued for cutting. They were the subject of Vincent Van Gogh's famous painting Sunflowers.

SWEET PEA
Lathyrus odoratus

At one time, sweet peas were the most popular flowering annuals grown in North America. Colonists and European immigrants were in the habit of growing these fragrant, colorful flowers in Europe. They continued to plant them in the United States and Canada year after year despite hot summers, which brought a quick end to the flowers. The popularity of sweet peas declined about 1930. It was caused by the inherent lack of heat resistance and spread of several destructive root-rot diseases. In addition, many native American plants, especially petunias, marigolds and zinnias, became popular at this time.

Sweet peas were commonly grown in England. Plant breeders there developed large-flower types in a wide color range. Then, European seedsmen discovered the Lompoc Valley of California, near Santa Barbara, where sweet peas could be grown better than anywhere else in the world. Soon California plant breeders were developing the best new strains. Today, American sweet peas are the best in the world, even though most areas of the United States are too warm for their growth.

Colors include white, pink, red, orange, purple and blue, with some bicolors. Dwarf kinds can be used for borders. Tall kinds can be used as a background and to climb on supports. But their primary value is as fragrant cut flowers. Flowers up to 2 inches across are borne four to six per stem. Plants grow to 5 feet high and spread 1 foot wide. Tall kinds need supports to climb. Native to Sicily.

Recommended Varieties—'Royal', mixed colors, have become the leading variety of climbing sweet pea. They produce flowers up to 20% larger than traditional varieties—clustered five and six to a stem.

'Bijou', mixed colors, is an established dwarf strain, 15 inches high. It can be grown without stakes. 'Snoopea' is a ground-hugging sweet pea that has no tendrils. It received 14 awards of excellence from the Royal Horticultural Society and other horticultural organizations. It has no tendrils to grip adjacent plants. It therefore remains low growing, producing a neat, ornamental effect when used in beds, borders and as a ground cover.

For coinnoisseurs, nothing compares to the old-fashion, heavily fragrant varieties available from British seedsmen. For mail-order sources, see page 38. What these rare sweet peas lack in flower size they more than make up with flower scent. Richness of the fragrance is unmatched in all the flower kingdom. A small spray of these on a bedroom vanity or a dining-

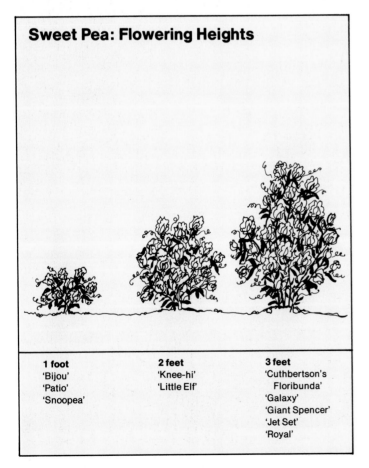

Sweet Pea: Flowering Heights

1 foot	2 feet	3 feet
'Bijou'	'Knee-hi'	'Cuthbertson's
'Patio'	'Little Elf'	Floribunda'
'Snoopea'		'Galaxy'
		'Giant Spencer'
		'Jet Set'
		'Royal'

room table will fill the room with a romantic fragrance. 'Antique Fantasy', mixed colors, is the name of one such collection of oldies.

How to Grow—Sow seeds outdoors directly in the garden as soon as soil can be worked in spring. Seedlings tolerate frost and require as much cool weather as possible to flower. Germination takes 10 to 14 days at 60F to 75F (16C to 24C) soil temperature. Improve germination by soaking seeds overnight in lukewarm water prior to planting. Plant seeds 1 inch deep—total darkness is needed for germination. For earlier flowers, start seeds indoors 4 to 6 weeks before time to plant outdoors.

Space plants 12 inches apart in full sun. In most areas where summers get hot, sweet peas should be sown indoors early in the season and transplanted. This gives them time to flower before heat kills them. Deep, fertile, loam soil enriched with organic matter and regular moisture helps encourage fast growth. In poor soils, prepare planting spot by digging trench 2 feet deep. Fill it with a mixture of compost and garden topsoil. Sweet peas can also be grown in planter boxes in a cool greenhouse to flower in early spring for cutting. In mild-winter areas, seeds can be sown in the garden in fall. They will overwinter and flower early the following spring.

Aphids can damage young growing tips of plants. Spray with Sevin or malathion chemical insecticide. Or wash plants with an insecticidal soap as an organic control. Root rots are difficult to control. Except for steam-sterilizing soil before planting, little can be done to protect plants. Powdery mildew can be controlled by spraying plants with benomyl.

Uses—Cutting to create beautiful, fragrant flower arrangements. Dwarf, spreading kinds are suitable for beds and borders.

Multiflora sweet peas near Guadalupe, California, are being grown for seeds.

SWEET SCABIOUS
Scabiosa atropurpurea

Flowers of sweet scabious resemble pincushions, and pincushion flower is one of its common names. These are hardy annuals native to southern Europe that have naturalized throughout California. Flowers measure 3 inches in diameter. Silvery gray, pollen-bearing filaments that look like pins protrude from the center. Flower colors include white, red, pink, blue and black. Plants grow 3 feet high and spread 1-1/2 feet wide. Do not confuse sweet scabious with the perennial *Scabiosa caucasica,* which has larger flowers and requires two seasons to flower.

Scabiosa stellata, 2 feet high, is an interesting plant, quite different from regular scabiosa. Flowers are white and insignificant, but soon develop into an exquisite, dried flower ball 1-1/2 inches in diameter. They are valued for use in dried-flower arrangements.

Recommended Varieties—'Giant Imperial', mixed colors, has the most popular blend of colors.

How to Grow—Sow seeds directly in the garden in early spring after soil warms. Seedlings are hardy and tolerate mild frosts. For earlier flowers, sow seeds indoors 4 to 5 weeks before time to plant outdoors. Cover seeds with 1/4 inch of fine soil. Germination takes 4 to 12 days at 70F (21C) soil temperature.

Space plants 12 inches apart in full sun. Soil should be fertile, loose and well drained, preferably alkaline.

Flowers of sweet scabious resemble a pincushion. They are commonly used for cutting.

Sweet sultan is popular for cutting to create flower arrangements.

Water moderately during dry spells. Pests and diseases are few. Plants sometimes succumb to aster yellows disease, spread by leaf hoppers. Control them with Sevin chemical spray or pyrethrum organic spray.

Uses—Background highlight in mixed beds and borders. Popular for cutting for use in fresh-flower arrangements.

SWEET SULTAN
Centaurea moschata

These hardy annuals produce fragrant, thistlelike flowers 2 inches across that bloom all summer. Colors include yellow, purple, rose-pink and white. Plants grow to 2 feet high and spread 1 foot wide. Native to the Orient.

Recommended Varieties—Not normally sold by variety name.

How to Grow—Sow seeds directly in the garden as soon as soil warms in early spring. Cover seeds with 1/4 inch of fine soil because they prefer darkness for germination. Germination takes 7 to 10 days at 60F to 70F (16C to 21C) soil temperature. For transplants, start seeds 6 to 8 weeks before time to plant outdoors. Because sweet sultans are hardy, you can plant them outdoors several weeks before the last frost date. Harden-off plants before setting them out. See page 42.

Space plants 12 inches apart in full sun in fertile, well-drained soil. Keep moist during dry spells. Remove spent flowers frequently to prolong flowering. Aphids may colonize tender stems. Control with malathion or Sevin chemical spray. Or wash plants with an insecticidal soap as an organic control. Leaf hoppers can spread aster yellows disease. Control with Sevin, malathion or pyrethrum organic spray.

Uses—Sweet sultans are admired as cut flowers. They are usually grown in cutting gardens or as clumps in beds and borders of mixed annuals.

SWEET WILLIAM
Dianthus barbatus

Sweet Williams are actually *biennials,* flowering the second season. Some dwarf varieties can be treated as annuals to flower the first year if seeds are started early in the season. Fragrant flowers are borne in tight clusters in white and shades of pink, purple and crimson. Some have mottling in the petals with contrasting eyes, creating a bicolor effect. Annual varieties are low growing, from 4 to 12 inches high, spreading 6 to 12 inches wide. Flowering continues for several weeks during cool, sunny weather. Native to the Pyrenees and other mountainous regions in Europe.

Recommended Varieties—'Wee Willie' begins to flower in 8 weeks when only 3 inches high. It remains extra dwarf. Flowers are single, available in many colors. Create a beautiful, low-growing carpet by planting them close together. 'Summer Beauty', mixed colors, grows to 12 inches high, producing flower stems long enough for cutting.

How to Grow—Sow seeds outdoors in early spring several weeks before your last frost date. For earlier flowers, start seeds indoors 6 to 8 weeks before time to plant outdoors. Cover seeds with 1/4 inch of fine soil. Germination takes 8 days at 70F to 75F (21C to 24C) soil temperature.

Space plants 6 inches apart in full sun. Plant in fertile, loose, well-drained soil. Cut plants back after flowering in early summer. New flowers will appear at onset of cooler weather in late summer and early fall. Although plants tolerate dry periods, they burn out during heat and high humidity unless soil is kept moist. Plants are subject to nitrogen burn. Fertilize seedlings with half the recommended application rate. Plants are rarely troubled by pests or diseases.

Uses—Beds and borders, especially as an edging. Effective in rock gardens and containers such as tubs and window boxes.

TAHOKA DAISY
Machaeranthera tanacetifolia

This wildflower is a hardy annual native to the western United States. It resembles a blue Michaelmas daisy. Summer-blooming flowers are 2-1/2 inches across and have golden-yellow centers. Plants grow 1 to 2 feet high and spread 9 inches wide.

Recommended Varieties—Not sold by variety name.

How to Grow—Surface-sow seeds outdoors after all danger of frost has passed. Or start seeds indoors 6 to 8 weeks before last frost date. Germination takes 4 to 10 days at 60F (16C). Seeds are sensitive to temperatures above 65F (19C).

Space plants 12 inches apart in full sun. Plants tolerate poor soil. Water regularly during hot, dry spells to keep the delicate fernlike foliage from burning.

Uses—Accent in mixed beds and borders, and for cutting.

Sweet William is sensational in spring and early summer for edging beds and borders.

Tahoka daisy is unusually hardy to cold.

Thunbergia, or black-eyed Susan, is a fast-growing vine that requires supports.

Flowers of tigridia, showing main assortment of colors available.

THUNBERGIA
Thunbergia alata

This fast-growing, tender annual is a popular flowering vine. The most common flower color is orange with a contrasting black throat. Yellow and white varieties are also available. Flowers are single, measuring up to 2 inches across. They are produced continually all summer until fall frost. Vines are heat tolerant.

Recommended Varieties—Tall, vining varieties generally are sold only in a mixture. A dwarf strain, 'Susie', has been separated into individual colors—orange, white and yellow. These are available with or without black eyes.

How to Grow—Sow seeds outdoors where plants are to bloom after all danger of frost has passed. Cover with 1/4 inch of fine soil. For earlier flowers, start seeds indoors 6 to 8 weeks before last frost date. Germination takes 5 to 12 days at 70F to 85F (21C to 30C) soil temperature.

Space plants 12 inches apart in full sun or part shade. Soil should be fertile loam or sandy. Keep moist by frequent watering. Provide a trellis or fence to support tall kinds. During periods of high heat and high humidity, flowers may dwindle. As soon as cooler conditions return, flowering will improve. The best displays are often seen in late summer and early fall. Generally not troubled by pests or diseases.

Uses—Tall, vining kinds are commonly used as a decorative screen to climb up trellis and fencing. Dwarf kinds are popular as hanging baskets and cascade beautifully from window boxes, tubs and urns.

TIGRIDIA
Tigridia pavonia

Tigridia is also known as *tiger flower, shell flower* and *jockey caps* because of the unusual, three-petal flowers. They are tender perennials but can be grown as tender annuals. Like dahlias, they are often classified as a summer-flowering bulb. But because bulbs can be expensive, it is better to grow them from seeds.

Tigridia is related to iris. Flowers are triangular, up to 5 inches across, with a cup shape in the middle. Colors include white, red, rose-pink and yellow. Most have spots in the center. Although each flower lasts only a day, flowers appear continually for several weeks during midsummer. Plants grow 2 feet high and spread 1 foot wide. Native to Mexico.

Recommended Varieties—Available only as a mixture of colors. Bulbs are available labeled as separate colors.

How to Grow—Sow seeds outdoors after danger of frost has passed. For earlier flowers start seeds indoors 8 weeks before last frost date. Cover seeds with 1/4 inch of fine soil. Germination takes 20 to 25 days at 70F to 85F (21C to 30C) soil temperature.

Space plants 12 inches apart in full sun. Plants prefer fertile loam or sandy soil. Water regularly and fertilize every 2 weeks with diluted liquid plant fertilizer. When frost kills leaves in fall, you can lift bulbs and store them in a cool, dark, dry location. Plant 4 inches deep in spring for repeat flowering the following season.

Uses—Rock gardens and at edge of streams or ponds on well-drained site. Also grown in beds and borders. Popular for cutting.

TIDY TIPS
Layia elegans

This California wildflower is a hardy annual popular in areas with cool summers. The 2-inch, daisylike flowers are bright yellow with white petal tips and golden-yellow centers. Plants grow 12 to 15 inches high and spread 12 inches wide.

Recommended Varieties—Not normally sold by variety name.

How to Grow—Sow seeds outdoors where plants are to bloom as soon as soil warms in spring. Germination takes 4 to 8 days at 60F (16C) soil temperature. Exposure to light aids germination. Seeds are sensitive to temperatures above 70F (21C).

Space plants 12 inches apart in full sun. Plants prefer loam or sandy soils and flower best during cool, sunny weather. Water regularly during dry spells. Generally free of pests and diseases.

Uses—Cutting and in wildflower plantings for coastal California and the Pacific Northwest.

TITHONIA
Tithonia rotundifolia

Also called *Mexican sunflower,* this tender annual is native to Mexico and adapted to high heat. Plants grow tall and leafy, producing deep-orange, sunflowerlike flowers that measure 3 inches across. Plants grow 4 to 6 feet high and spread 2 to 3 feet wide.

Recommended Varieties—'Torch', 4 to 6 feet high, won an All-America award for its reddish-orange flowers—the deepest color in tithonias. 'Sundance', 3 to 4 feet high, is an improvement because of its compact growth habit.

How to Grow—Sow seeds outdoors after all danger of frost has passed. Barely cover seeds with soil because some light aids germination. For earlier flowers, start seeds 6 weeks before last frost date. Seeds germinate in 4 to 8 days at 70F to 85F (21C to 30C) soil temperature.

Space plants 2 feet apart in full sun. Plants prefer fertile loam or sandy soil with good drainage. Plants are resistant to heat and drought, requiring water only when soil becomes dry. These are extremely trouble-free plants rarely bothered by pests and diseases.

Uses—Commonly planted as background. Flowers are also used for cutting.

Tidy tips is a California wildflower preferring cool, sunny conditions.

'Sundance' tithonia is popular background plant.

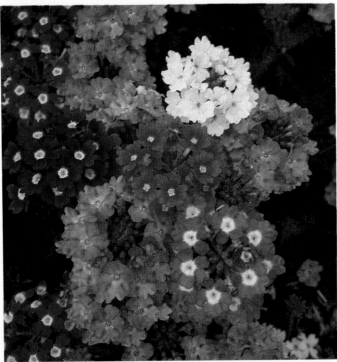

Venidium is native South-African wildflower that accepts heat.

VENIDIUM
Venidium fastuosum

South-African wildflowers introduced into cultivation are hard to surpass for dramatic color, and venidiums are no exception. They produce beautiful, daisylike flowers up to 5 inches across in brilliant orange. Inner petals are marked with black or dark-purple rings surrounding a black eye. Plants are tender annuals that grow 2 feet high and spread 1 foot wide. They flower continually during summer.

Recommended Varieties—Not normally sold by variety name, although some seedsmen list venidium as 'Monarch of the Veldt'.

How to Grow—Surface-sow seeds outdoors after all danger of frost has passed. For earlier flowers, start seeds indoors 6 to 8 weeks before last frost date. Barely press seeds into soil surface because they need light for maximum germination. Germination takes 10 days at 70F to 80F (21C to 30C) soil temperature.

Space plants 12 inches apart in full sun. Plants prefer fertile loam or sandy soil. Allow soil to dry between waterings. Rarely troubled by pests or diseases.

Uses—Beds and borders, also for cutting.

VERBENA
Verbena hybrida

These tender annuals have been greatly improved over the wild species. A rainbow of colors in every hue except yellow is now available. Most varieties are dwarf, spreading plants bearing clusters of primroselike flowers in red, white, pink and blue. Many have a distinctive white eye in the flower center. Plants grow 6 to 12 inches high and spread up to 2 feet wide. They tolerate heat and flower continually during summer. Native to the deserts of South America.

Recommended Varieties—'Springtime' mixture is an improvement over the popular standby, 'Ideal Florist Mixture'. It is more compact and flowers earlier in a wider color range. Among separate colors, the All-America award-winners 'Sangria', wine-red with white eye, and 'Amethyst', deep blue with white eye, are outstanding. Germination of 'Sangria' seeds is sometimes poor.

How to Grow—Start seeds indoors 10 to 12 weeks before planting outdoors. Plant after all danger of frost has passed. Germination takes 8 to 18 days at 70F to 85F (21to 30C) soil temperature. Exposure to light improves germination. Seeds are sensitive to overwatering. Some recently produced varieties of verbena have inherently poor germination.

Space plants 12 inches apart in full sun. Soil should be fertile loam or sandy. Plants tolerate heat but generally cease to flower during hot, humid spells unless watered regularly. Fertilize every 2 weeks during flowering with liquid plant fertilizer. Although verbenas are generally free of pests and diseases, they are susceptible to *chlorosis*. Leaves turn yellow, plants shrivel and die. For information on causes and treatment, see page 32.

Uses—Excellent for mass displays in beds and borders and for edging. Popular in rock gardens and containers such as window boxes and tubs.

Selection of 'Ideal Florist Mixture' verbena shows main assortment of colors available.

VINCA
Catharanthus roseus

The original botanical name for this tender annual, *Vinca rosea,* was recently changed to *Catharanthus roseus.* Most nurseries and seedsmen still sell it as vinca or periwinkle. The 1-1/2-inch, single flowers are white, pink or purple. Many have a contrasting eye in the center. Glossy dark-green leaves are decorative and appear to be evergreen, although they are not. Plants grow 9 inches high and spread 1 to 2 feet wide. They flower continually from early summer to fall frost. Vinca is one of the best flowering annuals for desert areas. Native to Madagascar.

Recommended Varieties—My favorite varieties are two All-America award winners. 'Polka Dot' produces brilliant white flowers with cherry-red centers. 'Little Linda' has deep rose-pink flowers. 'Polka Dot' is extremely dwarf, reaching no more than 4 inches high and spreading up to 2 feet wide. It makes an excellent, temporary flowering ground cover. 'Little Linda' grows 8 to 10 inches high, spreading 2 feet wide. It is distinctive because of its prolific and continual flowering.

How to Grow—Start seeds indoors 10 to 12 weeks before last frost date. Plant after all danger of frost has passed. Germination takes 6 to 23 days at 70F to 85F (21C to 30C) soil temperature. Light improves germination. Seeds are sensitive to drying out.

Space plants 9 inches apart in full sun or partial shade. Vincas tolerate a wide range of soil conditions—even poor soil—but do best in loam or sandy soil. Regular watering keeps plants blooming.

Plants are heat and drought tolerant and rarely bothered by pests or diseases. Young transplants are occasionally attacked by slugs and snails. Control by using slug bait or pick them off plants by hand.

Uses—Low-growing beds and borders. Excellent for hanging baskets and combined with other annuals in container plantings. Useful as a temporary ground cover, growing and flowering where most other annuals would die from heat and pollution.

'Polka Dot' vinca is resistant to air pollution. This planting is adjacent to a busy street and parking lot at the Los Angeles County Arboretum in Arcadia, California.

VIOLA
Viola cornuta

Violas are actually hardy perennials. Many cultivated varieties can be grown as hardy annuals to flower the first year. Violas resemble pansies but have smaller flowers and are generally more vigorous and longer lasting. Colors include red, white, yellow, blue, orange and purple. Some have black markings that resemble faces. Plants grow 6 inches high and spread 6 inches wide. Flowers appear for several weeks in spring during cool weather. Native to northern Spain.

Recommended Varieties—'Monarch', mixed colors, is a good, weather-resistant variety, producing large flowers in clear colors with some bicolors. 'Arkwright Ruby' is beautiful red with black blotches. Special class of violas called *Johnny-jump-ups* produce masses of small flowers in early spring. The most popular is 'Helen Mount'. It has three colors in flower petals—purple, lavender and yellow, plus black streaks at the center, resembling cat's whiskers.

How to Grow—Start seeds indoors 8 to 10 weeks before time to plant outdoors. Because plants are

Mixture of violas shows main assortment of flower colors available.

English wallflowers growing in garden near San Francisco.

Siberian wallflower growing in a garden near Atlanta.

hardy, they can be planted outdoors several weeks before the last frost date. Harden-off plants before setting them out. Seeds benefit from chilling in the vegetable bin in the refrigerator for several days to break dormancy. Cover seeds with 1/2 inch of soil. Germination generally occurs in 10 to 12 days at 70F (21C) soil temperature.

Space plants 6 inches apart in full sun or light shade. Plants prefer loose, fertile, loam soil. If soil is dry or stony, mix in plenty of organic matter to help retain moisture and keep soil cool. Water frequently. Flowering is best during cool weather. If plants stop flowering in summer heat, tops can be sheared. A second flowering usually appears when cool weather returns in fall.

Aphids are a common insect pest. Control by spraying plants with Sevin or malathion chemical sprays or wash plants with an insecticidal soap solution. Diseases include anthracnose and rust. Control by spraying with zineb fungicide.

Uses—Edging beds and borders. Use in rock gardens, window boxes and other container plantings. Plants bloom in spring before most other annuals have had a chance.

WALLFLOWER
Cheiranthus species

Wallflowers are hardy biennials. If seeds are sown early in the season, they grow as hardy annuals, flowering the first year in areas where summers are cool. Fragrant flowers are borne in clusters. English wallflower, *Cheiranthus cheiri,* offers an extensive range of colors, including red, white, yellow, cream, lemon, apricot, salmon, pink, purple and brown. The Siberian wallflower, *C. allioni,* is more heat tolerant and more widely used for spring bedding displays, even though its color range is limited to yellow and orange. Plants grow 2 feet high and spread 1 foot wide. Flowers appear during cool, sunny conditions in spring or summer. Native to Madeira and the Canary Islands eastward to the Himalaya Mountains.

Recommended Varieties—Among popular English wallflowers, 'Fair Lady' is considered one of the best mixtures, with mostly pastel shades. The best Siberian wallflower is 'Orange Bedder', widely used for spring bedding. It is often mixed with blue forget-me-nots to create a magnificent orange and blue companion planting.

How to Grow—Surface-sow seeds directly in the garden as soon as soil warms in early spring. Seedlings will tolerate mild frosts. For earlier flowers, start seeds indoors 8 weeks before time to plant outdoors. Germination takes 5 to 7 days at 70F to 85F (21C to 30C) soil temperature. Exposure of seeds to light improves germination.

Space plants 12 inches apart in full sun or partial shade. Plants tolerate a wide range of soil conditions—even poor soil. They do best in fertile loam. Keep soil moist by watering regularly. As a summer bedding plant, wallflowers prefer cool conditions such as those found in coastal and high-altitude locations. Plants also do well in frost-free locations as a winter-flowering bedding plant. For winter flowers, start seeds in late summer.

Most chewing or sucking insects such as beetles and aphids can be controlled by spraying with malathion or

Sevin chemical sprays, or pyrethrum organic spray. If bacterial wilt strikes plants, pull up affected plants and destroy them to prevent further infections. *Club root*—a disease usually associated with cabbage plants—can stunt wallflowers. The disease is not as common in neutral and slightly alkaline soils. Adding lime to acid soils can be helpful in preventing.

Uses—Bedding plants for mass display in beds and borders. Particularly attractive when interplanted with tulips. Timing of seed starting and planting is essential so that peak bloom occurs during cool, sunny weather.

WISHBONE FLOWER
Torenia fournieri

This neat, tender annual derives its popular name from the wishbone-shape structure inside the flower, formed by a pair of stamens. Flowers are dark purple-blue with a yellow throat. Plants grow 8 to 12 inches high and spread 8 inches wide. Native to Asia and Africa.

Recommended Varieties—Not normally sold by variety name. Large-flower varieties are being developed. New plants may soon be sold by variety name.

How to Grow—Seeds can be sown directly in the garden after all danger of frost has passed. Best to start seeds indoors 10 weeks before last frost date. Germination takes 8 days at 70F to 85F (21C to 30C) soil temperature. Light enhances germination. Cover seeds with just enough soil to anchor them.

Space plants 6 to 8 inches apart in lightly shaded location. Prefers fertile, moist, well-drained soil. If your soil is clay or sandy, add peat moss or similar organic matter. Plants can be grown in pots during winter in a greenhouse or sun room.

Uses—Popular for growing in shady locations, especially beds and borders and as edging. Plants do well in containers.

XERANTHEMUM
Xeranthemum annuum

Xeranthemums resemble strawflowers except colors are limited to white and shades of red or pink. Plants grow 2 to 3 feet high and spread 1 foot wide. Flowers appear for several weeks in summer. Hardy annuals native to the Mediterranean.

Recommended Varieties—Not normally sold by variety name.

How to Grow—Sow seeds outdoors after all danger of frost has passed. For earlier flowers, start seeds indoors 6 weeks before planting outside. Plants are difficult to transplant. Germination occurs in 10 to 15 days at 70F (21C) soil temperature. Barely cover seeds with soil because light aids germination.

Space plants 12 inches apart in full sun. Plant in loose, fertile loam or sandy soil. Water during dry spells. Do not disturb roots when transplanting or plants may wilt and die. Mealy bugs sometimes colonize tender stems. Spray with malathion chemical insecticide or wash them off with insecticidal soap.

Uses—Cutting to use in dried-flower arrangements.

Close-up of torenia displays the curious structure at flower center, the reason for its name—wishbone flower.

Xeranthemum shows two main flower colors available. Plants are popular for dried-flower arrangements.

'Rose Starlet' zinnia makes a beautiful low-growing border planting.

ZINNIA
Zinnia species

Zinnias are North America's most popular flower to grow from seeds. Flowers are mostly double, up to 7 inches across. They bloom all summer up to fall frost. Colors include white, yellow, orange, red, pink, purple and green. Some are bicolor. Most popular are the cactus-flower types, producing large, double flowers with quilled pointed petals. The dahlia-flower class is almost as popular, producing large, double flowers but with rounded, flat petals. They are available in a wide range of sizes, from miniatures 6 inches high, to giant-flower kinds up to 3 feet high. Plants can spread up to 2 feet wide. Tender annuals native to Mexico.

Recommended Varieties—Among cactus-flower kinds the hybrids have the largest flowers—up to 6 inches across. These include 'Zenith', 'Big Top' and 'Fruit Bowl', all growing to 3 feet high. In the dahlia-flower class, hybrids such as 'Gold Sun' and 'Red Sun' have terminal flowers that can grow to 7 inches across. 'Giants of California' is a popular, old-fashion mixture. See page 156. 'Envy', a green, dahlia-flower zinnia, is valued for use in flower arrangements.

Some bizarre, bicolor zinnias are available. Notables include 'Whirligig' and 'Candy Cane'. Both display ruffled white or yellow petals striped with red. 'Sombrero', a single bicolor, is popular with flower arrangers.

'Peter Pan' hybrids are the best bedding types. They produce large, 5-inch, dahlia-type blooms on dwarf plants that grow to 12 inches high. An outstanding non-hybrid is 'Rose Starlet'.

A class called *cut-and-come-again* zinnias have 3-inch blooms shaped like beehives. They grow to 3 feet high. 'Ruffles', a hybrid, is extremely early flowering, long lasting and cold tolerant. The more flowers you cut the more plants are stimulated into blooming. Also popular for cutting are the 'Mexicana' types such as 'Persian Carpet'. Growing 14 inches high, plants cover themselves with 1-1/2-inch flowers. These have pointed petals that are mostly white or yellow with red tips. A cactus-flower hybrid, 'Bouquet', does double duty for display and cutting.

Zinnia angustifolia creates an excellent ground cover. Sometimes listed as 'Classic', it grows 12 inches high and has bright-orange flowers. 'Thumbelina' remains a popular zinnia for edging. It flowers at 6 inches high, but is a weak plant highly susceptible to mildew.

How to Grow—Zinnias do not transplant well, so seeds are best sown directly in the garden after all danger of frost has passed. Barely cover seeds with fine soil because exposure to light improves germination. Seeds germinate in 3 to 7 days at 70F to 85F (21C to 30C) soil temperature. To grow transplants, sow seeds in individual peat pots 4 to 5 weeks before frost.

Space plants 12 inches apart except for miniatures, which should be spaced 6 inches apart. Plant in full sun in fertile loam or sandy soil. Keep soil moist until plants are established. Do not wet leaves because this encourages mildew disease.

Powdery mildew and alternaria blight can attack zinnias. Mildew can be controlled by planting resistant varieties and dusting plants with fungicides containing sulfur. To control alternaria, treat seeds with a fungicide before planting. Spray plants weekly with a protective fungicide such as maneb or zineb. Zinnia flowers

'Bouquet' mixed colors zinnia is stunning as mass planting.

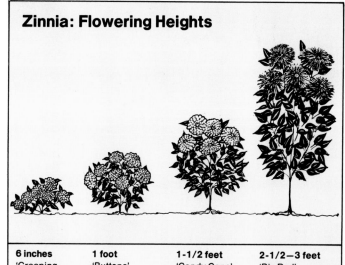

Zinnia: Flowering Heights

6 inches	1 foot	1-1/2 feet	2-1/2—3 feet
'Creeping Zinnia'	'Buttons'	'Candy Cane'	'Big Red'
'Mini'	'Classic'	'Chippendale Daisy'	'Big Top'
'Thumbelina'	'Cupid'	'Dasher'	'Burpeeana'
	'Fantastic Light Pink'	'Paint Brush'	'Cactus Flowered'
	'Persian Carpet'	'Rose Starlet'	'Dahlia Flowered'
	'Peter Pan'	'Small World'	'Fruit Bowl'
	'Tom Thumb'	'Sombrero'	'Giants of California'
			'Ruffles'
			'State Fair'
			'Zenith'

'Envy' zinnia is valued by flower arrangers because of its unique color.

'Sombrero' zinnia is a single-flower variety, popular among flower arrangers.

are a favorite food of Japanese beetles. Young plants also attract snails and slugs. Control Japanese beetles with traps. Control slugs and snails with bait or pick them from plants by hand.

Uses—Giant-flower types are spectacular in beds and borders. Cutting types are used for flower arrangements. Use spreading types for ground covers, rock gardens and hanging baskets. Miniatures and dwarfs are best for containers, low beds and edging.

DAHLIA-FLOWERED ZINNIAS

Mexicans have several common names to describe their native zinnias—*mal de ojo*—eyesores; and *sombreros*—the Mexican hat. These names are because of the raised flower center and mostly flat, magenta petals. Years ago, John Bodger, founder of Bodger Seeds, spotted a large *off-type* flower in a patch of zinnias—a mutation. He marked it for protection and had it tended until he could harvest seeds. A mule pulling the cultivator stepped on it once, but it survived.

After 5 years of growth, selecting the best plants from each generation for seed stocks, he put the plant on the market as 'Dahlia-Flowered Zinnia'. The year was 1919. In 1924, the Royal Horticultural Society of Great Britain awarded the zinnia a Gold Medal and an Award of Merit—a first for an American-bred flower.

In 1926, an improvement over the original 'Dahlia-Flowered Zinnia' was introduced by Bodger, sold as 'Giants of California'. They are still among the most popular zinnias grown today.

'Red Sun' zinnia has one of the biggest zinnia flowers, winning an All-America award.

'Fruit Bowl' zinnias create a dramatic island bed.

Index

Index